Reprints of Economic Classics

# THE PROGRESS OF SOCIETY

# THE PROGRESS OF SOCIETY

BY

ROBERT HAMILTON

[1830]

REPRINTS OF ECONOMIC CLASSICS

AUGUSTUS M. KELLEY · PUBLISHERS
*NEW YORK 1969*

First Edition 1830

(London: John Murray, *Albemarle Street*, 1830)

Reprinted 1969 by

AUGUSTUS M. KELLEY · PUBLISHERS

*New York New York 10010*

Library of Congress Catalogue Card Number

68-55729

PRINTED IN THE UNITED STATES OF AMERICA

*by* SENTRY PRESS, NEW YORK, N. Y. 10019

# THE

# PROGRESS OF SOCIETY.

BY

THE LATE ROBERT HAMILTON,

*LL.D., F.R.S.*

PROFESSOR OF MATHEMATICS IN THE MARISCHAL COLLEGE AND UNIVERSITY OF ABERDEEN;

AUTHOR OF "AN ENQUIRY CONCERNING THE NATIONAL DEBT."

LONDON:
JOHN MURRAY, ALBEMARLE-STREET.

MDCCCXXX.

# CONTENTS.

# INTRODUCTION.

The work now offered to the favourable reception of the public, being from the pen of the late Dr. Hamilton, of Aberdeen, and evidently composed with an eye to publication, stands in no need of a prefatory recommendation. A life extended beyond the ordinary limits, and passed chiefly in public and important situations, and in the course of which he published various valuable works, has made Dr. Hamilton well known to the greater number of those who are likely to take an interest in this volume. But as it is probable that no more of his writings will be submitted to the public, a short notice or memoir of the Author may not prove unacceptable to the community at large, and will be particularly gratifying to his friends and acquaintance.

Dr. Hamilton's grandfather was Dr. William Hamilton, well known as Professor of Divinity in the University of Edinburgh, and afterwards Principal of that seminary. He was a cadet of the family of Preston. His father was Gavin Hamilton, an eminent publisher and bookseller in Edinburgh, who was distinguished for his loyalty during the Rebellion of 1745. Mr. Hamilton married Helen, daughter of James Balfour, Esq., of Pilrig; and Dr. Robert Hamilton, the subject of this memoir, was the eighth child of that marriage, and was born on the 11th day of June, 1743.

In infancy Dr. Hamilton was of a delicate constitution, which improved as he advanced in years; and, with the exception of lumbago, to which he was much subjected in the latter part of life, and which occasioned his stooping very much, he scarcely had a serious ailment during his long life, till within three weeks of his death, which was occasioned by a total loss of appetite, and consequent decay of bodily strength.

He was an excellent scholar in every department of literature to which he applied, and his strong desire to acquire knowledge made him a favourite with all his teachers, and more especially with the celebrated Matthew Stewart, professor of mathematics in the University of Edinburgh, who was indignant when informed that his favourite pupil was intended for business.

Mr. Hamilton was always partial to a literary life; but, yielding to circumstances, he was induced to spend some time in the banking-office of Messrs. William Hogg and Son, in order to fit him for prosecuting that line, or for becoming a general merchant.

Soon after this, his father gave up business as a publisher, and retired to a paper-mill which he possessed in a beautifully romantic situation near Edinburgh.

About this time, the subject of this memoir formed several of his most lasting friendships, particularly with Dr. Charters, Dr. Wodrow, Robert Scott Moncrieff, Esq., &c. About this time also, he and some other literary young men formed themselves into a debating society, which existed for a season or two, and which led to the foundation of the present Speculative Society of Edinburgh.

It may not be uninteresting to notice, that he became personally acquainted with Lord Kaimes in rather a singular manner, but highly creditable to both. He wrote an anonymous criticism, in one of the magazines of the day, on one of the works of that celebrated author. This criticism attracted Lord Kaimes's attention so much, that he inserted a notice in the same periodical, requesting that if the author of the criticism in question was already known to him, he might have the pleasure of knowing him better; and, if he was a stranger, begging that he might have the honour of becoming acquainted with him. It was with much difficulty that Dr. Hamilton was persuaded to reveal himself to Lord Kaimes; and when he did so, his Lordship could scarcely believe that, in this young man, he saw before him his able critic. But so much was he pleased with the conversation of his new acquaintance, that he gave him a general invitation to his house as often as suited his convenience. Availing himself of this invitation, it proved the means of introducing Dr. Hamilton to many of the first literary characters of the time.

In 1766, the mathematical chair in Marischal College having become vacant by the death of Mr. Stewart, the earnest solicitation of Dr. Hamilton's friends prevailed with him, although reluctantly, being then only twenty-three years of age, to offer himself as a candidate for the office. He was unsuccessful (Dr. Trail being appointed); but the impression of Dr. Hamilton's talents and acquirements, which his appearance upon this occasion made upon the minds of the judges, was very strong, as several letters which are now before the writer of this memoir plainly show. One of these, from a most respectable professor in King's College, one of the examinators, addressed to Dr. John Gregory, of Edinburgh, it is hoped, may not prove unacceptable to the reader.

'Dear Doctor,

'Mr. Hamilton called upon me yesterday, but, 'having missed him, a due regard to that young 'man's merit obliges me to put you to the expense 'of a postage, that I may have an early opportunity 'of signifying my sentiments of the good appearance 'he made at the trial. In every exercise that was 'given the candidates, Mr. Hamilton discovered a 'remarkable genius for mathematics, and a justness 'of apprehension and perspicuity that is rarely to be 'met with. He is an excellent demonstrator; always 'planned out his demonstration with judgment, and 'apprized his audience where the stress lay, so that 'he brought it to a conclusion in the most perspicuous 'manner, and in such a way that no person of com-'mon understanding could miss it. All the exami-'nators were highly satisfied with the candour of his 'written performances, on which he never attempted 'to throw dust, or conceal where he was at a loss; 'and even upon those occasions, from the ingenious 'attempts he made to get himself disengaged, the 'judges formed the most favourable opinion of his 'ability. Mr. Trail was preferred to him; but 'justice requires that I should acquaint you, that he 'trode very closely at Mr. Trail's heels. I look 'upon it as a very agreeable circumstance of the trial, 'that I had thereby an opportunity of knowing a 'young gentleman of so much real merit, and every 'way so agreeable. If any more formal testimony 'can be of any service to Mr. Hamilton, I know that 'the least hint will procure it from all the examinators.

'I am, with great truth, yours,

(Signed) 'THOMAS GORDON.'

After this competition Dr. Hamilton became a partner in the paper-mill, and, his father having died the following year, the whole charge of the business devolved upon him. The concern being burdened with the shares of all the rest of the family, and the drudgery of it being foreign to his inclinations, and breaking in upon his literary habits and pursuits, he gave it up, having appointed a manager to take charge of it, and in 1769 obtained the rectorship of the academy at Perth.

In 1771 he married Miss Anne Mitchell, of Ladath, but had the misfortune to lose her in 1778. She left him three daughters, Anne, Helen, and Marian, all living at the date of this memoir. The eldest, to whom her father bequeathed his house in the country, is unmarried; the second is widow of Andrew Thomson, Esq., of Banchory, in the county of Kincardine; and the youngest is married to the Reverend Robert Swan, of Abercrombie, in Fife.

In 1779 Dr. Hamilton was presented to the natural philosophy chair in Marischal College, which is in the gift of the crown, and in the autumn of that year removed with his family to Aberdeen. For one session Dr. Hamilton taught the class to which he had been presented; but Dr. Copland having removed from the chair of this class to the mathematical chair, and neither finding themselves so much at home in the situations in which they were now severally placed, they arranged an exchange before the commencement of another session, and from that time forward Dr. Hamilton taught the mathematical class. It was not, however, till 1817, that he became, by presentation, professor of mathematics.

In 1782 Dr. Hamilton entered again into the married state, having espoused Jane, daughter of James Morison, Esq., of Elsick.

In 1814 Dr. Hamilton, finding the duty of teaching his three mathematical classes too laborious, engaged an assistant, with the permission of the Senatus Academicus, to which his age, and his long and faithful services, well entitled him. This assistant was Mr. John Cruickshank, who for many years instructed the two youngest classes, whilst the Doctor continued to teach the higher branches of the science himself; and so entire satisfaction did Mr. Cruickshank give both to Dr. Hamilton and to the other members of the college, that, on their joint application, the town council appointed him as assistant and successor to Dr. Hamilton, at the same time that the Doctor himself obtained a presentation to the mathematical chair.

In February, 1825, his second wife, by whom he had no family, died, leaving him again a widower. From this period, he passed much of his time at his cottage in the country, where his valuable life was terminated in the bosom of his family, on the 14th day of July, 1829, in the eighty-seventh year of his age.

Having thus briefly detailed the leading events of Dr. Hamilton's life, before attempting an outline of his character, it will be proper to notice his publications.

In 1777 the first edition of his 'Merchandise' appeared, whilst he was superintending the academy at Perth, and it has gone through several editions.

In 1790 he printed, for the use of his class, a set of Mathematical Tables.

In 1796 he published his 'Arithmetic,' which has been often reprinted.

In 1800 he published, for the use of his students, 'Heads of a Course of Lectures on Mathematics.' All his publications of a strictly professional character, being the result of a thorough acquaintance with his subject, and distinguished by luminous perspicuity, have been highly valued, and will ever retain a respectable place among works of that nature.

He published in 1790, without, however, affixing his name to it, 'An Essay on Peace and War.' In this short treatise, by exhibiting, in a clear point of view, the slender grounds upon which bloody and expensive wars are often undertaken, and the inadequacy of national advantages to compensate the loss of men and money incurred by the retention of foreign acquisitions, he ably combated that unbounded spirit of retaliation and conquest in which high-minded nations are too ready to indulge.

In 1813 the first edition of his work on the 'National Debt and Sinking Fund' was given to the public, and it has passed through three editions. This work has raised his name higher in the scale of political authors than any of his other publications, and must, indeed, render it immortal. It exhibited the fallacy of the arguments by which financiers had been blinded, and by means of which, for a considerable period, the nation had been kept in the dark; and it opened their eyes to the simple truth, that debts can only be liquidated by a surplus of income over expenditure.

Whilst noticing his printed works, we must not

omit to mention a valuable small pamphlet on 'Pauperism,' called forth by the state of the poor in Aberdeen, and an inquiry into the most eligible means of relieving their wants, without having recourse to poor's rates, to which last he was, on strong grounds, always hostile. In this pamphlet, he treats, with that perspicuity for which all his writings are remarkable, of the various claims of indigent persons on the charity of the public, and to what extent those claims deserve attention. The doctrine of this pamphlet is of general application, and ought to be widely diffused.

It may be noticed here, that Dr. Hamilton, although he did not send many of his works to the press, wrote at great length on various subjects connected with his favourite study of political economy. This appears from several essays found among his papers, viz.,—'On the American War'—'On Government,'—'On the Corn-bounty,' and others; and it is to be regretted that none of them are so far finished as to admit of being laid before the public.

From what has been said above, it will be readily anticipated that Dr. Hamilton's correspondence must have been extensive. Many eminent mathematicians received their education at Marischal College, who in after life acknowledged their obligations to Dr. Hamilton, in a manner highly gratifying to him, and his professional publications attracted the attention of many, both at home and abroad: this led to an extensive epistolary correspondence, which was greatly augmented by the force of reasoning displayed in his political essays. On the subject of these last, he exchanged many letters with Lord Lauderdale, Mr. Grenfell, and other members of the British parliament; and had also communications with Mons. J. Baptiste Say, and Baron Fahrenberg, of Carlsruhe, which last requested permission to translate his work on the 'Finances' into German, with a view to its publication in his native city.

Dr. Hamilton, in the midst of all his more momentous duties and avocations, with which he never allowed any other pursuit to interfere, devoted no inconsiderable portion of his time to the management of the college funds and bursaries, and still more disinterestedly to every subject connected with the good and prosperity of the town in which he resided. The demands upon him in the latter of these departments were numerous, owing to the confidence of those in office in his talents, and accuracy in business; and his opinion was uniformly listened to with deference and respect.

In 1807, in compliance with the deed of settlement of the late John Burnett, of Dens, an advertisement appeared in the newspapers, intimating that that gentleman had bequeathed a sum, not less than 800*l.*, to be paid for the best, and 400*l.* for the second best treatise on the following theme: namely, 'The 'evidence that there is a Being all-powerful, wise, 'and good, by whom everything exists; and this, in 'the first place, from considerations independent of 'written revelation; and, in the second place, from 'the revelation of the Lord Jesus; and to point out 'the inferences most necessary for, and most useful 'to, mankind.'

By the deed of settlement, also, the ministers of the established church of Aberdeen, the principals and professors of King's and Marischal Colleges of Aberdeen, and the trustees of the testator, were appointed to meet and make choice of three judges, to decide upon the comparative merit of such treatises as should be laid before them. This meeting took place in 1814, when the three judges elected were Dr. Gerard, professor of divinity in King's College, Mr. George Glennie, professor of moral philosophy in Marischal College, and the subject of this memoir. They accepted the office; and the number of treatises given in amounting to no fewer than fifty, the judges found that the task which they had undertaken proved extremely laborious, and the anxiety of Dr. Hamilton to ascertain with the strictest impartiality the respective merit of the writers was very great, as appears from the copious notes found among his papers, taken by him during the perusal of the treatises, which assisted, not a little, in enabling the judges to come to an unanimous decision.

As an elder of the church, he considered himself peculiarly called upon to give his attention to the management of the poor's funds, and the best means of rendering them efficient. In this capacity, too, he was frequently commissioned by his college to represent that body in the General Assembly of the Church of Scotland, and took a deep interest in their proceedings; and when he offered his sentiments on any subject of debate, which, from his innate modesty, was but seldom, he was listened to with profound attention.

No one understood better, and few indeed so well, all the details connected with the Church's Widows' Fund, or was more truly solicitous for its improvement and success.

A firm believer in divine revelation, Dr. Hamilton early became a member of the Auxiliary to the British and Foreign Bible Society formed at Aberdeen, and deeply deplored the intemperate manner in which the broachers of the apocryphal controversy carried it on, and the schism which it gave rise to.

He was shocked with cruelty, when exercised even upon the meanest of the inferior animals; and of slavery, and its dreadful consequences, both as they respect the bodies and the souls of mankind, he had a great abhorrence. Under the influence of this feeling, he was an original member of the Antislavery Society of Aberdeen, and was unanimously called to the chair as their president—a situation which he held till his death.

The above notices of Dr. Hamilton will serve in no inconsiderable degree to develop his character. Among his papers we find regulations for his future conduct in life, written when he was only twenty-two years of age, at which time he had the prospect of entering into business. They are extremely interesting, and embrace resolutions in respect to almost every situation in which he possibly might be placed in the course of Providence. They breathe throughout a most Christian and philanthropic spirit, and prescribe the most uncompromising rectitude of conduct, and the most open-handed charity; and although many of the supposed contingencies were never realized, on a review of his life we evidently perceive that he never lost sight of them.

Dr. Hamilton's talents were of the highest order, and sedulously improved; and it was a merciful dispensation for himself, as well as for the community of which he was so valuable a member, that his faculties were unimpaired to the close of life. Three weeks before his death, he attended a meeting of the Senatus of Marischal College, met on business connected with the royal visitation, and delighted his colleagues with the distinctness of his perceptions, and the importance of his remarks. And even many days after this, when his strength had greatly sunk under the pressure of disease, he was frequently employed in revising and correcting the work to which this memoir is prefixed.

Dr. Hamilton was naturally unobtrusive and retiring, and by strangers was considered as an *absent man*. Addison says, 'I distinguish a man who is '*absent* because he thinks of something else, from a 'man who is absent because he thinks of nothing.' In the latter sense, Dr. Hamilton was never absent; in the former, he might sometimes be said to be so, when what was passing before him was unimportant: when otherwise, he was so merely in appearance, from being silent, and withholding his opinion, which had he given would have been highly gratifying. This has not seldom been matter of regret to the writer of this memoir, who frequently had the happiness to enjoy his society.

Dr. Hamilton's favourite recreations were the cultivation of flowers, of which he was particularly fond, and making excursions with a few friends, most commonly to such parts of the island as he had not before visited; but it is remarkable that, in the year 1820, when in his seventy-eighth year, he joined a family party in a tour on the Continent. On such occasions he possessed the happy talent of shaking his mind loose from professional and other cares, and entering, with all his heart, into the pursuits of his party; exploring every object worthy of notice, and putting down his observations in a regularly-kept diary.

Dr. Hamilton's piety was rational, fervent, and unostentatious; in his charities, which were as extensive as his circumstances permitted, he was solicitous that 'his left hand should not know what his right hand did;' and his attention to his religious duties was uniform and unceasing. His affection for his family and relatives was of the warmest kind, and his friendships were steady and sincere. His talents, his virtues, and his devotedness to the duties of the respectable situation which he held in the University, as well as to the promotion of the best interests of the community at large, will be respectfully remembered by all who knew him even by character; and that these impressions may be handed down to posterity, it is highly creditable to the present generation, that they have opened a subscription for a monument to his memory, to which many respectable persons in both kingdoms have put their names.

THE

# PROGRESS OF SOCIETY.

## GENERAL PRINCIPLES.

THE earth and its produce, and the animals with which it is stocked, are the sources from which man derives every article that contributes to his maintenance or enjoyment.

These commodities, bestowed on man by the gift of nature, require, in general, to be modified by human art, before they be fit to answer the purposes to which they are subservient.

The effect of labour in preparing commodities for use is augmented by acquired skill, by division, by the use of tools, by the aid of the strength of animals, and of other powers, natural or artificial.

The division of labour is limited by the extent of the market, and, in a state unconnected with others by commerce, will be regulated by the extent of territory and population.

A considerable share of the commodities prepared by art and labour is not consumed immediately, but reserved for future use, or applied as the means of farther production. This constitutes wealth, or capital.

The wealth of a country depends on the fertility of the soil, the industry and skill of the inhabitants, and the accumulated capital transmitted to them by their predecessors.

The use of wealth is to furnish the means of enjoyment to mankind. The measure of enjoyment which it affords depends upon its distribution, as well as its absolute amount. An equal distribution of wealth is neither practicable nor desirable : but great inequality and accumulation of great fortunes is detrimental to general happiness.

Wealth is formed and increased by industry. It is diminished by any operative engine of destruction. Of these war is the most general and the most effective.

In war a large proportion of the inhabitants is withdrawn from the labours of useful industry, and engaged in military service, or preparing the apparatus requisite thereto. Another portion, in the country where the war is waged, is prevented from following their usual occupations.

The object of war is destruction. The fields are ravaged; cities demolished; villages burnt; noble works of art, whose construction was the labour of years, destroyed in an hour. It is the severest scourge to which humanity is subject, and tends most powerfully to impair wealth and enjoyment.

The acquisition of wealth which a victorious nation obtains from the plunder of the vanquished, seldom repays the expense of the war. The increased activity and prosperity of some particular classes in time of war is a delusive mark of general prosperity.

A nation of considerable extent may acquire, by industry and skill, a large share of wealth, without the aid of foreign commerce.

Commerce has been considered as a means by which one nation is enriched at the expense of another. Industrious, skilful, and enterprising nations have been supposed to gain from the indolent, the ignorant, and the timid. Were this a just view of the effects of commerce, it would not afford much ground of eulogium in its favour.

It would not promote the general welfare of the human race: but the view is altogether erroneous.

No commerce can be considerably beneficial to one nation, nor permanent, unless it be also beneficial to those nations with which it is carried on.

The advantages of commerce are to bring together the products of different climates into the same country, and thereby increase the means of human enjoyment.

It enlarges the effects of the division of labour by presenting a more extensive market.

It diffuses through the commercial world, on moderate terms, those articles in the fabrication of which different nations have acquired superior skill and dexterity.

By promoting an intercourse between nations of different manners, and in different states of civilization, it tends to the enlargement of knowledge, and the improvement of the intellectual and active powers of man.

In commerce a nation receives what it wants in exchange for what it has to spare. Export and import are reciprocal. The payment of a balance in money is a temporary measure, not much used, and of no advantage to the nation which receives it. The value in exchange of exports and imports is ultimately equal ; but the value in use of imports should be greater, otherwise commerce is not beneficial.

Commerce, in order to yield these advantages in the highest degree, should be subject to no restrictions ; neither should it, except in special and rare cases, be promoted by artificial encouragements.

Notwithstanding this, when a restrictive system has been long established and become incorporated with the constitution of the society, it cannot be suddenly relinquished without occasioning much distress to numerous classes of the community, and even impairing for a time its general prosperity ; and as human happiness is the object of wealth, an alteration of system, though ultimately beneficial, should be had recourse to cautiously and gradually.

A country of any considerable extent should be chiefly supplied with food from the produce of its own soil. So long as there is a sufficient supply of food in the existing state of agriculture, or in that which may be speedily obtained, there is no reason to desire a restriction in the number of inhabitants. If there be not something faulty in the general system, they will find employment, and obtain a share of the comforts of life.

Where there is not a sufficiency of food in the existing state of agriculture, or where employment cannot be found for the laborious in the existing state of society, emigration should be encouraged.

Emigration is a powerful means of conferring the blessings of civilized society on countries at present barbarous and comparatively desert.

There are at present on the earth extensive territories, of considerable fertility, uninhabited or thinly peopled, for the reception of emigrants; and this is likely to be the case for many succeeding ages.

Where a portion of the inhabitants have emigrated and established themselves in a distant land, a commercial intercourse between these settlers and the parent state may be established to their mutual advantage, and no other connexion is desirable. The attempt to draw a revenue from colonists in aid of that of the parent state has never succeeded; and the imposition of commercial restrictions depresses the progress and prosperity of the new states, and renders their commerce with the parent state

human welfare, that no other object ought to be brought into competition with it; and if any state of society appear clearly more favourable for promoting moral virtue than another, that state is entitled to a decided preference.

The improvement of our intellectual, inventive, and active powers may be ranked in the second place.

Thirdly, whatever contributes to the health and vigour of our bodies, and the due exertion of their various powers and operations,

Fourthly, the abundant possession and proper distribution of those articles, provided by nature and improved by art, which supply us with food, clothing, and habitation, or contribute in any way to the comfort and enjoyment of life.

Fifthly, the cultivation of the polite arts, and consequent improvement of these arts; viz.—painting, sculpture, architecture, music, poetry, eloquence, and the various branches of polite literature.

Sixthly, such an extent of population as is consistent with the comfortable subsistence of the inhabitants. It is desirable to procure the greatest practicable share of happiness to the greatest number of intelligent and sentient beings.

Along with all these it is necessary to maintain such political establishments and public force as may secure personal safety, and the protection of liberty and property, against foreign enemies or domestic violators of the public peace.

Inquiries of the kind now suggested are sometimes regarded as visionary and treated with ridicule. They are considered as the effusions of an enthusiastic imagination, and altogether inapplicable to the state in which mankind ever have been, and ever will be placed. It cannot be denied that some men, actuated by the purest benevolent motives, but not under the regulation of a sound judgment, have advanced extravagant doctrines, and proposed impracticable schemes. These, however, have done little harm, unless so far as they gave room for cavilling, to those who are disposed to sneer at every attempt for ameliorating the condition of mankind. It is evident that the state of society has undergone, and is still undergoing alterations; that it has sometimes improved, sometimes degenerated; and there seems no good reason to doubt that it is susceptible of higher improvement than it has hitherto attained. The belief of the perfectibility of human nature, and the attainment of a golden age, in which vice and misery have no place, will only be entertained by an enthusiast: but an inquiry into the means of improving our nature and enlarging our happiness is consistent with sober reason, and is the most important subject, merely human, that can engage the mind of man. No moral writer was ever censured for laying down as perfect a system of duty as he could, although it was not expected that this would be practised, even by the best, to its full extent.

## CHAPTER II.

### SKETCH OF THE PROGRESS OF SOCIETY.

In speculations relating to the progress of society, the occupations of hunting, of pasturage, and agriculture, are generally considered as the principal stages by which man advanced, from the state of rudeness ascribed to him in his original condition, to the high degree of civilization which he afterwards attained, and now in many countries possesses. The comparative merit and happiness of these states have been discussed, and there have not been wanting ingenious men* to embrace the cause of savage nature, and maintain its superior excellence, with all the powers of eloquence. These opinions, however, have never made any progress; and it may be doubted whether they ever obtained a firm hold on the minds of those who advanced them. Even on the supposition that the doctrine were not altogether unfounded in reason, it is too repugnant to the sentiments

* Rousseau, &c.

which men imbibe in an advanced state of society, to be embraced in earnest. It may float lightly on the imagination of a few, but it will not alter their character, or influence their conduct.

Speculations on this subject are necessarily involved in much obscurity. In the earlier stages, direct evidence is necessarily wanting. Until a very considerable progress has been made in art, men are unable to record any memorials which might transmit information to posterity. When an intercourse is formed between a civilized nation and a rude tribe, by means of colonization or otherwise, their association not only much accelerates the improvement of the latter, but may induce a change in their condition, by fewer intermediate steps, and in different order, from what would have taken place if they had been left to the unassisted expansion of their own powers. Ingenious men who have speculated upon this subject, have been generally addicted to hypothesis, and fond of raising an amusing theory on a slight foundation. Besides, we are ignorant of the original state of human nature. We see man in very different conditions, from the utmost degree of ignorance and rudeness, to a high degree of advancement in knowledge and refinement. Yet we may be wrong in pronouncing the first to have been his original state, or in considering the several intermediate stages as necessary steps for conducting him to that degree of civilization which he has now in many countries attained. Revelation does not favour this opinion; history does not prove it; the fables of the poets are unworthy of credit; and the reasonings which have been adduced in support of it are extremely conjectural.

The progress of society is, however, an undoubted fact; and its chief steps may be reasonably presumed to have taken place with considerable uniformity, and furnish matter for rational inquiry. Investigations of this kind should not be considered as merely tending to gratify curiosity and afford scope for ingenious conjecture. If we can conduct them aright, they will unfold principles of the highest importance to mankind in every condition, and furnish rules by which we may judge of the wisdom or folly of the systems and measures adopted in that state of society under which we live.

We must not attempt to trace this subject to

its source. As the origin of the human race eludes entirely the researches of our natural faculties, we must begin our speculations concerning man by viewing him as placed in some certain condition; and, however low this may be supposed, we shall be wrong unless we assign him powers and attainments superior to, and essentially distinct from, those of the inferior animals. The faculty of speech with which he is endued in the rudest state gives him a decided and inestimable superiority.

We find, in the present state of mankind, examples of tribes or nations in a great variety of situations; and history presents us with still greater variety.

The supply of food is the first demand of nature, and will therefore call forth the first exertions of human power, and may for a time, in a great measure, engross them. In this early stage of society, an important distinction in the conditions of man will arise from the climate under which he lives. His energies, his employments, and manner of living will be regulated in conformity thereto. It will have much influence in forming his character, not only in that early stage, but at every subsequent period.

A warm climate sometimes affords a sufficient quantity of food with little or no labour. The bread tree, the cocoa tree, and some others yield a supply of wholesome and palatable food, almost at every season. The inhabitants of such a climate derive their nourishment chiefly from vegetables, and procure it easily. As they are not urged to severe exertions, nor exposed to frequent dangers, their character inclines to indolence and gentleness, and the nature of the climate is favourable to these dispositions. A considerable number can procure subsistence in a territory of moderate extent. They are therefore likely to increase rapidly, so long as they find a sufficient supply of food, and to acquire a relish for social intercourse, and be stimulated by those desires which spring up in the bosom of society.

As a cold climate without culture affords little food for man, his chief dependence is upon the animals he can catch by hunting. This employment requires severe exertion, frequently exposes him to hazard, and after all his success is precarious. He therefore becomes accustomed to brave danger, to undergo hardships, and endure hunger. His dispositions are harsh and unsocial. A large extent of country is necessary for his range, and therefore a country of hunters is thinly inhabited.

The superiority of man's understanding, in contriving means for accomplishing his ends, is conspicuously displayed in the invention of tools for the various purposes to which his exertions are directed. As none of the inferior animals appear capable of this expedient, and as it is practised in some degree by the rudest of mankind, it has been considered by some as the distinguishing characteristic of the human species, and man has been quaintly defined *a tool-making animal.* Without some kind of tool the hunter could hardly procure food. Although he acquires by habit a degree of swiftness, rarely attained by those who are more advanced in civilization, he cannot equal that of many of the animals; and the few which he might sometimes catch by surprise would afford too precarious a supply. To aid his natural defects, the use of the dart is universal, and that of the bow very common. In the management of these the savage acquires a dexterity which men bred in different habits can seldom equal.

The materials which a savage is possessed of

for constructing his tools are scanty. He points his arrows with sharp bones and flints. His axe is formed of the same materials. With this axe he cuts the bough of a tree, and shapes it into various instruments. He uses a tough animal fibre as a string to his bow. Yet, in the construction of these weapons, he displays a degree of ingenuity which, under the same disadvantages, we should find it difficult to equal.

In countries bordering on the sea, and on the banks of rivers, men have generally obtained a part of their subsistence by the occupation of fishing. The apparatus requisite for this purpose is more complex than that used in the employment of hunting. It cannot be carried on to advantage without boats or canoes. These are formed, sometimes by excavating a tree, sometimes by constructing a wooden frame and covering it with skins. These boats are managed at first by oars or paddles, and in the course of time sails are employed. By these means men were emboldened to venture on the watery element, and the first rudiments were laid of an art, which has since attained an immense magnitude, and produced most important effects on the condition of mankind.

Even in the earliest periods of society and in the most unfavourable climates, the whole of a man's time is not required for procuring food, and some parts of it are employed in supplying his other wants, of which clothing and habitation are the principal. These wants are not equally urgent in every climate, and travellers mention some savage tribes that go entirely naked: yet, with few exceptions, a considerable part of human labour and ingenuity has been employed in supplying these articles.

In warm climates, the materials for clothing as well as food are chiefly obtained from the vegetable kingdom. Leaves of trees sewed together formed the first garments, and afterwards bark prepared with more or less art. The labours of the loom were not introduced till a later period. In a country of hunters, the hides and furs of animals killed for food afford a sufficient stock of materials for clothing.

The habitations of mankind also vary with the climate. In cold climates defence against the storms of winter is the most important object; and, for attaining this, cavities are sometimes dug in the earth, especially in the sides of mountains*. In warm climates shelter from the heat of the sun and from the rains that prevail at certain seasons is chiefly regarded. The woods supply the materials. A sufficient number of stakes are driven into the ground, and the interstices wattled with branches and covered with leaves. The roofs are formed in a similar manner. In some places the huts are constructed of turf or clay. The manufacture of bricks from clay mixed with straw, and dried in the sun, or by fire, was an early invention.

Fuel may hold the next place among the necessaries of life. In cold climates mankind can hardly subsist without it; and even in warm climates the practice of preparing victuals by fire is so general that it cannot easily be dispensed with. In every country, except the coldest, which are hardly inhabitable, there is, previous to the introduction of agriculture, a sufficient quantity of wood for fuel as well as for other purposes, at hand, and nothing is wanted but the labour of cutting and breaking it. The working

* Our navigators in the most inhospitable regions have lately discovered that even ice and snow are used as materials for habitation during winter.

of coal-mines belongs to a later period of society, after wood has become scarce in consequence of the extension of agriculture.

Another source of exertion arises from the necessity of defence against ferocious animals, and against hostile tribes of men. The arts and means of defence are similar to those employed by the hunter in procuring food, but more circumspection is required, and the united efforts of numbers is necessary.

If the desires of mankind had been limited to a supply of food and necessary clothing, habitation, and fuel, his progress in art would have been very limited, and the expansion of his faculties much circumscribed. But a desire for convenience and a taste for ornament is congenial to his nature, and manifests itself, at a very early state of society, in the decorations, however rude, of the dress and utensils of the savage. This improves, as society advances, into elegance, and afterwards degenerates into the caprices of fashion and fantastical refinement.

These secondary desires have been improperly called artificial. Under different modifications they are universal, and they have a considerable influence in drawing forth the inventive and active powers of man. Their energy, however, depends much upon education and external circumstances. It is cherished by plenty, and repressed by hardship. Hence the exertions of mankind in a cold climate are chiefly urged by necessity. In a warm climate they are drawn forth by the influence of new desires, which expand according to the measure of the comfort and security they enjoy.

Although the objects which gratify these desires are valued on their own account, the pursuit of them is much invigorated by variety and emulation; by a desire of shining in the eyes of others, and of excelling others. A gentleman would be little interested in the elegance of his house and equipage, a lady would pay little attention to her dress and ornaments, were these never to be admired by others, or compared with those of their neighbours.

Emulation, in its various forms, is one of the most powerful principles of human nature. Its earliest direction is to a display of superior bodily strength, or a superiority in those exercises and exertions which have room to operate in a savage state. When art and elegance are cultivated, it is directed to a display of superior art and elegance. When distinction of property takes place, it is directed to a display of superior riches. This direction, the most reprehensible of any, in a degenerate state, almost engrosses every other. The superiority of one man above another is estimated by the extent of his possessions, and a display of splendour is set forth, not on its own account, but as a proof of the wealth of the possessor.

In the earlier stages of society there is little distinction of rank or fortune. These are introduced with the increase of wealth and the progress of art, and, increasing as these advance, attain a great magnitude, though considerably diversified in their attending circumstances. In some states a considerable share of the comforts of life is within the reach of all ranks; in others the labouring classes are restricted to mere necessaries, and in too many they are held in slavery. In some states there is a progressive gradation from the lowest to the highest rank, and every man has a hope of rising by exertion above his original station. In others there are only two classes, the noble and the vulgar, and their separation is marked by barriers almost insurmountable.

## CHAPTER III.

### OF WEALTH AND INDUSTRY.

ALTHOUGH the possession of wealth is not the most important article in the estimate of human happiness, it holds a principal place in the speculations of the political economist, not only as being the chief object to which the exertions of mankind, individually or collectively, are generally directed, but as being, in a considerable degree, the instrument by which the different states of society operate on the human mind, and produce effects, good or bad, on the condition of mankind.

Wealth has been defined as consisting in the abundant possession of those corporeal articles which are necessary, useful, or agreeable to mankind. This definition, if not altogether free from objection, is sufficiently accurate for every useful purpose.

The materials of all we possess are supplied by nature: but the quantity of many of them is greatly increased by human industry, and the rude materials which nature furnishes are thereby prepared and adapted to the various purposes which contribute to the support or accommodation of human life.

The amount of our wealth, therefore, depends on the fertility of the country we inhabit, and the quantity and skilful direction of the labour employed in cultivating the earth, and working up its produce for the supply of our wants, and the gratification of our luxuries.

Industry lays the foundation of wealth. The disposition to industry is very different in different communities, and also in different members of the same community. Some ascribe this to natural, and some to moral causes, and both may have their efficacy. A climate moderately cold, which braces, but does not chill the human constitution, which does not afford abundance of spontaneous fruit, but yields a liberal return to the labours of the husbandman, is naturally favourable to industry. A system of polity which allows every man to follow the employment most suitable to his genius and inclination, and in the place in which he can carry it on to most advantage, and secures him the safe possession and free disposal of what he acquires, promotes it by its moral tendency.

At the same time, so remarkable a diversity is observed in the disposition of different nations towards industry, that some have been led to believe there was an inherent difference in the races of men, as there are in the breeds of animals; and ascribe the superiority which some possess to a native energy granted to certain tribes, but denied to others.

However this may be, the industry of man in his actual state can only be drawn into exertion by the motives which influence human nature. Although it be true that a life of industry is happier than a life of idleness, it is no less true that some motive of hope or fear, some good to be enjoyed, or some evil to be avoided, is necessary to call forth his activity.

The West Indian slave is compelled to labour by the lash of the overseer. The European labourer may be forced by the dread of starving, or he may be swayed by the more cheering motives of procuring for himself and family a competent share of the enjoyments of life.

Although these incitements to industry may in some degree be blended, it is of importance to determine which ought to predominate ; whether the exertions of the labourer should be chiefly forced by necessity, or induced by the hopes of ameliorating his situation.

These systems will not entirely coalesce. If compulsion be resorted to for obtaining labour, the utmost exertions of the labourer will be required to afford him subsistence, and there is little more he can expect. If comfort and a share of affluence be the reward of much industry, a moderate share of industry will be sufficient for procuring necessaries, and sometimes no more may be exerted.

Arguments said to be founded on experience are adduced in favour of the harsher system. It is alleged that in time of plenty less labour is performed ; that a man who can earn subsistence by working three days in a week will not easily be induced to continue at work for six days ; and that an increase of wages, from whatever cause, leads to intemperance.

If we extend our views to the improvement of human nature and the promotion of general happiness, there cannot be room for hesitation. A system which condemns the most numerous and useful part of mankind to earn a scanty subsistence by hard labour, without hope of improving their circumstances, or cheering the intervals of labour by a share of the comforts which nature and industry afford; a system which considers that portion of our fellow creatures as mere machines, to be employed in gratifying the luxury, or soothing the caprice of their superiors, for whose service they were formed; a system which tends to stifle every generous sentiment, and call forth the malignant passions of envy and hatred, or reduce the mind of the labourer to the lowest degree of abasement,—such a system cannot be reprobated in terms of too great severity.

It may be thought this picture is overcharged. Perhaps it is so: but the bad effects of the system are only limited by the impracticability of carrying it fully into execution. Its tendency is to produce the evils abovementioned, and it only falls short of doing so because it cannot be enforced completely.

If we confine our attention to the quantity of work performed as the only valuable object, even in that limited point of view, there are sufficient reasons for preferring the more generous system. Hope is a more enlivening and active principle than fear. If a man's prospects be confined to procuring necessaries from day to day by hard labour, his spirits are depressed, and his exertions enfeebled. Hope, indeed, is so natural to the human mind, that it can hardly be eradicated by any treatment, however severe: but so far as the coercive system is established, hope is damped, with all the energy that springs from it. Let industry be rewarded by competency, and we need not fear but industry will in general prevail.

The man who can procure necessaries by part of the labour which he is capable of performing, will seldom stop at that point, but will endeavour by further exertions to obtain a share of such things as contribute to his present gratification, or to lay up a store for future exigencies: yet labour, when carried too far, either in severity or duration, is oppressive to human nature, and every man will stop at a certain point. This will be different in different men, not only from the inequality of their bodily strength, but the difference of their spirit, activity, and habits, and the force of their acquired desires; but all will stop at a lower point than if they were labouring to keep themselves from starving. It does not, however, follow that a smaller quantity of work will be done under cheering views, than when the labourer is forced to exert his strength to the utmost. Such compulsion may produce a greater temporary effect; but it exhausts the powers both of body and mind, and brings on imbecility and premature decay.

A man is induced to continue at labour by the prospect of obtaining a reward for it; he is inclined to discontinue it by fatigue. The stronger motive will prevail. Whatever adds to the force of the former, or weakens that of the latter, will increase the quantity and produce of labour.

The strength of the motives to labour depends upon the quantity of desirable articles which that labour can procure, and the relish which the man has for the enjoyments they afford. He will exert, if he can thereby procure a certain measure of wealth. If the acquisition within his reach be lower, he may give way to indolence. Every improvement in art and skill which renders labour more productive, adds to the quantity of labour performed by offering a higher reward for it. It is, therefore, an erroneous system to tax the luxuries of the poor, and lessen their enjoyments, with the design of forcing their industry. For necessaries a poor man will exert himself to the utmost, but in regard to luxuries he will balance the fatigue of obtaining them against the gratification they afford. It is absurd to suppose he will work more for the sake of obtaining a smaller than a greater share of enjoyment. Things, not in themselves necessary, become so in a great measure from habit; and when the habit is acquired, a man will exert himself much rather than forego his wonted gratification. Tobacco is at first a nauseous drug; but those who are accustomed to use it cannot easily dispense with it, and will work hard rather than go without their tobacco.

The industry of the labourer is best drawn forth by cherishing those desires which it will require all his exertions to gratify: and this does not require any delicate management. They spring up naturally, if obstructions be not thrown in the way. The savage Indian has no relish for the enjoyments of civilized life: but a taste for these enjoyments begins at an early period of society, and increases at every step of its progress. To be well fed and comfortably clothed and lodged; to have a sufficient supply of fuel in a cold climate; to be able to engage in the connections of a family at that age when the propensities of nature are strongest; to maintain and educate one's children in a decent manner; to lay up some provision as a resource for sickness or old age; these are desires sufficiently powerful and universal to excite industry, and sufficiently diversified to give it ample scope.

Industry is promoted by the following means.

By directing education and early habits in a manner that tends to increase bodily strength and reconcile the mind to application and perseverance;

By placing within the reach of the labourer a competent share of those enjoyments which are suitable to his station;

By affording him, at all times, an opportunity of exerting his industry to advantage;

By securing him the free possession and enjoyment of what his industry has gained;

By offering, not only a share of the enjoyments of life, but respectability and an advancement in the scale of society, as a reward for successful industry.

The case of an isolated individual has seldom, if ever, existed. Such a being, if placed in a favourable climate, and possessed of a few tools, might not only continue to live, but might procure some small share of the comforts of life. This is well illustrated in the excellent fictitious history of Robinson Crusoe, which is said to be founded on the real fact of one Alexander Selkirk having been left several years in a desert island. Mankind, in every condition which falls under our view at present, or of which we have any authentic records, have been associated in tribes more or less numerous, and have possessed some weapons and other implements. Their union in society has given rise to various expedients which increase the efficacy of labour in the production of commodities, and it is instructive to trace these, as far as we are able, from their rudiments, and mark their progress.

By the mere co-operation of a number of men many things are done which exceed the power of an individual. Heavy bodies are removed from places where they are cumbersome, or brought to places where they are useful; works of magnitude are constructed. A single man could not build a modern house of the better kind, though he were bred to the employment and supplied with the usual tools. He could not make or navigate a ship, nor dig and labour a mine.

Among the means which have contributed, successively or collaterally, to the increase of wealth, some of the more remarkable are, division of labour and exchange of commodities; application of the strength of animals and other natural powers; use of metals; machinery of every kind; appropriation of land; use of money; lending on interest; paper credit; foreign commerce; colonization, and foreign settlements. Some of these are coeval with society, and find place in the smallest and simplest communities. Others cannot be introduced till large states be formed, and mankind have made considerable progress in arts and civilization.

Division of labour is justly reckoned among the most efficacious means of rendering it more productive, and has been much attended to by writers on political economy. It commences in a very early state of society. Cain, we are told, was a tiller of the ground; but Abel kept a flock of sheep; and Tubal Cain was an artificer in brass and iron. Its scope is much enlarged by the progress of art. A man constantly engaged in any ordinary mechanical profession performs more and better work than another who applies to a variety of employments by turns; and in the nicer works of art, the man who gives all his time and attention to a single manual operation acquires a high degree of despatch and dexterity. The advantage gained by the division of labour in the pin manufactory is estimated to increase its efficacy at least some hundred times, and instances might be adduced in which its effect is still more considerable. This principle, however, is not equally applicable to every kind of labour, and some of the cases in which it is carried farthest are comparatively trivial. In the labours of agriculture, the most important of any, its application is considerably limited.

Exchange of commodities, either by barter or sale, and division of labour, accompany each other. Without exchange of commodities there could be no division of labour; and there would be little room for the former, unless different commodities were placed in different hands by means of the latter. Without recurring, as some have done, to a natural instinct inclining men to traffic, the utility of the practice is sufficient to account for its early and universal adoption. When traffic is carried on by the exchange of commodities, without the intervention of any medium or a reference to any, it is called barter; and as this is the simplest, it was the earliest kind. It still takes place in the transactions of civilized nations with those in a state of comparative rudeness, as well as in the latter among themselves. The European barters his wares with the Indian of North America for a certain number of furs; and our navigators trafficked with the inhabitants of the South Sea islands by purchasing their hogs in return for iron, feathers, and toys. So universal is the practice, that savage tribes produce their commodities on the arrival of strangers, and carry on a traffic by signs, when neither of them understand a word of the language of the other.

It is not by his personal labour alone that man supplies his wants. He causes the stronger and more tractable animals to labour for him. He causes the elements of water, wind, and steam, to labour for him.

The operations of agriculture were at first performed by manual labour. Shovels only were used in those parts of America where agriculture was practised, when that country was discovered. But the training of cattle, and application of their strength to plowing, carriages, and other purposes, was introduced at an early period. Oxen were used for these purposes in Egypt in the time of the patriarchs, and in Arabia in the time of Job. The horse, the most useful animal, seems not to have been had recourse to so soon. The ass, the camel, the rein-deer, and some other animals, are employed in climates to which their nature is adapted.

The first natural element that man made subservient to his purposes was fire. Universal as this now is, and necessary as we deem it, there is sufficient evidence that some tribes, in their earliest state, were entirely ignorant of it; and in some which have lately been discovered it was equally wanting. Besides its use in cherishing the human constitution in cold climates, and in the preparation of food, many of the most important arts almost entirely depend on it. The smelting, refining, and working of metals, glass-making, brick-making, pottery, sugar-baking, brewing, and many others, fall under this description.

The application of water to work for man was not a very early invention. Corn-mills were wrought by manual labour, and afterwards driven by cattle, before water was applied to that purpose. This invention seems to have been made in Asia about the time of Mithridates, or earlier. Water-mills were known in Rome in the time of Augustus, but were not then common. They had become so in the reign of Justinian, as appears from his Code; and the knowledge of them was soon extended to all the nations of Europe. The earliest application of water-mills was for grinding corn, and it is still the most important. But they are now also employed for sawing timber, hammering metals, and many other purposes. Water-wheels are commonly driven by the impulse of falling water; but they are also constructed on flowing rivers, or placed on the sea-beach so as to be driven by the flowing and ebbing of the tide. Modern improvements in hydraulics have led to other ways of employing the power of water in places where water-wheels could not be used with advantage.

Wind, a more unmanageable element, has also been employed to work for man. The invention of wind-mills is later than that of water-mills, and its origin is not well known; but they seem likewise to have been an eastern invention, and to have been brought into use in Europe about the time of the Crusades. These mills are chiefly used in countries, such as the Netherlands, where a sufficiency of running water for driving water-mills cannot be procured, and have been brought there to the greatest perfection.

The very important use of the power of wind in navigation will fall under our consideration in another place.

The power of water can only be procured in certain places; that of wind is only supplied by nature at certain times. Another power, that of steam, has been had recourse to, which is neither limited in regard to place nor time, but may be applied wherever fuel can be provided, and is completely under management. The application of this power is a recent invention. It is less obvious than the other natural powers, and requires a more intricate apparatus: but now threatens to supplant them all. It has hardly been in use a century; and for a considerable part of that time was applied to no other purpose but that of raising water from mines. Of late years the machinery requisite for its operations has been much improved by Mr. Watt and others; and engines have been constructed on every scale, from a fraction of a horse-power to those of above an hundred, and applied for almost every kind of work. In the earlier engines the pressure of the atmosphere was properly the acting power, steam being only used for producing a vacuum; but in the present ones the elasticity of the steam also acts as a power. The immediate effect of this power is to produce a vibratory motion; but mechanical means have been found of deriving from it a rotatory motion, nearly as uniform as that produced by a water-wheel.

One of the latest and most useful applications of steam is that of giving motion to shipping. This was first done in America, about twenty years ago, and is now in common use in Britain and other countries. It is particularly suited to passage vessels, whose arrival at their place of destination, when impelled by this power, may in general be accurately depended on. By this means the navigation of the river Mississippi, which was formerly very difficult, is so much facilitated as to promise to open the means of improvement to an immense tract of country, hitherto almost secluded from communication with civilized nations.

We may also notice another artificial power—that of gunpowder, which is used in some mechanical operations. The principal one is the splitting of hard rocks, which can scarcely be effected by any other power whatever.

The use of metals is so important, that the progress of a nation in wealth and comfort depends considerably on the measure in which it possesses them. Some nations are entirely destitute of them, and their rank in the scale of society is of consequence very low. The substances from which metals, especially the more useful ones, are obtained, are generally so hidden in the earth, and bear so little resemblance to the metal in its perfect and useful state, and require such intricate operations to be brought to that state, that it is difficult to account for their discovery by means merely human. The most useful metals were, however, known to the nations of the ancient world at an earlier period than authentic history reaches to. Gold and silver seem to have been first known, as might be expected, from their being frequently found in their metallic state. They are, however, too soft, and are obtained in too small quantities, to be useful for general purposes. Copper was next in order. Iron, the most useful of any, being more recondite, was a later discovery. The operations of smelting the ores, and forging the metals, if inventions merely human, are surprising efforts of human ingenuity. No less so is the art of multiplying, in some measure, the number of metals by mixture; thus forming alloys, more useful for many purposes than the simple metals of which they are composed. Among these, brass, a composition of copper and zinc, and bronze, a composition of copper and tin, deserve particular notice. The art of converting iron from the untractable state in which it comes from the forge, to a malleable substance fit for ordinary purposes, or into a harder substance, steel, for weapons and tools, is no less remarkable. At the discovery of America, the more advanced nations were possessed of gold, silver, and copper; but not of iron, tin, or lead. The ruder tribes had no metals whatever.

Akin to the discovery of the metals, is that of glass-making; so useful for furnishing the more convenient method of introducing light into our houses, and for many other purposes. This art is later, but is of great antiquity, though it has been much improved in modern times.

The art of pottery, also very ancient, affords many articles which contribute to the accommodation of mankind.

Man can do little by his labour without the aid of tools. We find no tribe entirely unprovided with them; but their number has been much enlarged, and their structure improved, by the progress of art. In agriculture, the shovel and the rake have been succeeded by the plough and the harrow; and the first rude and simple forms of these instruments have been succeeded by others more commodious. The scythe, the sowing and drilling machines, the fanners, have been introduced in their proper places; and the very recent invention of the thrashing-mill has nearly superseded the hard manual labour by which that operation was formerly performed.

The use of tools in mechanic arts is still more extensive. In timber-work, the axe, the adze, the plane, the saw, and the turning-lathe, enable the artificer to shape his material into innumerable forms with facility. The last-named instrument has been much diversified, and applied to the speedy and accurate execution of many of the most curious works of art.

In the department of clothing, the use of the distaff and simple loom, by which the first webs were formed, was a considerable advance above the condition wherein skins and leaves were the only materials used for that purpose. The spinning-wheel followed—the loom was improved. Yet, from these, as they were constructed some centuries ago, to the machinery of Arkwright, and the complex looms which fabricate damask and imitate tapestry, how vast is the distance!

The department of hardware presents us with examples of ingenuity no less remarkable. By the complicated machinery in the workshops of Birmingham and Sheffield, an immense variety of articles, ornamental or useful, are formed with ease, despatch, and accuracy. We have tools to make tools, in several successive gradations.

Though we can only mention a few instances, we cannot forbear taking notice of that very valuable instrument, the printing-press, by which writing is indefinitely multiplied, and whatever is valuable in science or literature communicated to the public and transmitted to posterity. The general circulation of newspapers in the present time, however improperly they are sometimes conducted, has a powerful effect in the dissemination of knowledge among every rank of men.

# CHAPTER IV.

## OF REWARDS FOR INVENTIONS.

As the produce of labour depends so much on the direction it receives from human ingenuity, whatever contributes to excite or enlarge the inventive powers of man, is valuable from the increase thereby afforded to the materials for human enjoyment, as well as for the more important purpose of advancing the powers of the human mind to a higher degree of improvement.

Some rare instances of superior inventive talents have occurred in nations still in a rude and ignorant state. But in general these talents expand, and become eminently useful, in a more advanced period of society. Nature has endued a sufficient number of mankind with such a share of genius, as, with moderate culture, or at least if not depressed, will exhibit itself in useful discoveries, and will sometimes break forth in spite of much discouragement.

Errors in polity may check the natural development of genius and retard the consequent improvement of art. If a large portion of the community be held in actual slavery, or reduced by oppression to a state not much better than slavery; if a man be obliged to follow the occupation of his forefathers; if aristocratical maxims raise an insurmountable barrier between different ranks, and deny any countenance to genius struggling to emerge; if the useful arts be held in contempt; if the prevailing sentiments favour an attachment to ancient practices, and dislike to innovation; under such discouragements genius languishes, and the progress of art is slow.

It is the duty of Government to counteract these errors. It has little power to call forth genius by direct institutions, yet what little can be done with a view to this ought not to be neglected.

An adequate reward for useful discoveries is a debt due by the public. This reward either arises from public esteem, or is of a pecuniary nature.

It is a common observation that men given to scheme, although great benefactors to the public, often injure their own fortunes. The observation is just, and the fact much to be regretted. One useful discovery may fully repay the debt which every man owes to the wealth of the community: but among ten schemes nine are generally unsuccessful. The expense of the unsuccessful experiments falls on the projector, and there is a risk of his being a loser even by those which succeed. Before he brings his discovery to perfection he bestows much time, and makes many trials, and after it is known and adopted by the public, it affords him little further emolument.

There are three ways by which a useful discovery may afford an advantage to its author; —by his keeping it a secret; by obtaining an exclusive patent for exercising it; or by his receiving a direct pecuniary reward from the public.

The method of concealment is not applicable to every kind of discovery; an operation in chemistry may be kept secret; but improvements in agriculture and mechanics, if practised, must be known. Even when concealment is practicable, there is always a risk of discovery, and then there is an end of the inventor's reward, at a period entirely undetermined, sooner or later, as chance may order it. But the principal objection to this mode of reward is drawn from the injury the public sustains. The inventor is deterred by the fear of discovery from exercising his art so extensively as the public service may require. He may be inclined to confine it to a narrow scale, such as he can manage personally, or with few assistants, and there is a risk of the invention being lost to the public at his death.

The second method of rewarding discoveries, is by granting a patent for a monopoly. If this be limited to a moderate duration, it does not deserve the censure sometimes bestowed on it. During the currency of the patent, the public are gainers to a certain extent, for it is the interest of the patentee to bring the subject of his invention to market on moderate terms; and, when the patent expires, the public have the full benefit. It is, perhaps, the most unexceptionable mode of rewarding useful discoveries: as the article for which the patent is granted must find its own way to public use, the reward can only attach to articles by which the public is benefited, or supposes itself to be so, and the extent of the reward will generally be in proportion to the value of the invention.

Patents may sometimes be granted for trifling articles which are introduced by fashion into general use, and become highly lucrative to the patentee. When this happens, an individual gains without deserving it; but the public can hardly be deemed to sustain an injury. The gain of the patentee is a tax on the caprice of those who use the article. A patent for a paltry improvement on shoe-buckles is said to have made the fortune of the proprietor.

The restrictions under which patents are granted by the laws of Britain, seem to remove every objection to which this mode of reward is liable. The duration is limited to the term of fourteen years, the applicant is obliged to give a full specification of his invention, and the patent is set aside if the specification be imperfect, or if it appear that his claim to the discovery is not well founded.

In a few instances a patent of longer duration has been granted by Act of Parliament. This is exceptionable in regard to precedent and departure from general principle. It would be better, if in any case, from peculiar circumstances, a patent for the usual term be insufficient, to aid it by a pecuniary reward.

To this head we may refer the right which authors have to the exclusive publication of their works. This is now extended for a longer term, and in all cases subsists during the life of the author.

The third method is that of a direct pecuniary reward granted by the public. This method is exceptionable from the risk of partiality in bestowing it. Sometimes through error, sometimes through favour, rewards may be given for pretended discoveries, or such as are of small value. At other times they may be refused, or sparingly bestowed, and the inventors may be driven to the expedient of concealment. It is hardly possible, even with the best information and utmost impartiality, to apportion the reward so well to the utility of the invention as patents do. There are cases, however, where this method should be had recourse to: when a valuable discovery is of such a nature that it is hardly possible to prevent it from being generally practised. A new plough may be the subject of a patent; but a new method of ploughing must be rewarded by a premium, or not at all. The discovery of a method for recovering decayed trees was a proper subject for a premium, being effected by a composition which, when known, every gardener could make and use. Rewards are proper when, from the nature of the invention, patents are not applicable, or where there is a strong call to communicate the full benefit of it at once to the public. The rewards offered for discovering the longitude at sea are proper. The physician who introduced the practice of vaccination, received most deservedly, a liberal reward from the public.

Societies have been established for promoting agriculture and useful arts, by bestowing premiums on useful discoveries, or on the best articles of produce or manufacture exhibited, or on the performance of ordinary operations in the best manner. These societies, well conducted, as they generally are, may do considerable good: for the small rewards they bestow are accompanied with a higher honorary gratification, and it is hardly possible they can do any harm. Suppose premiums granted for introducing modes of agriculture into a district of the country, which are practised in other districts with advantage. These may be unsuitable to the climate, and may not succeed. But if among many trials a few be successful, the public is amply recompensed for the expense of them all. The farmer is restrained from experiment by local prejudices, as well as by the real risk of failure, and stands in need of the encouragement of a premium. It is in some measure owing to this, that the valuable improvements of raising sown grass, and other green crops, have been introduced into some parts of the country, and plantations, especially of the hardy larix, cover many of our hills that were accounted unsusceptible of improvement.

But premiums should never be extended beyond the term requisite for the introduction of a practice into a place where it was unknown before. A farmer may be prevented from sowing turnips by ignorance or timidity, till he see his neighbour do it with success. But the practice, if proper, when once introduced, will make rapid progress. To continue premiums for raising any article on an extensive scale, and during a long course of years, is not only a useless but a pernicious expenditure of public money. It is forcing a species of culture which does not suit the climate. The large sums bestowed in Scotland for many years, in premiums for promoting the culture of flax, seem liable to this censure.

Societies formed for the promotion of science, conducted upon principles entirely honorary, are entitled to the highest respect, and seem exempted from any risk of misapplication. Eminent genius may not require their fostering care, and if a few be engaged by their means in pursuits for which nature did not intend them, the public hardly feels the loss; yet experience concurs with reason in evincing the advantages which result from the association of ingenious men in their philosophical researches.

Useful as the art of printing is, there are many nice points in the application of art to its various purposes which are better taught by exhibition, accompanied by oral direction. Hence the utility of public lectures where the application of science to practical purposes is illustrated by experiment. These lectures may aim at the development of the abstruser parts of science, or they may be of a more superficial nature, and both are useful to different classes of hearers, and deserving of encouragement.

The efficacy of labour is carried to the utmost extent by the vast stock of practical knowledge accumulated in a succession of ages. Art and skill are progressive, but their progress, in different ages and nations, is very unequal. In China some of the more useful arts were known at an earlier period than in Europe, but they have never attained the same perfection. The human mind exerts an energy at certain periods which political institutions cannot do much to forward, nor can its causes be fully investigated by human sagacity.

But there is little risk, as society is now constituted, of losing what is once attained. By means of the press and of oral instruction every discovery, whether the result of investigation, or the effect of accident, soon becomes generally known, and is introduced into general practice. Every improvement in agriculture, in metallurgy, and the other practical branches of chemistry, in mechanics, enlarges permanently the power of man over the material world.

The conquest of the civilized world by barbarous nations is the only event that could cause the loss of what has been acquired. Something of this kind took place when the Roman empire was subverted, and when the polished nations of Asia were overrun by hordes of Tartars. Modern Europe is little exposed to a similar hazard. There does not now exist an extent of territory in a barbarous state sufficient to furnish numbers for the conquest of what is civilized, and the more general diffusion of knowledge among the moderns would even secure the permanency of any after conquest. The entire extermination of the former inhabitants is impracticable, and the conquerors would acquire the arts and adopt the manners of the survivors. This has happened several times in China, which has been subdued by Tartars, without losing the civilization it had attained.

# CHAPTER V.

## OF CAPITAL.

To obtain distinct views of the progress of wealth it may be proper to inquire, first, into that measure of it which a community of a less or greater extent may acquire by the resources of its own industry and skill, when unconnected with the rest of the world, or surrounded with a wall of brass, as Bishop Berkeley supposes; and afterwards into the effects produced by a commercial intercourse with other countries.

In a former chapter we have taken a cursory view of the means of acquiring wealth. The fruits of human industry are seldom entirely consumed by that generation which produces them. A part remains for the benefit of succeeding generations. Even in the rudest state, the hut which a man has built, and the simple tools he has made, are useful to his children and successors; and, for the most part, every generation transmits a larger share of wealth to its posterity than it received from its ancestors. The wealth thus accumulated is called CAPITAL.

The stock of practical knowledge above mentioned is an inheritance of great value; but seems rather to be a means of increasing the power of acquiring wealth, than to constitute any part of it. A more tangible inheritance is handed down in every age to posterity.

Improvements in agriculture constitute a valuable part of this wealth. The earth, even in the more favourable climates, requires to be cultivated in order to yield any considerable quantity of food. The effect of the labour bestowed on it does not always terminate with the succeeding crop, but often renders the soil more productive for a long time after. The operations of ploughing and manuring, indeed, only answer a temporary purpose; but those of clearing, draining, levelling, and inclosing, are beneficial for ages. Some of these improvements can hardly be lost by neglect, and all of them can be preserved by a much less portion of labour than was requisite at first for their execution.

A person advanced in life is struck with pleasing astonishment when he observes the improvements that have taken place during his own time; barren heaths converted into fertile fields, rich pastures, or smiling gardens; wretched modes of husbandry giving way to a spirited and far more productive system; the cattle more vigorous; the peasants exhibiting higher indications of plenty and comfort. If he could compare the present state of the country with that which it presented some centuries ago, the contrast would be still more remarkable.

To this head we may refer the stock of useful plants which are cultivated in their present state of perfection. Some of these, as wheat, are so much ameliorated by culture, that we are hardly able now to trace their native climate. Others, as potatoes, have been introduced more lately, and therefore their history is better known, but they form an accession no less valuable to the produce of the soil. To this head also belongs the stock of domestic animals, which, through the gift of nature, have been multiplied and improved by human care, and by the attention given to the choice of breeds.

Some countries are covered with wood by the luxuriant hand of nature, and must be cleared to render them healthy and fit for cultivation. Others do not contain, at least in modern times, a sufficiency of wood for shelter and other purposes; and industry is requisite for supplying the deficiency. The labour exerted, whether in planting or clearing, so far as it renders the country more fertile or more commodious, is alike beneficial, and is the means of transmitting a better inheritance to posterity.

The working of a mine, in some sense, exhausts the stores of the earth. Yet as these hidden stores only become useful by discovery, whether accidental, or the result of laborious search, the stock of general wealth is augmented by known mines; and the operations necessary for setting a mine agoing constitute part of its value.

Highways, bridges, and navigable canals, by facilitating conveyance, promote all kinds of improvement, and add much to the value of a country.

The other parts of accumulated wealth consist chiefly of the following articles :—

The great variety of tools used in manufacture, engines and mills of every kind, with their appendages, wheel-carriages, furnaces, apparatus for experimental philosophy.

All buildings, whether appropriated for places of manufacture, for private dwelling, or for public purposes; churches, halls, colleges, schools, theatres, hospitals, granaries, warehouses, prisons.

The quantity of corn, and other provisions, laid up in store.

The whole stock of articles intended for future consumption, whether completely prepared for use, or requiring further manufacture; wool, flax, cotton, silk, leather, metals, and other materials, and all the commodities into which they are formed.

The shipping belonging to the country, artificial harbours, and improvements of natural ones; light-houses; boats, and implements for fishing.

Nor must we omit those articles which, though not, strictly speaking, convertible to use, become objects of desire by gratifying taste or caprice. Under this head we may comprehend pictures, statues, and other works of elegant art. Musical instruments, libraries, and books, wherever kept, claim a very respectable place in our lists. The lowest should be assigned to those which only contribute to ostentation, or are sought after for their rarity; diamonds and other precious stones, and uncommon productions of nature or art.

What place shall we assign to the precious metals, to which alone the multitude consider the character of wealth as belonging? These metals are applicable to some purposes in life, and in this view they have a value, though not a very high one. In point of real utility, silver is much inferior to iron, and gold still more so. But the precious metals derive their chief value from their universal use as a medium of commerce, and representative of every kind of wealth. When applied to this use they become MONEY, the nature and advantages of which require a particular discussion.

# CHAPTER VI.

## OF MONEY.

We have already mentioned barter, or the exchange of one commodity for another, as the simplest and earliest mode of traffic. It labours, however, under great inconveniences. A. has a commodity to spare, and B. wants it. A. stands in need of a different commodity, with which B. cannot supply him, though he is possessed of others for which A. has no occasion. A. is possessed of a perishable commodity, and as he has no immediate wants to supply, he is desirous of parting with it, provided he can thereby acquire a power of receiving afterwards what his future occasions may require. B. wants something to afford him present subsistence, or enable him to carry on his labour till the article he proposes to give in return be fit for use. In these cases commercial intercourse cannot be carried on by barter alone. Confidence and credit may in part supply the defect: but this will be done more effectually and universally by means of some standard article which is considered as an equivalent for every kind of commodity. Whoever possesses a sufficient quantity of that standard may obtain any thing which his wants require, and the country affords, in return: and therefore every man is willing to accept of that standard, in exchange for what he has to spare. The standard upon which the public has fixed this value, and which is actually applied to these purposes, is called MONEY.

The essential requisites of the materials for money are rarity, durability, and susceptibility of minute and accurate division. If their external properties be splendid, and if they be previously used for purposes of ornament and magnificence, they will more readily acquire that popular value which is necessary to give them circulation. All these qualities are united in gold and silver, which, therefore, with few exceptions, have been employed as money in civilized nations in every age. Copper or brass was used in Rome in the earlier ages, for want of gold and silver, and is still in general use for articles of small value. Iron was had recourse to in Sparta, with the design of banishing luxury. In some parts of Africa and India, certain species of shells are employed as money.

The use of money commenced at so early a period, that we are not to expect, nor do we meet with, a distinct history of its introduction. It appears to have been known in the age of the patriarchs, and probably, like other institutions of powerful efficacy on the state of society, it was not a contrivance of speculative wisdom, but derived its origin and reception from occasional circumstances. An estimation of the precious metals for other purposes preceded their use as money. Abraham sent jewels of gold and silver by his servants who went for Rebecca. The affixing a stamp on money, or forming it into pieces of a certain weight, were improvements of a later period. Money was weighed, not numbered, in the earlier transactions.

Money may be considered as an engine or tool by which commerce is facilitated, and a very powerful one. It contributes, perhaps, more than highways and canals, to an easy exchange of commodities. Gold and silver, therefore, being the materials of money, constitute, as such, a part of the public wealth. We are at present inquiring into the wealth of a country considered as detached from the rest of the world, and in that view we apprehend the quantity of money is of no consequence whatever. The money value of commodities depends upon the proportion between the quantity of money in circulation and the quantity of commodities brought into the market. Although money be a tool, it differs in this from every other tool, that the effect is produced alike by a greater or a lesser quantity. If the quantity of money in an isolated country were doubled, other circumstances remaining the same, the only effect would be to double the nominal price of labour, of corn, and of every other commodity. If the quantity of money be diminished, prices would fall in the same proportion. The effect of circulating paper, used as a substitute for money, is in this respect the same.

Commercial transactions may be carried on without money or other circulating medium, but not with the same facility, and therefore, probably, not to the same extent. As commerce is a principal source of wealth, any incumbrance upon commerce tends to lessen the general wealth; and want of money, or an effective substitute, is of that nature. But the degree in which money facilitates commerce is the measure of its value as a constituent part of wealth, and this bears a certain proportion to the mass of commodities brought to market, though it is not easy to assign what that proportion is. A small quantity of money, when prices are settled, is sufficient to answer the purpose, and the greatest quantity can do no more.

The value of the precious metals arises, as we have observed, partly from their utility or estimation as commodities, and partly from their universal reception as a circulating medium of commerce. The latter part is by far the more important. If their use for that purpose were discontinued, their value would greatly fall. We may conceive the existence of an article possessing the properties of rarity, divisibility, and durability, but applicable to no useful purpose, and entirely unfit for ornament or magnificence. Such an article might be adopted as money. Though the supposition be imaginary, it may assist us in distinguishing the value which the precious metals derive from being used as money, from that which arises from their application to other purposes.

The exchange of commodities cannot easily be effected without referring their value to some common standard, though nothing of this kind be received or delivered in the transaction. This standard may be a certain quantity of gold or silver, reckoned by weight or tale, a bushel of corn, a yard of cloth, a bar of iron, a pound of tobacco, or a mere denomination. *Makutes* * are said, by Montesquieu, and some other writers, (perhaps erroneously) to be of this kind. The inhabitants of the coast of Angola, according to their account, settle the relative value of the articles which they exchange by affixing to each that of a certain number of makutes, although there be no such material article as a makute in existence. However the fact may be, the supposition implies no absurdity. It may be doubted, however, whether the assumption of such a standard be not too refined an expedient to have occurred to men in that simple state of society which preceded the use of gold and silver.

An imaginary standard might facilitate bar-

* A Makute is now understood to be the name of a kind of net-work used by the Africans for clothing. Mr. Park mentions a bar of iron, as used in other parts of Africa for a general standard. Neither of these are usually received or delivered in their transactions.

ter, but could not serve the purpose of money. A person who delivered goods to another without receiving goods in return, would only have the credit of the buyer to trust to for being recompensed at a future time. A payment in money gives him an immediate and certain equivalent *.

A prejudice in regard to money as constitut-

* We have ventured, on this subject, to differ from the doctrine laid down in the Edinburgh Review, in their strictures on an Essay on the Theory of Money and Exchange, by Thomas Smith, October, 1808. The able writer of that article, after pointing out the impracticability of finding an actual standard of invariable value, and ridiculing the recourse to an ideal one, puts the question, " When you go to market with a guinea, does it not purchase in proportion to the *value of the metal* contained in the guinea ? " And observes, that " selling a sheep for a piece of gold, or a piece of silver of a certain weight, is visibly the same species of transaction as selling it for a certain weight of salt, or of corn. The gold is the commodity purchased with the sheep, in the one case ; the salt or corn is the commodity purchased with it in the other. It is the barter of two commodities, the value of which are equal. The one party has bought a sheep, the other party has bought a quantity of gold. Money is nothing but a commodity bought or sold for its value, like other commodities ;" and a good deal more to the same purpose. We apprehend that an important distinction is overlooked in this view of the subject. The sheep, the salt, the corn, and other commodities which might have been mentioned, have an intrinsic value, as being required for the sustenance or comfort of human life. The value of the gold is arbitrary, arising chiefly from its use as a medium of commerce. Discontinue its application to that purpose, and its value will shrink into very little.

ing wealth is so general, that some further illustration of our views on the subject may not be improper. On this occasion, some tautology may be more excusable than too much brevity.

The stock of wealth belonging to a community is the aggregate of whatever affords subsistence or enjoyment, or furnishes the means of procuring or increasing them ; land, with all its improvements, highways, corn in store, mines, materials for manufacture, manufactured goods, tools, buildings, shipping, and the like. All these contribute, directly or indirectly, to supply our wants or gratify our desires, natural or acquired. The more of these a country possesses, it is the richer, and, so far as external things contribute to happiness, the people are the happier. But money, as such, does not contribute to the stock of enjoyment, and ought not to be accounted wealth; and if the inconsiderable use of gold and silver for plate and like purposes be set aside, it is a matter of indifference whether the quantity of these metals be great or small, or whether they be wanting altogether, provided commerce could be carried on as well without them. Land and goods of every kind are wealth to their respective proprietors; and the aggregate of their several portions constitutes the mass of general wealth. A. has corn, B. has cattle, C. has wine, D. has manufactured goods, or tools and materials for manufacture; E. has money, with which he can purchase corn or whatever he has occasion for, at the usual price. The situation of E. is equally eligible as that of any of the others; and in reckoning the wealth of the whole, why should not the money of E. be included, as well as the corn of A., the cattle of B., the wine of C., and the manufactures of D.? If the money of E. were annihilated, still the quantity of corn, cattle, wine, and manufactures appropriated to the use of this small community is the same; but E. has no share in it, and depends on the generosity of the others. That he may not be exposed to this hardship, let us suppose that he purchases part of the commodities belonging to the others, till the money be equally distributed among them, after which let the money be annihilated; nothing is thereby abstracted from the means of maintenance and enjoyment which these five persons command, and they ought not to be accounted poorer. If a community consisted only of five, or even if it were extended to fifty persons, their commercial transactions with each other could be carried on without money; and in so narrow a community, unconnected with the rest of the world, money would be of no use. But in large communities, as commodities cannot be exchanged without commerce, so commerce goes heavily on without a circulating medium. Money enables us more easily to obtain a supply of our wants in return for what we have to spare. It therefore renders our property more valuable, and may be accounted to increase the general wealth in so far as it relieves commerce from embarrassment.

But the advantages arising from a circulating medium have only a limited value. Commerce, without money, is practicable, though attended with difficulties; and a certain proportion of the general industry would be applied for counteracting these difficulties. Let us suppose that the industry required for that purpose is equal in value to one-twentieth part of the commodities annually produced and exchanged, and let the value of these without money be denominated M; let an amount of money, less or more, be introduced; then the embarrassment to commerce being removed, and the industry applied to counteract it set free, the annual produce of the community will be raised to $M + \frac{1}{20} M$. If the quantity of money introduced be five millions, M will be equal to one hundred millions, and the value of the annual produce of the community will be augmented to one hundred and five millions. If ten millions of money had been introduced, the value would have been two hundred and ten millions, yet the real wealth of the country would be the same in the one case as in the other. It is not the wealth of the country that has increased, but the value of the currency that has diminished, when the nominal value is raised from one hundred and five to two hundred and ten millions, by the introduction of an additional quantity of five millions of currency.

Since the discovery of America, an immense quantity of labour and capital has been expended in mining operations, attended with no small waste of human life and infliction of human misery. If the acquisition of the large quantity of the precious metals from these mines has been attended with no other consequence than the increase of the nominal price of commodities in all commercial countries, how much is this misapplication of capital and labour to be regretted! Little has been done for the improvement of the countries which supply these metals, though they be very susceptible of it. What a different appearance would they have now exhibited if the same capital and labour had been expended in purposes of real utility!

# CHAPTER VII.

## OF VALUE AND PRICE.

THERE is no subject which has given occasion to more controversy among writers on political economy than that of *value.* This arises partly from the loose manner in which the term has been applied; and from its being used not unfrequently by the same writer in different senses, without his remarking, or seeming to observe, that he had done so.

The term *value* is sometimes applied to express the measure of sustenance or enjoyment that a commodity affords to its possessor. A man may apply the articles he has produced, or in any manner obtained, to his own maintenance or comfort, and the benefit he derives from them has been called *their value in use,* or *absolute value.* Some commodities have a natural superiority to others, as contributing more to these purposes: corn is more essential than wine. A good house contributes more to comfort than the possession of a diamond. Value taken in this sense is nearly the same as wealth. Although its attainment and enlargement is, or should be, one of the chief objects of political institutions, this is not the sense in which the term *value* is commonly used by writers on political economy.

After the establishment of traffic and division of labour, it is generally only a small part of the commodities that the producer retains to himself. The great mass is exchanged for other commodities, and, according as he can command more or fewer of these in return, his commodity is of greater or less value. This has been called *value in exchange;* and as this is the common acceptation in which it is used by political economists, when the term is used simply,—it ought to be applied in this sense, unless some other meaning be specially assigned to it.

The value of a commodity applied to the use of the possessor is incapable of being reduced to any standard. It depends upon his necessities, his taste, and his caprices, and no two men would agree in regard to it; but the value of the commodities which he brings to market is ascertained by a steadier standard. It is measured by the amount of what he can receive in return. The quantity of one kind of commodity that can be obtained for a given quantity of another ascertains their *relative value.* As this is the only meaning that can be applied to the term, if that of the *value in use* be set aside, the prefix *relative* may be omitted as superfluous, and as leading to error by suggesting the notion of an *absolute value in exchange.*

In exchanging commodities, or transferring them to the possession of others, upon condition of receiving an adequate return afterwards, it is convenient and usual to express their value in a numerical manner, referring to certain pieces of the precious metals which compose the currency of the country, or perhaps to a mere denomination. The value of a commodity expressed in this manner is called its *price.*

The relative value of commodities at any given time is accurately expressed by their price; but money is not on that account more a standard of value than any other commodity. If the price of a yard of silk be equal to that of five yards of linen, it will also exchange for five times as much corn, wine, or any other commodity. The corn or wine given in exchange may, therefore, be considered, as well as the money, as measures of the relative value of the silk and linen;

though money, being commonly used, or at least referred to in these transactions, furnishes the common way of expressing the value of commodities.

The price of a single commodity gives no information in regard to its value. If the price of a horse be twenty pounds, and that of a quarter of wheat two pounds, we know that ten quarters of wheat are of the same value as the horse, and may be obtained in exchange for it, and this holds without any regard to the nature of the pound, whether a greater or less quantity of gold or silver, or a mere denomination. But if we are only told that the price of the horse is twenty pounds, this gives us no information so long as we are ignorant of the price of other commodities; nor does it add much to our knowledge, though we be shown the quantity of gold or silver that is denominated a pound.

The notion of an absolute value (we speak of value in exchange) has given rise to considerable errors. To raise the value of commodities has been considered as a desirable object, and some have gone so far as to hold the raising the value of all commodities to be a most beneficial measure. Nothing can be more absurd. Value being relative, you cannot increase that of one commodity without depressing that of others. If you raise the value of corn, you depress the value of the articles for which it is exchanged. If you raise the price of all commodities in the some proportion, you depress the value of the currency, but make no alteration in the value of commodities. The raising the value of a particular commodity may be beneficial or otherwise. It may enrich some individuals at the expense of others, but it does not promote the public welfare upon any general principle.

A standard of value has been sought for by political economists. The value of all commodities is subject to fluctuation, though in very different proportions, and the desired standard, were it attainable, would ascertain the comparative value of any articles at different periods of time, or in different nations at the same time.

Corn has been considered by some as a correct standard. The value of a commodity, it is said, may be estimated in all ages and nations by the quantity of corn that can be obtained for it. This doctrine requires some modification.

As food is the first article of human want,

and corn the most universal kind of food, if any single article be fit for a general standard of value, no doubt it is corn. Now, suppose a value in corn has been affixed by general consent upon all commodities brought to market, and that afterwards, by improvement in machinery or otherwise, some commodity, say cloth, can be manufactured with less labour, and, therefore, more of it brought to market, and given in exchange for corn, or other commodities, than formerly, while others retain the same corn price as before. Then he who possesses wine can get as much corn for it as formerly, but his wine goes farther in purchasing cloth. His wine is, therefore, of more value than formerly. It is not corn alone that men have occasion for when they go to market. If they can procure a larger share of articles subservient to comfort or luxury along with a sufficient supply of necessaries, the value of the articles which they give in exchange for this aggregate is augmented. As corn, or other common food, is an article of prime necessity, and bears a considerable proportion to the whole, it ascertains, in a great measure, but not solely and exclusively, the value of every other commodity. This depends upon the returns that can be obtained for them, of whatever kind. If by a change of circumstances a greater share of any other commodity can be obtained for mine, the value of mine is in some measure increased. If a lesser share of a different commodity can only be got for it, the value of mine is in some measure diminished, and its ultimate value depends upon the aggregate of all other commodities that it will exchange for, regard being always had to the quantity of each that is wanted. This estimate, indeed, is too complex to admit of being brought to an accurate determination.

Dr. Smith proposes as a standard of value the quantity of labour that it can command, as labour may be applied to the supply of almost every want, and even to that of corn. Mr. Malthus proposes a medium between corn and labour; and since maintenance and a command of the services of others are the chief desiderata of mankind, this medium is, perhaps, as accurate a standard as can be attained.

To attain a standard that will answer in all ages and nations is impracticable, for all commodities alter in value. Of all standards, that of the precious metals is the most fallacious. Most commodities have a *value in use* which influences, though it does not exclusively determine, their *value in exchange.* But gold and silver have little value in use, and derive their value almost entirely from being assumed as a medium of commerce, which is a device altogether political and arbitrary, and which may be effected by any quantity of these metals, whether great or small. Accordingly we find that the prices of commodities have been very different in different ages. They also differ considerably in different countries at the same time, though they have a tendency to assimilate, if the countries be connected by commercial intercourse.

A determination of the causes which regulate the price or relative value of different commodities, is a point of much importance in political economy. On this two opinions have been advanced.

The first is, that the price of commodities is regulated by the quantity of labour required for their production, or rather by the expense of production, of which expense, labour, either past or present, generally constitutes the greater part. This has been called *the natural or necessary price.*

The second is, that price is regulated by the proportion of the supply of a commodity brought to market with the effective demand for that commodity. This is called *the market price.*

Though these doctrines have been considered as opposed to each other, it will not be difficult, by a little consideration, to reconcile them.

An isolated individual must perform every operation requisite for his life and comfort the best way he can. Robinson Crusoe was his own huntsman, agriculturist, carpenter, tailor, potter, and basket-maker. If several persons be placed in some spot where they have no communication with the rest of mankind, they will not long continue to work each for himself, as the isolated individual does. They had, perhaps, before being placed in this situation, been bred to different mechanical occupations, the articles supplied by each of which are needed by every member of this small community. The carpenter, the blacksmith, the shoemaker, will each supply that article which, from education and practice, he can produce in less time, and of better quality than the others can do, and will receive from the others in return those commodities, in the production of which they possess a like advantage. There seems to be no other rule for regulating these transactions than that every article be exchanged for another which requires an equal quantity of labour for its production. A day's work of the shoemaker, or its produce, will be given for a day's work of the carpenter; or, what comes to the same thing, each member of the community will receive a share of the whole commodities produced in proportion to the quantity of labour he has contributed to their production. The natural and market-price will thus be the same in the situation here supposed; nor will they deviate much even when the community is considerably enlarged, due allowance being made for such circumstances as assign higher wages to some kinds of labour than to others. These are chiefly the following:—

1st. Some kinds of labour are more severe, more disagreeable, more dangerous, more unhealthy than others, and therefore will not be undertaken without a higher reward. For some or all of these reasons the wages of labourers employed in mines is always higher than of those employed in agriculture.

2d. Some employments require superior abilities, natural or acquired, or an extensive course of education; others require dexterity and skill, which long practice only can confer. A skilful surgeon receives a higher reward for the time he is employed than an artist, and an ingenious artist more than an ordinary mechanic.

3d. In some employments there is almost a certainty of accomplishing the object intended. In others the success is very precarious. In some mechanic arts the operator is exposed to the constant risk of breaking his work, while others are nearly exempt from that hazard. Agriculture is a surer means of procuring subsistence than fishing; the profits of mining are still more precarious. The projector is exposed to the greatest hazard of any; and, therefore, when his schemes succeed, and prove beneficial to the public, he is entitled to a liberal reward, though he does not always receive it.

4th. Another circumstance which considerably affects the value of labour is the time which elapses before the article on which it is exerted be fit for use. In many mechanic arts the article is ready so soon as the labour is performed. In agriculture the greater part of the labour precedes the reaping of the crop by several months, and much labour is often exerted when no return is expected for several years. If a plough till five hundred acres of land before it be worn out, the labour of making the plough is part of the labour of tilling five hundred acres. But it may be employed ten years before it perform that quantity of work, and the average time between making the plough and deriving advantage from its use is five years. The same takes place in mining and in some complicated manufactures. An additional reward is due to such labour on account of the delay before any return be received. This belongs to the article of interest, the principles of which require a separate consideration*.

Any circumstance, natural or artificial, which facilitates the production of an article, diminishes its natural value. Any circumstance which obstructs or retards its production increases its natural value.

But in large communities the exchange of commodities is not always regulated by the expense of their production. A deviation from that proportion frequently takes place both in

* See this subject more fully treated in Dr. Smith's Inquiry, part i., chap. 10.

the exchange of manufactured commodities for rude produce, and in that of one manufactured article for another, owing to the unequal measure of the supply of commodities to the wants of those who have something to give in return. The proportion of the different commodities wanted by the whole community is nearly fixed by their established habits, and if the quantity of each kind brought to market be in the same proportion, those which require equal measures of labour for their production will be exchanged for each other, and the market price will be the same as the natural. If a greater quantity of cloth be brought to market than those who frequent it have occasion for, when acting according to their usual habits, a proportion will remain in the hands of the manufacturers after the first demand is supplied; and, rather than carry this home, where he can turn it to no present advantage, he will give it in exchange for other commodities that required less time for their production. This induces the other frequenters of the market to purchase a greater quantity of cloth than they intended, and supply their families more liberally with that article, or lay up a part of their purchase for future use.

Thus the price of cloth falls. On the other hand, if the quantity of cloth brought to market be less than is wanted, those whose wants are most exigent, when they perceive a difficulty of obtaining a supply, will offer a larger share of their own productions in return; and others whose wants are less exigent or have less to offer in return, must go away unsupplied. Thus the price of cloth rises. If more corn be brought to market than is required to supply the consumers during the time they usually provide for at once, the farmer, rather than carry back the surplus, will offer it at a lower rate, and this will induce the purchaser to lay in for a longer time, and the price of corn will fall. On the contrary, a deficiency in the supply will cause the price of corn to rise by the converse of this operation.

The deviation of the market price from the natural one may take place in a considerable degree even in articles of internal produce and manufacture, and much more so when a great part of the supply or demand proceeds from foreign commerce.

The market price, however, has always a tendency to approach to the natural one, at least in articles of home production. If the supply of any article exceed the demand, and the price, in consequence, fall, the production of that article will be lessened or discontinued till its price rise so as to obtain the usual reward of labour. If the demand exceed the supply, and the price rise, more of that article will be produced and brought to market, till the price fall to its usual rate. A deficiency in articles of prime necessity may occasion a great rise in their market price above the natural one. A deficient crop, though necessarily accompanied with a rise in the natural price of corn (as a smaller quantity is produced by the same labour, in a bad season), may increase the market price in a higher proportion. For food must be procured, if it can, at any price. A deficiency in materials for clothing is not likely to produce this effect in the same degree; for many will rather cause the clothes they have at present to serve, till a supply on reasonable terms can be procured. Perishable commodities fall very low in price by what is called a glut in the market, as they must be consumed immediately, or lost. Those of a more durable nature may be withdrawn from the market, in hopes of a rise.

The natural value has in most cases a present

effect on the market price, and this latter, therefore, does not depend altogether on the proportion between supply and demand. So natural does this appear, that a rise in the expense of production, occasioned by a new tax, or any other cause, likely to be permanent, *immediately* raises the price of the article to which it is applied, although it cannot, for some time, alter the supply or demand in the market.

The supporters of these opposite doctrines in regard to value seem to differ only in degree. Those who argue for the natural price, as depending on the expense of production, acknowledge that the market price differs frequently, and sometimes greatly from it. Those who argue for the market price, as regulated by the proportion between supply and demand, acknowledge that this will be modified in time by the effect of the natural price. The length of time required to produce an equalization seems to be the only point of difference between them. This depends on the facility of procuring materials, and the time required for the production of the article, including that of constructing the requisite machinery and tools, and of acquiring the requisite skill for their use.

Relative value is continually varying. At one time three yards of cloth may be obtained for a quarter of wheat; at another time only two yards. When this happens, shall we say that the value of the wheat has fallen, or that the value of the cloth has risen? To answer this question, we observe that at the former time the quarter of wheat would exchange for a certain quantity of butcher's meat, wine, furniture, fuel, or other commodities, and three yards of cloth would then exchange for the same quantity of these commodities. At the latter time, two yards of cloth will purchase as much of these commodities as a quarter of wheat will do. Either, therefore, a greater share of other commodities, taking them in the aggregate, will be obtained for the yard of cloth, or a smaller share for the quarter of wheat than before. In the former case, the value of the cloth has risen; in the latter case, the value of the wheat has fallen. It may happen that the alteration in the relative value is occasioned partly by the rise in that of one of the commodities, and partly by the fall of that of the other.

The estimation of the value of a commodity by the quantity of labour required for its production, is not the same as that estimated by the labour that it will purchase when produced, though they in some degree tend to assimilate. The former is the natural value; the latter, which Dr. Smith assumes as a standard, is the market value.

# CHAPTER VIII.

## OF THE COMPONENT PARTS OF VALUE.

THE price of commodities, considered as regulated by the expense of their production, is resolved by political economists into three parts, —rent of land, profit of stock, and wages of labour; to which may be added any special taxes they are charged with. The profits of stock may be again resolved into former rent, and former labour; the larger part being former labour.

To ascertain the proportion of these different parts, as well as the amount of the whole, compared with the population under existing circumstances, is an object of considerable importance.

In that state of society, where land is not yet parcelled out and appropriated, the whole value of commodities arises from the labour required for obtaining them, and preparing them for use. But subsequent to the appropriation of land, there is scarcely any article, the whole value of which can be resolved into labour. In estimating the expense of the production of any commodity, the price of the material must be added to that of the labour bestowed upon it; and so far as this does not arise from former labour, it arises from rent. The farmer is employed in raising corn, and his implements are made by artificers bred to their several employments: but the rent of the wood which furnishes timber for his carts and ploughs, and the rent of the mine which supplies them with iron, as well as the rent of the land which he cultivates, must all be paid by the price of his corn. The price of wool forms a part of the price of cloth; and this is almost entirely resolvable into rent, as the labours of the shepherd are inconsiderable. The price of butcher's meat also arises chiefly from rent. The price of houses is partly composed of the rent of the quarries which supply the builder with stones. In the more exquisite works of art, the value of the material bears so small a proportion to that of the labour, as almost to escape observation. The value of the balance-spring of a watch exceeds by ten thousand times that of the steel which it is made of; yet the rent of the mine from which the steel is obtained forms a part, though a very small one, of the price of the balance-spring. The property of animals obtained by hunting and fishing, in places where these occupations are permitted freely, is another instance where little is assignable to rent. Yet if the hunter use a gun, or even a bow, the rent of the land which furnishes wood, or of the mine which furnishes metal for these weapons, composes a part of the price of the game he kills. A very trivial example, mentioned by Dr. Smith, of property arising entirely from labour,—that of pebbles gathered on the sea-shore, and afterwards wrought into trinkets, is the only one we at present recollect.

A catalogue somewhat larger may be adduced of articles whose value arises from rent only: this includes all the spontaneous productions of the earth. The extent of these is very different in different climates.

The value of the far greater part of commodities is composed jointly of rent and labour, present or former; and for the most part labour contributes the greater share.

The use of tools is necessary for the execu tion of work; and the materials must be supplied, and the labourers maintained, during the time the commodities are preparing. The proprietors of the tools, the materials, and the food, have a right to a share of the manufactured commodity; or what is more common, may assume the property of the whole, on paying the labourer an adequate consideration in name of wages. The value of the article produced is divided between the owner of the capital and the labourer; and the equitable rule of distribution seems to depend on the proportion between the former labour expended in raising the capital, including an allowance for rent, and the present labour employed in making the commodity. In ascertaining this proportion, we should estimate all the labour that has been exercised, directly or indirectly, in producing the article, making due allowance for the time which has intervened between the exertion of each portion of the labour and the full accomplishment of its object. The actual distribution, however, will frequently be different, in the same manner as the market price of commodities is different from the expense of their production.

If the labourer provide his own tools, or

maintain himself while the work is carrying on, he is so far a capitalist, and what he earns belongs to the head of profit of stock, as well as wages of labour.

Mr. Ricardo makes the supposition, of a machine which costs twenty thousand pounds, and lasts an hundred years, during which time it produces commodities without the aid of human labour. Chimerical as this supposition appears, it is useful in analyzing the component parts into which the expense of production is resolved.

# CHAPTER IX.

## DISTRIBUTION OF THE PRODUCE OF BRITAIN.

We cannot treat of this subject, without stating specific sums, in the estimation of general wealth. We are aware, however, of the difficulty of obtaining accurate statements: a difficulty arising partly from the extent and variety of the subject, and partly from the continual fluctuation both of the mass of wealth, and the value of the standard in which it is estimated. All we can expect is such an approximation as may assist our views, without leading to any important error.

The necessary or ordinary expenses of the labouring part of the community in Britain*, including men, women and children, may be taken at sixpence a day, or nine pounds in a year

* We have made these statements in regard to Britain rather than the United Kingdom, because we have not authentic information of some particulars respecting Ireland, and also because the circumstances of the countries are different in essential points.

each. Sir Frederick Eden estimated the annual expense of the English cottage, in the year 1796, at 6*l.* 4*s.* a head. This is too low for the present time, and the expense of tradesmen and manufacturers in towns is greater than that of country cottagers. If we take the average expense of all ranks at double that of the labourer, we may not be far from the truth. The number of inhabitants in Britain, by the last census, was about fourteen millions. Their expenses, therefore, at eighteen pounds a head, amounts to two hundred and fifty-two millions.

If the wealth of a country remain stationary, the annual income of the whole community, or value of the productions applicable to the use of man, is equal to the annual expenditure. If the amount of productions exceed the expenditure, so much is added to the public wealth in agricultural improvements, houses, furniture, machinery, or some other form *. If the expenditure exceed the income, so much is deducted from the public wealth.

* Some have erroneously stated money saved and lent as an addition to the national wealth. When there is a lender, there is a borrower. The interest which the one receives the other pays. The general mass of wealth is no ways affected by these transactions.

It is difficult to ascertain the alteration in the mass of general wealth, but the quantity added to it, or deducted from it, in any year, never exceeds a small proportion of the produce of that year; the greater part of what is produced being always consumed within the year. It is certain, however, that in Britain there has been an increase of wealth, more or less, for many years. This is obvious from the better cultivation of our fields, and greater extent of cultivated ground, the increase and improvement of our houses and furniture, the superior machinery in our manufacturing establishments, and other indications of wealth which strike our eyes, to whatever quarter we turn them.

Suppose eighteen millions added annually to the national wealth: the annual income then amounts to two hundred and seventy millions; and this is divided among the landholders for rent, the capitalists for profits, the labourers for wages, and those who participate of the public revenue. Some share is given in charity, to those who have no property, and are incapable of labour.

This sum of two hundred and seventy millions comprehends the value of every article produced or in any way obtained within the year, for the maintenance and accommodation of mankind, and also the annual value of things not produced within the year, but which remain useful for a length of time, as houses and the like. But it does not include the value of the services of professional men, and of those who contribute to amusement. If it be thought proper to include these, an addition must be made to the foregoing sum, and an alteration will be requisite in some of the following statements.

As the labouring part of the community seldom accumulate much wealth, their annual earnings are nearly equal to their annual outgoings. This we have stated at nine pounds a year each. If a family consist of five persons, a man, his wife, two children who can do some labour, and a young child, their aggregate expense amounts to forty-five pounds. If the man gain eighteen-pence a-day, for three hundred working days, his wages amount to twenty-two pounds ten shillings in the year, and if the wife and two children gain as much among them, the requisite sum is made up. They can procure food, clothing, lodging, furniture, and other articles to the extent which that sum will purchase. This may be an average case*. If the man possess a small capital, or if he can practise some art that is paid above the common rate, he may live so much better, or save something. If he have a large family of young children, he will be liable to save little or nothing, and his fare will naturally be worse.

To persons in these circumstances food is the principal article of expense. According to Sir Frederick Eden, it amounts to three-fourths of the whole. The income of a labourer is burthened with a part of the taxes which supply the national revenue. He pays little in direct taxation, but he pays indirectly, in the price of beer, leather, candles, soap, tobacco, and other articles. If these commodities were not taxed, he would be better fed, clothed, and lodged, for the same nominal expenditure. Among families in better circumstances the proportion required for food is smaller. In those of middle rank it may be about one-half; and in those of higher rank much less. Such families require the personal service of one or more of the inferior

* Perhaps we should be still nearer the truth, if we stated the average wages of the labourer a little higher, and that of the other members of the family a little lower.

classes. Those in affluent circumstances generally employ a large number of menial attendants. When we estimate the average expense of each person in Britain at eighteen pounds, we include the food, dress, houses, furniture, establishment, travelling and miscellaneous expenses of the rich, but not the wages and maintenance of their domestics. These form a part of what the average of eighteen pounds is composed of, and would be twice reckoned if each domestic were charged separately as an individual, and at the same time collectively as a part of the establishment to which be belonged *. The annual

* It may be objected to this method of statement, that we estimate the wages of the tradesmen who supply the wealthy with commodities in determining the average, but not the wages of the domestic, though both are maintained at the expense of the employer. The cases, however, are not the same. A number of the most necessary tradesmen may unite to supply themselves with lodging, furniture, and clothing, each furnishing the article which the employment he is bred to enables him to produce. If to these be associated a sufficient number of farmers on like terms, all the members of such a society would be fed and otherwise accommodated with considerable fulness, provided they were possessed of land and capital requisite for their several employments. But if these be wanting, they must give part of what they produce and manufacture, or its value, to the owners of the land and capital, and be satisfied with inferior fare and accommodation. The mass of the productions of such a society would be divided into two parts, one given to the landholder and capitalist, the other retained for their own use, and each part would have its distinct value. There is nothing similar to this in the case of domestic servants

income of two hundred and seventy millions comprehends the produce of the land which is appropriated to the use of man, or of horses kept for pleasure, or which supplies materials for manufacture, but not that part of the produce required for seed, or for maintaining horses or other cattle employed in agriculture, which is immediately reabsorbed. It includes also the produce of our mines, woods, and fisheries, and all that is added to the value of the raw materials by our various trades and manufactures; also the profits of our foreign commerce, and whatever is drawn by persons residing in Britain from their properties in our colonies*.

A large share of this mass of wealth is intercepted by public burthens of various kinds. The taxes paid to government, and constituting the revenue of Britain, amounted, on an average of three years preceding the 5th of January 1823, nearly to fifty-five millions, including the expense of collection, but deducting what was repaid in drawbacks and bounties. During the late war

who produce nothing, but are retained to indulge the indolence, or gratify the vanity of their masters.

* We propose, in general, as the distinctest way of conducting these inquiries, to consider separately the internal sources of wealth, and that acquired by commerce or colonization. It was necessary, however, in the general estimate here given, to comprehend the whole national income, from whatever source arising.

it sometimes amounted to upwards of seventy millions.

Of this revenue about twenty-eight millions and a half are paid to the public creditors in dividends and annuities, and about one million and a half for interest on Exchequer bills. About five millions are applied for the reduction of the national debt; and the remainder, amounting to twenty millions, is expended on the army and navy, and the payment of public functionaries of every rank, from the sovereign to the meanest clerk.

The other public burthens are tithes, poor-rates, and county and other local assessments.

The tithes, exclusive of those belonging to lay impropriators, which should be accounted a species of land-rent, may amount to about four millions.

The poor-rates, when highest, exceeded seven millions and a half. They are now (1823) under seven millions.

The county and other local assessments, as far as can be ascertained, may amount to one million and a half.

These burthens, which, that we may be within bounds, we shall estimate at twelve millions, are generally paid, in the first instance, by the farmer; but are immediately devolved on the proprietor of the land, who receives so much less rent from the farmer as these burthens amount to. It is not clear that the landholder can reimburse himself by devolving these burthens on other classes of society. In regard to tithes* and local assessments, there is no reason to believe he can; and if poor-rates were only applied to their proper purpose, the maintenance of those who are disabled, by age or otherwise, from labour, they would also fall on the landholder without reimbursement. If they be applied in such a manner as to reduce the wages of labour, this system, however exceptionable, by lessening the farmer's expenses, enables him to pay a higher rent, and thus affords the landholder compensation to a certain extent.

The sums levied by taxes of any kind may be beneficially applied for the public welfare. It is true they may also be excessive, or misapplied.

* The tithes are here considered as a part of the rent paid to the titheholder, instead of the landholder. Some respectable writers maintain that tithes do not partake of the nature of rent, and that their tendency is rather to increase than to lessen it. We shall consider this opinion more fully in a following Chapter. However this may be, it does not affect the following statements, which proceed upon the rent as it actually is, when modified by all the circumstances that tend either to increase or lessen it.

But the people are obliged to pay them, whether they consider themselves as deriving equivalent advantage from them or not; and this constitutes an essential difference between that part of the national expenditure, and the part which is voluntarily paid to that class of the community who are accounted unproductive labourers.

The distinction between productive and unproductive labour was, we believe, first pointed out by Dr. Smith, and it appeared to him clear and important. Some later writers have endeavoured to represent it as futile, and their argument chiefly rests on the adduction of cases, in regard to which it is difficult to say whether they should be assigned to the one class or the other. This may be admitted, and it nevertheless may be true, that the distinction, in most cases, is sufficiently marked. It is well known that, in every branch of science, classification is useful, and even necessary: yet the different classes, by whatever rule we arrange them, sometimes approximate so much, that we cannot always determine whether a particular subject should be referred to one class or another.

The sovereign, and all concerned in public

administration, judges and magistrates, tax-gatherers, the army and navy, the established clergy, are all unproductive labourers whom we are obliged to pay, and who, therefore, may be overpaid. Under this head we may also class, in England, the poor, whom we are obliged to pay, though they may not labour at all.

Physicians, who do or should afford us health; schoolmasters and dissenting clergymen who give us instruction, lawyers who assist us in the protection of our property, musicians and other public performers who supply us with amusement, and the numerous body of domestic servants who contribute to our accommodation, are unproductive labourers whom we pay voluntarily, and who are not, therefore, likely to receive more than a suitable recompense for their services.

We resume our attempt to calculate, as nearly as we can, in what proportion the income of two hundred and seventy millions is distributed among the various classes of the community. We shall first consider the whole as distributed among the proprietors of land, the capitalists, and the labourers, and then consider to what extent these are burthened with national or other taxes, the produce of which is applied to the maintenance of other classes of the community.

The circumstances which give rise to and regulate rent will be the subject of a separate discussion. At present it is only the amount of it with which we are concerned.

| | |
|---|---|
| The rents paid by the farmer for land applied to the purposes of tillage and pasturage, including the value of what is retained in the actual possession of the proprietor, whether applied to these purposes or laid out in pleasure-grounds, and including also the tithes in the hands of lay impropriators, may amount to | £40,000,000 |
| But if the farmers were exempt from tithes, poor-rates, and other public burthens, they would pay so much more rent. We estimated these at twelve millions; but as part of this falls upon other classes, the part which falls on the land may be stated at . . . . | 10,000,000 |
| Rent of mines, fisheries, woods, &c. | 5,000,000 |
| Gross income of landed proprietors | £55,000,000 |

| | |
|---|---|
| The number of families chiefly employed in agriculture, by the last census, 1821, was . . . . . | 978,656 |
| Of those chiefly employed in trades and manufactures . . . . | 1,350,239 |
| | 2,328,895 |
| Families of all other descriptions . | 612,488 |
| Whole number of families . . | 2,941,383 |

And the whole number of inhabitants, exclusive of the army and navy, was 14,072,331, being about four and three-fourths to a family, or more accurately 4.784.

The proportion of persons belonging to the families of the agricultural and manufacturing classes is about eleven millions, and this would be the number of labourers and their families if they were all employed as such.

But this is not affirmed to be the case, and it is obvious that these families must include many who derive part of their income from the profits of capital. It includes farmers, master tradesmen, and manufacturers, and others of like description.

We may, therefore, deduct one million, and there remains ten millions of labourers and their families, whose income, at 9*l.* per head, amounts to . . . . . . . . . . £90,000,000

| | |
|---|---|
| Gross income of landed proprietors | 55,000,000 |
| And there remains for the gross income of the capitalists, not including the public creditors, whose income will be allowed for otherwise . . . . . . | 125,000,000 |
| | £270,000,000 |

This gross sum is liable to the following deductions:—

| | |
|---|---|
| National revenue . . . . . . | 55,000,000 |
| Tithes, poor's rates, and other local taxes . . . . . . . . | 12,000,000 |
| | £67,000,000 |

which sum is to be deducted from the several classes, but in very different proportions.

The labourers are hardly subject to any local taxes, and the greater part of their expense, being for simple food, is not liable to taxation. We may state the duties upon any taxable articles they consume, and any other small taxes that may fall upon them, at 1*l.* per head, or . . . . . . . . . . £10,000,000

| | |
|---|---|
| The landed proprietor pays, exclusively, the land-tax, the unredeemed part of which at present is about . . . . . . . . | 1,200,000 |
| And the remainder falls upon the other classes, nearly in proportion to their incomes . . . . | 43,800,000 |
| | 55,000,000 |

Of this last the public creditors pay their share, as do also persons in public office, and others who participate of the public revenue: but as a large part of the revenue is applied to the pay of the private men in the army and navy, and to other objects which yield little or no return, we shall state the part of the public expenditure which yields a return at ten millions. The clergy also contribute their share.

The proportion of taxes falling on the different classes of society will be, in round numbers, as follows:—

| | £ | £ |
|---|---|---|
| On proprietors of land, in proportion to an income of . . | 43,800,000 | 9,100,000 |
| On capitalists, in proportion to an income of . . . . . . . . . . . | 123,000,000 | 25,600,000 |
| On public creditors, in proportion to an income of . . . . . . | 30,000,000 | 6,200,000 |
| On others who participate of the public revenue, in proportion to an income of . . . . . . | 10,000,000 | 2,100,000 |
| On the clergy, in proportion to an income of . . . . . . . . . . . | 4,000,000 | 800,000 |
| | £210,800,000 | 43,800,000 |

And the net income of the different classes will be as follows:—

| | | |
|---|---|---|
| Proprietors of land, gross income . . . . . . . . | | 55,000,000 |
| Deduct tithes, poor's rates, and other local taxes. . . . . . . . . . . | 10,000,000 | |
| Land-tax . . . . . . . . . . . . . . . . . . | 1,200,000 | |
| | | 11,200,000 |
| | £ | 43,800,000 |
| Deduct also their proportion of other taxes . | | 9,100,000 |
| Net income . . . . . . . . . . . . . . . . . . . . . . . . | | 34,700,000 |
| Capitalists, gross income . . . . . . . . . . . . . . . . | | 125,000,000 |
| Deduct their proportion of local taxes . . . . . | | 2,000,000 |
| | | 123,000,000 |
| Also their proportion of public taxes . . . . . . | | 25,600,000 |
| Net income. . . . . . . . . . . . . . . . . . . . . . | | 97,400,000 |
| Labourers, gross income . . . . . . . . . . . . . . . . | | 90,000,000 |
| Proportion of public taxes . . . . . . . . . . . . | | 10,000,000 |
| | £ | 80,000,000 |

| | | £ |
|---|---|---|
| * Net income of proprietors of land ....... | | 34,700,000 |
| ,, of capitalists .............. | | 97,400,000 |
| ,, of labourers.............. | | 80,000,000 |
| | | 212,100,000 |
| Dividends to national creditors | 30,000,000 | |
| Public expenditure for army, navy, civil list, &c.. ....... | 20,000,000 | |
| Applied to the reduction of the national debt ............ | 5,000,000 | |
| Amount of public revenue.... | 55,000,000 | |
| Tithes, appropriated to the maintenance of the clergy. . | 4,000,000 | |
| Poor's rates, and other local taxes................... | 8,000,000 | |
| Amount of public burthens . . | 67,000,000 | |
| Deduct the part which falls upon the national creditors, public officers, and clergy. . | 9,100,000 | |
| | | 57,900,000 |
| Amount of national income.......... | £ | 270,000,000 |

We have not stated the income of professional men in the allotment of national income. These are paid voluntarily by the landed proprietors, and capitalists; a small part by the labourer, in return for services received.

* The sums here assigned as the net income of the several classes, are those which would remain for their expenditure if they paid, directly, those taxes, which fall upon them indirectly, by being laid upon the commodities they consume.

We do not undertake to affirm, that the sums in these statements are exact. Some of them may be considerably otherwise; and we rather apprehend we have stated the public income, and also the expenditure of the different classes too high, when the alteration occasioned by the late increase of the value of the currency is taken into consideration. We may also have stated the annual increase of the national wealth too high. An arrangement, such as given above, in elucidating our views of the subject, may, however, be useful, and the sums only require such correction as fuller information may supply, or as may be necessary to adapt them to a future time; most of the articles being in a state of continual fluctuation.

We trust, however, they are sufficiently near the truth to warrant the following inferences:—

That the income of the capitalists (not including the public creditors) exceeds that of the labourers.

That the income of the landed proprietors is much inferior to that of the capitalists or labourers, not amounting, probably, to one-half of the latter.

That the amount of general taxes is not less

than one-fifth of the national income, and the whole amount of taxes, general and local, not less than one-fourth. As a small part of these taxes falls upon the labourer and small capitalist, a much larger proportion than above-mentioned falls upon the more affluent part of the community.

That in the latter part of the last war the public taxes alone exceeded one-fourth part of the national income.

That the income of the public creditors is inferior to the net income of the landed proprietors.

Some particulars are omitted in the foregoing statements, which may nearly compensate each other. The part of the dividends on the national debt paid to foreigners is a deduction from our national income; but that is now fully compensated by the investment of British capital in foreign funds.

The design of this treatise is rather to state our opinions on the important subjects it relates to, and the principles on which they are founded, than to enter into controversy with those who maintain different opinions: but the doctrines advanced by Mr. Simon Gray, are so opposite to our's, and have gained so much reception, that a brief parallel statement seems requisite. We shall begin with a statement of the opinions which we entertain ourselves.

It is agreed on all hands, that it is necessary mankind should be sufficiently fed, and desirable that they should be well clothed, lodged, and provided with other articles that afford comfort and enjoyment. It is also desirable they should be instructed, properly attended when in sickness, gratified at suitable times with music, and other recreations. The persons who supply the former are called productive labourers, and those who supply the latter are called unproductive labourers, by such as admit of that distinction.

We do not dispute the value of the latter articles. They are requisite for human happiness, and for raising human nature to that rank and respectability of which it is susceptible, and for which it was intended. The exertions of a certain number of the community are directed to the supply of these objects, and therefore something is deducted from the number of those who furnish the tangible articles, and consequently from the amount of these articles, supposing the industry and skill of those who produce them equal. But this deficiency, if confined within due limits, is amply compensated by the benefits which these unproductive labourers confer. Still, however, productive labourers are more indispensably necessary, and the services of unproductive labourers, if carried too far, degenerate into caprice, and do not promote human happiness at all.

Though nature supplies the materials for tangible articles, it is human industry that prepares them for use, and the whole amount of these articles that society can enjoy, depends upon the measure and skilful application of industry, aided by tools and other contrivances. Every man wishes to be well clothed, lodged, and provided with other comforts, and it is desirable all should be so as far as possible. Why is not every man as well lodged, clothed, &c. as a lord? For this obvious reason, that the utmost exertion of human labour, aided by every possible contrivance, could not produce a number of fine houses, a quantity of elegant furniture, and other articles sufficient for that purpose. Were the product of a given quantity of industry susceptible of indefinite augmentation, there would be nothing to prevent every man from being as well supplied as the lord, except in regard to those wants, chiefly capricious, which require the personal service of others.

In the present, or in any supposable state of society, the industry of a considerable number, perhaps one-third, of the community is required for providing food. It is desirable that another proportion, not a very large one, be employed in the duties of instruction, and in affording amusement and other gratifications. These are unproductive labourers. The rest of the community may and ought to be employed in providing houses, clothes, furniture, and whatever besides renders human life comfortable, and the quantity of these articles depends entirely upon the number, industry and skill of the labourers, aided by capital which has been amassed by former labour. Its distribution among the different classes of the community is an object of separate consideration. It may be proper or improper. This mass of articles forms the general wealth, and the measure of enjoyment which a given quantity of wealth affords depends much on the propriety of its distribution.

Before an article be fit for use, the material

supplied by nature generally passes through several hands in its way to the consumer. The wool of which our cloths are made is transferred from the shepherd to the woolcomber, and from him successively to the spinner, the weaver, the fuller, the dyer, and the tailor, before it reaches the wearer. Each of these labourers makes a visible alteration on the article, and brings it nearer to the state in which it is useful. There are other labourers, however, who, though they make no visible alteration on the article, yet, as their aid is required to facilitate its progress, may, without impropriety, be classed with those above-mentioned. Such are the carrier, and the retailer. By the joint operation of all these persons, the wool of the shepherd is brought in the form of a coat to the wearer. But what is the advantage of its passing through so many hands? Merely that which arises from the division of labour. If the same person could do as much, and as good work, when he applied himself successively to the operations of woolcombing, spinning, weaving, fulling, dyeing, and tailoring, it would save a great deal of trouble in transferring the article from hand to hand.

We do not, however, overlook a great advantage, independent of the preparation of the article, which arises from its passing through different hands. The human mind derives its chief improvement from the association of mankind with one another, and though there be other principles which lead men to associate, that of commercial intercourse holds a considerable place. Skill is cultivated, and activity brought forward in the course of commercial transactions.

As wealth is the result of industry properly applied, it is promoted by whatever puts industry in motion. In the present state of society, a large proportion of the community earn their subsistence by labouring for others, and therefore depend upon a demand for their labour. Their employers set them to work, and, by doing so, indirectly occasion the production of wealth. There is, however, an essential distinction between the function which these perform, and the industry which produces the articles that constitute wealth. While we state this distinction, we include those who exercise the offices of superintendence and direction among the number of productive labourers, as much as those by whose manual labour the article is found.

Neither is the unproductive labourer and the idler, though they contribute their share in giving employment to the productive labourer, entitled, on that account, to any peculiar merit. The whole mass of commodities annually produced, or its value, is vested in the hands of the various orders of the community in the form of rent, salary, wages, interest, or some other, and the far greater part is annually expended, and gives employment to labour. It matters not to the labourer from what quarter the demand comes. A stagnation of demand may occur from special circumstances, and occasion much distress: but this is an unnatural state, and is seldom lasting; and is not less likely to occur where a large proportion of the general wealth is vested in the hands of idlers and unproductive labourers. If their share be less, more will remain for the industrious, who will expend more, and thus give employment to other classes of labourers.

Having stated our own opinions as clearly as we can, we shall next state those of Mr. Gray, as well as we are able to apprehend them.

*Circulation,* or that which is to be circulated, is an object of principal importance in political science, as, perhaps, a full moiety of human happiness or misery depends upon it. Under this head is included land—whatever depends principally on the mind, as literary composition, —or on the body, as manual labour—or jointly on both—and also raw materials. It is circulation alone that gives value to things. The value of circulation arises from the utility of the thing circulated in exchange. Each circulator through whose hands it passes makes a charge upon it, and thereby adds to its value. The amount of these values, enhanced by successive changes, constitutes a *general fund which is inexhaustible.* The more rapid and extensive the exchanging or circulation is in any district or country, the more wealthy that district or country becomes. Some kinds of circulation are more necessary than others, but all of them are sources of wealth, because by all of them men become circulators, and are enabled to charge on the general fund. The price of things is the amount of the charges made by all the circulators through whose hands they pass. Whatever is added to the price of things is an addition to the wealth of the nation. It is paid, nominally by all, and really by none. We are nominally all payers, but it is through the medium of charging one another which is common to all. By drawing and re-drawing on the common fund, it is continually increased; and out of this *inexhaustible mass,* each takes, by means of others, what he can, but only to replace it largely by means of others.

Suppose twelve circulators, whose average of circulation is 20, and that a rise of one-twentieth part takes place in the price of commodities. To meet this, each circulator draws on the common fund, not only for this twentieth, but for another twentieth to increase his means of living well. The quantum each draws is now 22, and the amount, instead of the former 240, is 264. The difference, which is 24, constitutes an additional fund. Who then loses? The truth is, all are benefited by the change. Every circulator makes use of the rise to procure what he wants. The various branches of circulation are the means by which all are enabled to charge one another, and together they form the common fund from which all circulators are supplied, and to which they all contribute.

The distinction between productive and unproductive classes is futile. There is no meaning in the assertion, that cultivators create revenue, and other circulators only use it. The income made by each is so much added to the general stock. A tax-gatherer who earns 300*l.* a year, adds as much to the general stock as the farmer who earns the same sum. The tax-gatherer contributes as really to the farmer as the farmer to the tax-gatherer. The wealthy, however, reputed drones, are in reality the most productive. They are the agents whom nature employs, by means of circulation, to diffuse a greater quantity of wealth through all classes. The quality by which circulation tends to increase wealth, is not any peculiarity of form or character, but the power of enabling its possessor to charge for it. A lawyer, a player, a musician, a soldier, a schoolmaster, a tax-gatherer, or a pensioner, who earns 400*l.* a year, brings more wealth to himself and the country, than a farmer who earns only 300*l.*

The more expensive the style of living of a nation, the richer will it be, because the great mass of circulators, by means of rapid circulation, are enabled with more ease to draw their increasing charges from the common fund. Every unprejudiced person observes that, under increasing expenses, the whole population enjoy a more comfortable style of living. What can account for this, but a common fund on which each charges and draws for his additional expenses?

# CHAPTER X.

## OF RENT.

As rent forms a part of the expense of the production of almost every commodity, and a large part of that of the most useful ones, it is of importance to ascertain from what source it arises, and by what principles it is regulated.

Rent presupposes the appropriation of land, and naturally results from it. To inquire into the origin of the appropriation of land is rather the office of the lawyer, or the antiquary, than of the political economist. It is sufficient at present to take it as established. Occupation for a length of time is the title by which most of our lands are now held, and when this is accompanied, as it generally is, by improvement, it constitutes the best of titles, and is most beneficial to society. If property in land were not established and secured, little improvement would take place, the produce of the land would be small, the population scanty, and that scanty population poorly supplied with the comforts and necessaries of life.

In the present state of society all our land, whether cultivated or not, is appropriated. Our mines and quarries are appropriated; the maritime plants on our shores are appropriated; the fishings on our lakes and rivers are appropriated, and though some of these are little susceptible of improvement, they all afford a rent to the proprietor.

A part of the rent of land is the return paid for the labour which the proprietors, or their predecessors, have bestowed in bringing it to its present state of fertility, and partakes of the nature of the profit of capital: but the whole cannot be ascribed to this source, as is obvious from the rise of rent which often takes place without any labour or expense on the part of the proprietor. Improvements in agriculture are followed by an increase of rent. The soil is rendered more productive, and part of the profit accrues to the landlord*.

* Mr. Ricardo advances a doctrine directly opposite to this, and maintains that improvements in agriculture, both those which augment the produce of the soil, and those which enable the farmer to raise it at less expense have a tendency to diminish rent. It is obvious, that if the farmer sell his produce at the same price as formerly, he will be able to pay more rent in consequence of either of these kinds of improvement; and as he will not be able to draw more benefit from his capital and

It is that portion of the produce of the earth which is paid to the proprietor for the use of the original powers of the soil, which constitutes rent in the most proper sense. As this is blended with the allowance made for improvements, and both paid by the farmer to his landlord at the same time, they are not generally distinguished, nor is it of importance that they should. But as there are some who consider rent as an injurious burthen imposed upon the community at large, for the benefit of a privileged few, it may not be amiss to remind them how large a proportion of rent, in its popular sense, is assignable to labour, the best founded of all claims, and the

labour for any length of time than the general rate, he will be obliged to do so. The only circumstance which can counteract this, is the fall in the price of produce. It does not seem likely that a saving in the farmer's expense would have this effect. An increase of produce would lower the price, if the population remained the same: but if the population increased in the same proportion as the produce, which is likely to be the case, the price would remain as before.

As far as experience can be depended on, Mr. Ricardo's doctrine is untenable. Rise of rent and agricultural improvement have gone on hand in hand for a long course of time. But as other causes have co-operated in the rise of rent, this argument may not be deemed altogether conclusive.

Mr. Ricardo's arguments are founded on the assumption that all rent is derived from the inequality in the fertility of different portions of the land; a doctrine which we are to consider in the subsequent part of this chapter.

violation of which would be attended with incalculable mischief to society.

It has of late been a prevailing doctrine that rents proceed, in a great measure, or entirely, from the difference in the quality of different portions of the soil. As this is a point of much importance, we shall transcribe what is adduced in its favour, in the words of one of its ablest supporters*.

"Grain is in no case raised without a certain degree of labour or expense, which must be repaid to the grower: otherwise he cannot afford to produce it. This may be said in the strictest sense to constitute the intrinsic price.

"Money being accounted the common measure of value, this price will be affected by the quantity of money that can be obtained for labour in general, in that place, at that time. The farmer must give those he employs, wages in proportion to what they can get in other employments, so that if these wages be high, the farmer's charges must be high likewise, and the intrinsic price of his corn must rise as the rate of this charge is augmented.

* The Bee, a periodical work, by Dr. Anderson, vol. vi. p. 273, &c., published at Edinburgh in the year 1791.

"Thus do we perceive that there must be a necessary connection between the price of grain, and the prosperity of manufactures, and the degree of emolument to be derived from them; so that any attempt to advance the one at the expense of the other is contrary to nature, violent in its operation, and must be transitory in its effects.

"The intrinsic price of grain, however, all other circumstances being alike, must vary with the fertility of the soil on which it is produced. On a rich soil, less labour and less seed will produce a given quantity of grain than they would do on a soil that is less productive: so that, strictly speaking, this intrinsic price of corn, when considered only in this point of view, would be different in almost every different field. How then, may it be asked, can the intrinsic value be ascertained over a vast tract of country, possessing a diversity of soils of various degrees of fertility, and how shall matters be so managed, that all the rearers of it shall draw nearly the same price for their grain, and have nearly the same profits? All this is effected in the easiest and most natural manner by means of rent. Rent is, in fact, nothing else than a simple and ingenious contrivance for equalizing the profits to be drawn from fields of different degrees of fertility, and of local circumstances which tend to augment or diminish the expense of culture. To make this plain, a few elucidations will be necessary.

" In every country where men exist there will be an effective demand for a certain quantity of corn. By effective demand, I mean a demand which can be supplied, so that the inhabitants may be properly subsisted. It is this demand which in all cases regulates the price of grain: for the quantity of grain required in this case must be had, and the price that is necessary for producing it must be paid, whatever that price may be. These calls are of such a pressing nature as not to be dispensed with.

" For the sake of illustration, we shall suppose that the soils are arranged into classes, according to the degree of their fertility, which classes we shall at present denominate by the letters A. B. C D. E. F. G. &c. Let those comprehended in the class A. be richer than in the class B., and so on, decreasing in fertility for each class as you advance towards G. Now, as the expense of cultivating the least fertile is as great or greater than that of cultivating the most fertile field, it must happen that if an equal quantity of grain, the produce of each class of fields, can be sold at the same price, the profit on cultivating the most fertile fields will be greater, if no precaution be used, than could be obtained by cultivating those that are less fertile; and as this profit must continue to decrease as sterility increases, it must happen, whatever be the price of corn, that the expense of cultivating some of the inferior fields may be equal to, or exceed the value of the whole produce.

"This being admitted, let us suppose the effective demand was such as to raise the price of grain, say to 16*s*. per boll, and that the fields included in F. could just admit of defraying all expenses, and no more, when corn was at that price; that those of the class E. could admit of being cultivated when the price was at 15*s*., and that in like manner the classes D. C. B. and A. consisted of fields which could be respectively cultivated when the prices were 14*s*. 13*s*. 12*s*. and 11*s*. per boll.

"In these circumstances, it would happen that the persons who possess fields in the class F. would be able to afford no rent at all, nor could any rent be afforded for those of G., or other more sterile fields, *for the purpose of raising corn;* but those who possessed fields in the class E. could not only pay the expense of cultivating them, but could pay to the proprietor a rent equal to one shilling for every boll of the free produce. In like manner those who possessed the fields D. C. B. and A. would be able to pay a rent equal to 2*s*. 3*s*. 4*s*. and 5*s*. per boll of their free produce respectively. Nor could the proprietor of these fields find any difficulty in obtaining these rents, because the farmers, finding they could live equally well upon these soils after paying such rents as they could upon the class F. without any rent at all, would be equally willing to take these fields as the others. Thus it is that rent equalizes the profits on different soils in the most natural and easy manner, without tending in any way to affect the price of grain.

"Let us now suppose once more, that the produce of all the fields A. B. C. D. E. and F. were not sufficient to maintain the whole inhabitants of that district. In that case one of two things must happen, either the price of grain must rise to 17*s*., so as to induce the owner of the fields in the class G. to bring them into culture, or a supply must be brought from some other place to answer the demand. In the first case, the fields G. being brought into culture, those in the class F. would now be able to afford a rent of one shilling per boll of the free produce, and all the other classes would admit a similar rise. Now then we clearly perceive that it is the price of grain which affects the rent, and not the rent which affects the price of grain, as has been often mistakenly alleged.

" The natural effect of such increasing demand for grain and augmentation of price, is the converting of barren fields into corn lands, which otherwise would never have become such.

* * * * *

" I must not, however, conclude, without taking notice of one particular, which was purposely kept out of sight, not to embarrass the demonstration. I have taken notice of land that might produce corn without affording any rent. But that, though a physical possibility, cannot practically happen. Land, in every case, when in pasture, can afford some rent, and when the pasture is rich, among a luxurious people, it can afford more rent in many circumstances than while in corn. This rent must always be deducted, whatever it is, before such land comes to the state in which our reasoning above is philosophically just*. If, therefore, the prices of grain be unreasonably depressed by injudicious regulations, while the price of live stock increases, a wonderful diminution of the quantity of grain raised may take place, so as to occasion phenomena that may appear very inexplicable to short-sighted men, and occasion alarms that are altogether unfounded."

Such is the origin of rent, according to Dr. Anderson, and it is a doctrine which has met with a pretty general reception. Others have taken into account the successive portions of capital and labour bestowed upon the same land to render it more productive. When the demand for corn increases, instead of cultivating inferior soils, a better return may sometimes be obtained by employing additional capital upon land already in culture; and though this may yield less return than what was obtained from the capital formerly employed, it may still be beneficial to the

* "This rent, in fact, ought to be accounted part of the expense of cultivating the soil, as it must be sunk when it is subjected to the plough."

proprietor, and if he do not undertake such improvements himself, he may obtain a rent from another for permission to do so. A third portion of capital will generally yield less additional produce, and therefore will procure less additional rent; and so on till farther expenditure of capital ceases to be profitable, and therefore will procure no rent at all. The gradation of produce obtained by the application of different portions of capital is similar to that which proceeds from the different qualities of the soil; and the reasoning above stated in regard to the latter is also applicable to the former. As the last quality of ground brought into culture, so the last portion of capital expended, affords, according to this doctrine, no return to the proprietor.

This doctrine, however, is not to be received without limitation. It is incontrovertible that the price of corn must be sufficient to defray the expense of cultivation on the meanest soils employed, and therefore those of superior quality will afford a rent equal, at least, to the value of the difference of the produce: but it does not follow that the whole of the rent arises from this source. Rent is said to be an equalizer. What would happen if all the land in an appropriated country were of equal fertility? It will hardly be affirmed that, in that case, all rent would cease. If F., and other inferior lands, could be raised to the same degree of fertility as A., the quantity of corn, so long as all the ground was cultivated, would increase; and this, if there were no increase of inhabitants, and no foreign demand, would lower the price of corn, and bring down the rent of land; part of which would soon be left uncultivated. But if the improvement of land were attended with a proportional increase of inhabitants, the rent, when all was brought to an equal fertility, would be the same as that of the highest before.

As the agriculturist pays the same rent for F., when under tillage, that the grazier does when under pasture, it is likely to be partly in the one state and partly in the other. The rent of A. is equal to the sum of the rent of F. and the value of all the additional corn which A. produces more than F., including that which arises from the superior quality of the corn raised on the better soil. More cannot be obtained for A., as the farmer, rather than give it, would have recourse to the cultivation of F., and if A. were offered for less, the farmer would run after it, and raise the rent by competition. The rent of F., compared with that of A., depends upon the net market value of all the corn, cattle, and other produce that can be raised on the one or the other, after deducting expenses. If the value of the cattle reared on twenty acres of F., when brought to market, after deducting the expense of pasturage, be equal to that of the corn raised on one acre of A., after deducting the expense of tillage, then the rent of an acre of A. will be equal to that of twenty acres of F.

To render this as clear as possible, we shall state an example which will illustrate the principle, although the numbers may not correspond to existing circumstances. Suppose the produce of an acre of land of the best quality to be ten bolls, or rather a quantity of corn whose value is equal to that of ten bolls raised on inferior soils, and that the necessary expenses, including the farmer's profit, are defrayed by the sale of three bolls. Then the rent which the farmer can afford to pay is seven bolls, or their value: but the grazier who holds a possession of the quality F., pays a rent per acre equal to one-twentieth part of the rent of an acre of A., or $\frac{7}{20}$ of a boll; and therefore, if a farmer cultivate land of that quality, he must pay as much; and as his expenses and profit require the value of three bolls, he must raise $3\frac{7}{20}$ on an acre. If he cannot raise so much he will discontinue to cultivate. Now, as A. produces 10 bolls, the surplus quantity above the produce of F. is $6\frac{13}{20}$ bolls, to which add the rent of F., or $\frac{7}{20}$ of a boll, the whole rent of A. is 7 bolls, the same as before. If the cultivation of F. be discontinued, the supply of corn being lessened, the price will rise, and this will alter the proportion between the value of land under culture and in pasturage, and produce a new arrangement.

From the produce of all cultivated land, a quantity nearly uniform must be reserved for the seed of the following crop, the maintenance of the farmer and his family, his servants and labouring cattle. The surplus must be sold at a price sufficient to pay his servants' wages, and other expenses of cultivation, his own profits at the ordinary rate, and his rent. This last will vary according to the fertility of the soil, and may in some cases be little or nothing. If the demands of an increasing cultivation force inferior soils into cultivation, the surplus produce must be sold at such a price as to yield a sum equal to what was obtained from the surplus of better land before, providing all other expenses remain the same, and the farmer live and thrive as well as before. It is the proportion of the surplus produce, not the proportion of the whole produce, that in this case regulates the price.

But circumstances naturally resulting from the case supposed may alter this adjustment. In a country where there is a sufficient quantity of land, of nearly equal and considerable fertility, the labour of a small proportion of the inhabitants only is required for cultivating the land and raising the necessary food. In the discussions relative to West Indian slavery, it has been affirmed that the labour of thirty or thirty-five days in a year, on the provision-ground allotted to the slave, was sufficient. If this were true, the labour of one man could raise provisions for ten. This representation is probably exaggerated, and at any rate it is an extreme case. We shall come nearer to what takes place in the most fertile soils of Europe, if we suppose the labour of one-fourth part to be required for agriculture. The labour of the other three-fourths will be exerted for procuring the comforts and conveniences of life, and will afford a liberal measure of them: but if from a deficiency of fertile land, or increase of inhabitants, it becomes necessary to cultivate inferior soils, perhaps the labour of one-third part of the inhabitants may be required for agriculture, and that of two-thirds only will remain for other purposes. This will afford a less share of the conveniences and comforts of life; and this decrease will be more felt as worse land is had recourse to. Thus the inhabitants of a fertile country are more affluent than those of a barren one, if their industry and skill be the same. Those of the latter will be worse clothed, lodged, and otherwise accommodated, and not fed with the same fulness: but the deficiency is not likely to fall equally upon every class of the community.

So long as every man had good land to cultivate for nothing, there would be little difference of circumstances between individuals, except what arose from the difference in their measure of industry, skill, and bodily strength. The more fertile the soil, the larger share of affluence would be enjoyed by every member of the community. But when inferior soils are had recourse to, though the whole wealth of the community is proportioned to the average fertility, the measure of it which falls to the share of those who have no property in land is only in proportion to the fertility of the worst land in cultivation. If the land, at an average, require the labour of one-half of its inhabitants, but the worst land in cultivation require the labour of three-fourths, for raising food, the inferior ranks will have only one-fourth to provide themselves with other articles. It is the same to them as if no better land existed. The benefit arising from the more fertile land is intercepted, in the form of rent, by the proprietor.

A gradation in the value of uncultivated land, according to the advantages it possesses in fertility or situation, may be traced on the same principles. Uncultivated land derives its chief value from the pasture it affords to cattle, and very sterile land will answer for rearing any number of cattle if the extent be sufficiently ample. If there be any land so sterile as to afford nothing for cattle, or so little that no cattle are kept on it, such land may be considered as not existing, and does not affect our reasoning on the subject. To re-assume Dr. Anderson's method of illustration: Let the worst land upon which cattle are kept be denominated Z. Such land, according to circumstances, may yield a small rent, or none at all. A grazier maintains a hundred cattle on a range of ten miles. If he can procure better land, and maintain the same number on a range of five miles, he will derive considerable advantage from this circumscription, and will cheerfully pay a rent for it in addition to that, if any, which he paid for Z. In the most fertile pasture lands, a certain extent is required for maintaining a hundred cattle; but there are various considerations which raise the value of the requisite portion above that of the ten miles of barren pasture. The cattle can be kept with less labour, and fewer attendants; they are nearer to markets; they are exposed to less hazard of suffering by destructive animals and severe seasons; and the grazier himself enjoys the advantage of residing in a more populous and cultivated part of the country. For some, or all of these reasons, an additional rent will be allowed, so often as the pasture land becomes better or more eligible; and thus the rent advances regularly from land of the quality Z. to that of the quality G., or the best that is never brought into cultivation.

In a country not fully settled, pastures of the worst quality, or in the most inconvenient situations, yield no rent. An extent of ground is occupied in pasturage, sufficient for the purposes of the community; and that is preferred which is thought most eligible, on the joint considerations of fertility and situation. Such land yields a rent; but rather than give any for the worst, the grazier, unless prevented by political appropriation, would retire to more remote lands, as yet unoccupied, which he can possess for nothing.

So long as the country remains in this situation, the rent of Z. is nothing: but, when all the land is appropriated and occupied, a certain rent may be obtained for Z. If the state of the country be such that the expense of rearing cattle on the worst pasture is barely equal to their value when reared, such pasture may be occupied, but can afford no rent. If the value be less, such parts will be deserted.

When rent is allowed for Z., it depends upon competition, and this upon the value which the produce will afford in the market. The rent of Z. regulates, upon steady principles, that of all pasture lands of superior quality to G. or F., and the rent of F. regulates that of all arable lands to A. If G. coincide with Z., the rent of the worst arable land may fall to little or nothing. If the number of intermediate gradations be considerable, the rent of F. will rise accordingly. The rent of F. is composed of the rent of Z. and an addition for every intermediate class between Z and F.; as the rent of A. is composed of the rent of F. and an addition for every intermediate class between F. and A.

The quality of the land F., or the degree of sterility which is the limit of cultivation, depends on the following principles. Let us suppose, for a moment, that the price of animal and vegetable food were proportioned to the sustenance they afford, and that both were equally agreeable to the human appetite.

Land susceptible of cultivation affords a greater quantity of sustenance in vegetable than in animal food. It has been said, that the same extent of good ground which maintains one man upon butcher meat will maintain twelve men upon wheat, and seventy men upon potatoes. This statement seems overcharged; but certainly the difference is great. If population be the only object, the whole arable land, and all that is capable of being rendered such, ought to be in tillage. If the sterility of the ground diminish the quantity of animal and vegetable food in the same proportion, corn will still afford the greater quantity of nourishment from the most barren soil; but the expense of cultivating such soil increases with the extent required to afford a given quantity of food, or even in a higher proportion. There is, therefore, a limit at which cultivation ceases to be profitable. Land, in order to be cultivated, must yield a quantity of food sufficient to maintain the labourers, and also to maintain those who supply them with other necessaries. It must also maintain the labouring cattle, and replace the seed, and afford an overplus for the farmer's profit equal to that obtained from uncultivated land.

The above supposition, however, does not apply to the state of society under which we live. A certain mixture of animal and vegetable food seems most congenial to the human constitution; at least those who can procure such a mixture almost universally prefer it, and the proportion of animal food * is considerable. The ground appropriated to pasture, on the foregoing principles, is insufficient. The pressure of demand raises the price of animal food, and as pasture land becomes more valuable the limit of F. takes place at a higher degree of fertility; at the same time, the rise of the price of animal food restricts the use of it among the lower ranks, and prevents the place of F. from rising

* The price of butcher meat may be to that of bread as four to one. If the pound of bread be at a penny, the price of beef is, perhaps, at four-pence, and so in proportion. It is certain that more nourishment is obtained from a pound of meat than from a pound of bread, though physicians and others differ greatly in estimating the proportion. Mr. Gray reckons five quartern loaves a week a full allowance for an average of all ages, when fed altogether upon that article. This amounts to about twenty-one and a half pounds weight. The allowance to our seamen, till lately, was a pound of meat per day, or seven pounds a week†; and if we suppose the nourishment it affords double to that of an equal weight of bread, it is equivalent to fourteen pounds of bread. But their food is not altogether of meat. They also receive an allowance of bread, cheese, butter, and other articles. If we suppose the quantity of these equal to one-third of the bread consumed by those who live entirely on it, the amount of nourishment is nearly the same to both. Our sailors, indeed, are more highly fed than the average of mankind: but this may be compensated by the allowance of one-third for the other articles being too small. On these suppositions the expense of living on butcher meat is double that of living on bread. We rather apprehend the difference is greater.

† By a late regulation the allowance of meat to our sailors is reduced to three-quarters of a pound, and an addition made to their allowance of other articles.

so high as it would otherwise do. The quantity of land in pasture is therefore regulated by the appetite for, and consumption of animal food, and consequently by the number of persons who are able to afford that indulgence. It is greatest in that state of society in which persons of every rank could afford to purchase a quantity of animal food at an advanced price suited to their desires, natural or acquired.

It does not affect this argument, that arable land produces more food on the whole by being sometimes in grass, and that sterile pastures are only capable of rearing, not of fattening cattle. The price of butcher meat consists of two parts; that of the lean animal, reared on our mountains, which may be considered as a rude material; and that of the fatness superinduced; when they are brought by the grazier to our richer pastures. The foregoing reasoning, though it has a more direct reference to the former, is also applicable to the latter; for the quantity of arable land actually cultivated will be regulated by the proportion of the profit obtained by raising corn, and by fattening cattle.

We may notice, by the way, that there is a stage in the infancy of agriculture, when the quantity of corn raised does not afford the proportion of vegetable food most agreeable to the human appetite, and is in this respect the reverse of our present situation. This seems to have been the general state of Europe for some centuries after the subversion of the Roman empire, and is still realized in the case of the wandering Tartars and Arabs, and of some tribes of North America, who are well supplied with animal food by hunting, pasturage, and fishing, but whose feeble attempts in agriculture furnish only a very scanty allowance of corn. In such a state corn is more in request than animal food, and is therefore dearer.

In Dr. Anderson's illustrations, it is laid down that the price of corn must be equal to the expense of raising it on the most sterile cultivated land, and that this expense includes the rent of such land when not cultivated, which value must be sunk when it is subjected to the plough. He is therefore not correct when he affirms, that rent forms no component part of the price of corn.

The proposition *announced* by those who embrace his doctrine is, that *all rent* arises from the inequality of the productive quality of the soil, and that the rent of the best land is equal to the difference between the value of its produce and that of an equal extent of the worst land under cultivation.

The proposition which they have *demonstrated* is, that this difference forms a *necessary part of rent*, and as the price of corn must be sufficient to defray the expense of raising it on the most barren soils on which it is raised, it is a matter of indifference to the rest of the community, whether this be paid to the landlord or retained by the farmer who possesses better land; who, if he did so, would become the proprietor of his own possession.

In the elucidation of their argument, they cannot dispense with bringing into view another part of rent, the value of ground when uncultivated. This, they say, is part of the expense of raising the crop; but it is a part not arising either from present labour, or from capital accumulated by former labour. It therefore resolves itself into rent, as much as the difference of the value of the produce arising from the different qualities of the ground.

The rent of uncultivated land, or of the poorest cultivated land, which regulates that of all of superior quality, partakes of the nature of a monopoly, though limited in its operations by peculiar circumstances.

It is an assumed principle in regard to price, that every man will strive to obtain the highest price he can for every article he brings to market. There may be some exceptions to this; but they bear too small a proportion to the whole to require any notice in general speculations. The price which the seller can obtain is that which the buyer is willing to give, and this depends on two circumstances: whether he can procure the article cheaper elsewhere; and whether he can, and be willing to dispense with the use of it rather than give the price demanded. The first of these is excluded in the case of a complete monopoly. If the value of an article arise chiefly from the labour and skill employed in its production, that of the rude material bearing only a small proportion, and if the right of producing it be open to all, the price cannot much exceed that by which a like quantity of labour and skill applied to other purposes is usually rewarded. But if an exclusive right of producing that article be vested, by legal power, in a few, or in one individual, he or they may raise the price, till the community discontinue the use of the article, or at least use it so sparingly, that the patentee loses more by the diminution of his sales, than he gains by the highness of the price. This is monopoly in the strictest sense of the word.

Another kind of monopoly is, when some material, necessary for the production of the commodity, is in the hands of one, or a few individuals, who, by combination, may raise the price to a high amount, especially if it be an article the use of which cannot be dispensed with. If all the iron-mines in a country were in the hands of a few proprietors, and no means afforded of obtaining a supply by commerce, they might raise the price of iron very high. But, the greater the numbers of proprietors, the more difficult is it to raise the price by combination, and the more likely is a fall of price by competition. If the number of proprietors be very considerable, their power to raise the price by combination is very small, though still the article partakes in some degree of the nature of a monopoly.

The connexion between the rent of land and the price of corn is obvious. Land is necessary for the production of corn. The proprietors of land are very numerous. In settled countries, however, they are not the whole, and generally not the majority of the community. They possess, therefore, in some measure, though in a low degree, the power of the monopolist. Mr. Malthus calls this power a partial monopoly.

The indispensable necessity of the article, supposing foreign supply not admitted, strengthens the monopolizing power; but it is limited, on the other hand, by what the labourers can afford to give. They must be able to procure by their wages a supply sufficient to support nature and procure other necessaries: otherwise they will starve or emigrate, or rise in mobs, and seize the corn by violence from the granaries of the monopolists.

The rent of land is also restricted by competition among the proprietors. Where there is no exportation of corn, the extent of land in culture is limited by the demands of the existing population. In most countries the extent of land susceptible of cultivation is greater than the demands of the population, and as it is the interest of every proprietor to have as much of his land cultivated as he can, a competition takes place, attended with the usual effect of its being let upon lower terms.

As the rent of land can never fall so low as to allow nothing for that of the quality F., on the other hand it can never rise so high as to allow nothing but absolute necessaries to the agriculturists. If this were the case, every other employment must be reduced to equal indigence, otherwise the profession of agriculture would be deserted, and the profits of stock reduced to the lowest possible rate, or all stock vested in the hands of land-owners. Such an unnatural state of things, for obvious reasons, can never take place, though it is sometimes approximated more nearly to than it ought to be. For examples of this we need not have recourse to the state of the boors in Russia and Poland: we shall find one nearer home in the wretched condition of the Irish peasantry.

Inasmuch as corn partakes of the nature of a monopoly, its price is raised, and the rent in money raised. The price received by the farmer for the crops he raises is partly retained by him to enable him to pay the labourer and other expenses incurred in raising the crop, including his own profit, and partly paid by him in rent, for being permitted to use the productive power of the soil. He will not be able to retain more than the usual recompense for the labour and capital employed in cultivation. The rest he must give away, and it may be accounted rent, whether it be paid to the proprietor of the land, to the tithe-holder, or to the tax-gatherer. The amount is limited by the power which these possess of raising the price of corn, and whatever share the tithe-holder and tax-gatherer draw, the less remains for the proprietor. Some peculiar consequences, however, result from drawing part of the rent in the form of tithes, which shall be considered afterwards.

A part of our cultivated land is applied to raise other crops than corn. The price of these crops is regulated by that of corn. If a crop of flax be less profitable, that plant will not be cultivated till the price rise. If it be more profitable, more land will be sown with it till the price fall. The effects of commerce are at present out of the question.

The rent of wood-lands is modified by the slowness of the growth of timber. An acre of full-grown wood, upon general principles, ought to pay the rent of the ground during the time it has been growing, and other expenses, with interest, a deduction being made for the value of the young trees taken out for thinning, and of the pasture among the growing wood. There is something, however, so discouraging in the length of time before returns are expected, that few would plant on these terms. A man knows, when he plants, that he will not live to see the trees at perfection, or derive profit from them, and the concern which he takes in the affairs of posterity is comparatively languid. Accordingly the value of a full-grown wood generally exceeds the estimate of its cost, with every allowance of rent and interest. Even this expectation would be insufficient if mankind were not led to plant by other inducements. A certain quantity of wood is ornamental to the country, and long before the trees have attained their full size, the appearance of a plantation is delightful. Our bleak heaths, which present an uncouth aspect, and hardly admit of cultivation, are often well adapted for planting. A proprietor sees a thriving young wood rising in his vicinity, advancing in beauty every year, and engages in extending the agreeable scene.

The slowness of the growth of timber prevents the quantity from being easily adapted to the demands of the country. If too much or too little ground be appropriated to an annual crop, if too much be in tillage or in pasture, the evil cures itself in a few years; but if the quantity of wood be too small, the want can hardly be supplied, without the aid of commerce, to the present generation. The price of wood, and the profits of wood-land, depend upon the state of the country at least half a century ago.

Orchards and vineyards hold a middle place between corn-lands and wood-lands. Their returns are slower than the former, but much quicker than the latter.

The price of metals consists in part of a rent paid to the proprietor of the mine. The residue is a recompense for the capital and labour employed, and the risk incurred in the business of mining. If the number of known mines be fully sufficient for the supply of a country, the rent to the proprietor will be little. Still it is something. The rent increases with the scarcity of the mines. It is limited by the price which the community is willing to give for the article. Iron is the only metal, the use of which, in considerable quantities, cannot easily be dispensed with; but it is also, by the wise appointment of nature, the most plentiful, and therefore the rent drawn for iron mines is not very great. Copper, lead, and tin, are comparatively rare, and therefore, though far less useful, their mines are more lucrative to the proprietor. Quarries of lime, free-stone, and slate, generally yield a rent, though, in remote places, they yield but little. In mountainous countries abounding with granite no rent is drawn for that article, except in favourable situations.

In cold countries, fuel holds a considerable place among the necessaries of life. The articles chiefly used for that purpose are wood, turf, and pit-coal. The first of these only can be increased without limitation, and may by proper care afford an inexhaustible supply, if the others should fail. Of the second, our whole store is at once exposed to view, and by proper management it may, in some measure, be regenerated: yet still it is liable to be exhausted in length of time. The third admits of no known renovation; but the extent of undiscovered stores cannot be known. It is the most easily transported, and its price is regulated by the same principles as that of other minerals. It is limited, however, by the price of wood, which can be raised in all places, and would supersede the use of coal if its price were cheaper. The use of coal adds to the general wealth, by saving the ground that would be required for wood, and allowing our mosses to be converted into arable land.

The rent of appropriated fisheries depends on the quantity of fish they supply, and the notion entertained of their delicacy.

# CHAPTER XI.

## OF TITHES.

We return to the consideration of the burthen generally imposed on the farmer, in this and many other countries, by the abstraction of a determinate part of his produce for the payment of tithes.

We are not at present to take into view the purpose to which tithes are applied, or the persons by whom they are levied; the duty of providing a suitable maintenance for the clergy, the propriety of doing so in the way of tithe, or the objections which may be and have been urged against that system. The present question is, upon whom do tithes, when exacted, fall? Whether, according to some, do they fall on the proprietor of the land, who receives so much less rent from his tenant; or whether do they, according to others, fall upon the community at large, constituting a part of the expense of raising corn, and enhancing its value accordingly?

A tax upon land, of an invariable amount in money upon each estate, falls upon the landlord, who can never devolve it on the tenant, or any other part of the community. This proposition, so far as we know, has not been controverted. If it does not extend to tithes, this must be owing to some specialty connected with the latter. It can make no difference, in regard to either, whether they be in the first instance advanced by the farmer, or paid directly by the proprietor. The only specialty in regard to tithes is their variableness, being generally a certain proportion of the crop of the current year, or, at most, an annual sum of money considered as equivalent, on an average of a small number of years.

In some cases the proprietor is also the tithe-holder. In other words, some lands are tithe-free. It is believed no such proprietor ever drew from his tenants a part of what they paid him in the form of tithe, and the rest in the usual way of rent, or that he could derive any advantage from doing so. In the former chapter we stated the circumstances of extent of land, fertility, population, and competition, upon which rent depended; and apprehend that, while these remain the same, it is not in the power of the proprietor to obtain more from his tenants by having recourse to a capricious system. If he do so, he is more likely to injure both himself and them, by laying restraints on the most eligible modes of cultivation.

If the proprietor cannot draw more from the tenant on the whole, by taking so much for tithe, and so much for rent, it is difficult to conceive how it is possible to draw more when these portions are paid to different persons.

A large portion of rent, and according to some the whole, arises from the superior produce of fertile land above that of the most sterile in cultivation. So long as no tithe is drawn, the whole of this surplus goes to rent; but after tithing, it is only the surplus of what the tithe-holder leaves that is applicable thereto; and, as more is withdrawn from the fertile land, this surplus is less than before, and so far the rent estimated in corn is lessened, and the landlord bears the burthen of the tithe without remuneration.

It is argued, that the farmer who cultivated land of the quality F., previous to the establishment of the tithing system, could pay a rent equal to what land of the same quality yielded when uncultivated; the corn, when sold at the market-price, being sufficient to afford it: but if tithe be exacted, one-tenth of the produce being withdrawn, the remaining nine-tenths, when sold at the former price, would be insufficient; and therefore the farmer would discontinue to cultivate such land unless the price of corn rise, and, as the demands of the population require its cultivation, the price will rise.

But the farmer may continue to cultivate and sell his corn at the former price if his rent fall; and if the proprietor had no other way of disposing of his land, the rent would fall to the requisite extent. In existing circumstances, the rent is not likely to fall so much, and the price of corn may rise: but this is entirely owing to the imposition of a burthen, which falls exclusively on land under culture, and, by its inequality, deranges that appropriation of land which would otherwise take place, to the joint purposes of agriculture and pasturage.

The exaction of tithes is a discouragement to the raising of crops which require an expensive cultivation, because they fall upon the gross and not upon the net produce. The expense of cultivating an acre of hops is much greater than that of cultivating an acre of corn, but the value of the crop is generally so much greater as to afford a sufficient remuneration to the raiser. Suppose 20*l.* value of hops raised on an acre at the expense of 15*l.*, and 10*l.* value of wheat raised on an acre of like ground at an expense of 5*l.* So long as it remains tithe-free there will be a surplus of 5*l.* for rent and farmer's profit; but when tithe is exacted, viz., 2*l.* from the hop-acre and 1*l.* from the wheat-acre, there remains only 3*l.* from the former, but 4*l.* from the latter for rent and farmer's profit. Thus the cultivation of hops is discouraged, unless the price rise. The same applies to the cultivation of flax, perhaps in a smaller degree. It would also apply to the cultivation of corn, the expense of which is greater than that of pasturage, even though tithe were exacted on the produce of pasture land, to the full extent; and when we revert to the actual case of land in pasture generally paying no tithe at all, the advantage it possesses under a tithing system is much greater. If a burthen were imposed on pasture land, which pressed as much on it as tithes do upon cultivated land, there would be no rise in the price of corn, and the tithe, though advanced by the farmer, would fall on the proprietor.

Land of the quality F. is supposed to yield an equal surplus produce, after payment of all expenses, whether applied to the purposes of tillage or pasturage, and to pay an equal rent. So long as no tithe is levied, all this rent is paid to the proprietor; but if tithe be levied, so much of the produce of the land in tillage is transferred to another person, and the remainder only paid to the proprietor, while he continues to draw the full rent for pasture land as before. He therefore will not let such land for the purpose of tillage, unless the price of corn rise so much as to yield him the same money-rent as before, after satisfying the demands of the tithe-holder.

Let us resume the supposition, that land of the quality A. produces 10 bolls per acre, and that of the quality F. 3 $\frac{7}{20}$ bolls, and that the expense of cultivating an acre of either is the value of 3 bolls. The rent of A., so far as it depends on surplus produce, when no tithe is exacted, is 6 $\frac{13}{20}$ bolls. When tithe is drawn, which amounts to 1 boll from A. and $\frac{67}{200}$ of a boll from F., there remain 9 bolls of the produce of A. and $3\frac{3}{200}$ of that of F., and the difference applicable to the rent of A. is $5\frac{197}{200}$ bolls, or one-tenth less than before. The tenant of F. requiring 3 bolls for expenses, can only pay $\frac{3}{200}$ of a boll in rent; and if the tithe-holder, who draws $\frac{67}{200}$ of a boll from F. when in culture, drew the value of a like quantity from it when uncultivated, it would be impossible for the proprietor to obtain more than the very small rent above-mentioned for F. But, as no tithe is drawn from F. when uncultivated, none of it will be cultivated till the price of corn rise. As the cultivation of the usual portion of F. is required to afford the former supply to the population, a rise of price will take place, and if it rise one-tenth, the money-rent will be the same to the proprietor as before, while his corn rent has fallen one-tenth part.

It formerly required the price of three bolls to pay the farmer's expenses. A less quantity, sold at an advanced price, will give the same return in money. It will require only $2\frac{7}{10}$ bolls when the price has advanced one-tenth; and after selling that quantity to defray expenses, and having $\frac{67}{200}$ of a boll abstracted by the tithe-holder, there will remain $\frac{63}{200}$ of a boll for the landlord's rent. He received before $\frac{70}{200}$, but the smaller quantity, sold at an advanced price, will give the same return in money as the larger quantity did before.

A still higher rise in the price of corn would be required to put the farmer on his former footing, if his rent be not abated. All the corn raised is not sent to market. A part of it, nearly uniform, must be retained for the maintenance of the farmer's family and servant, and his labouring cattle. Suppose $1\frac{7}{20}$ bolls retained for these purposes, there remain 2 bolls previous to tithing, and $1\frac{133}{200}$ after tithing, to be taken to market. These must be sold for equal sums, to afford an equal allowance to the farmer for his miscellaneous expenses and profit; and if such a rise took place, the money rent of the proprietor would be increased.

But it is not probable that the price would rise to that extent. Any rise that takes place is occasioned by an additional quantity of F. being offered to the grazier, in consequence of which the rent of such land applied to pasturage will fall, and the price of corn is likely to settle at some intermediate rate between the former and that which would give the farmer a full equivalent for the tithe.

A derangement of the natural price of the produce of land, when under tillage or in pasturage, is thus occasioned by the exaction of tithes from the former, and not from the latter. To illustrate this further, we shall state an imaginary case. Suppose a country entirely agricultural, where the only crops raised are wheat and barley, and where the land, being all appropriated, is rented at a higher rate than that resulting from the difference of fertility. The prices of these two kinds of grain, and the quantities raised of each, will be regulated by the general expense and produce of an acre of each, and the relative demand for them: these points being adjusted when the land is tithe-free, let us suppose a tithe imposed on the wheat, but not on the barley. What would be the consequence? The farmer could not continue to cultivate wheat and sell it at the former price and pay the former rent. The price of wheat would rise, or the rent of wheat-land would fall, or both these alterations would take place to a certain extent. But, as land of the same quality would be let by the proprietor at the same rent, whatever purpose the farmer applied it to, the rent of barley-land would also fall; and the expense of raising that crop being the same as before, the natural and consequently the actual price of that grain would fall, and from the difference of price, it is likely that a smaller quantity of wheat and a larger quantity of barley would be consumed by the inhabitants than before. The demand and supply being the same as formerly, the whole rent paid by the farmer, tithe included, will also be the same, the portion drawn from wheat-land by the tithe-holder being compensated by the general fall of rent paid to the proprietor.

If a deficiency of one-tenth of the usual crop of corn be occasioned by blight, this, unless a supply can be procured by importation, must occasion a more parsimonious consumption, and the price will rise. But if importation be permitted, and a sufficient supply procured from a country where corn is raised at less expense, the price may not rise. The effect upon the market will be much the same, whether the tenth of the usual crop, being destroyed by blight, be supplied by the foreigner, or whether, being withdrawn in tithe, it is immediately poured into the market by the tithe-holder. The only difference is, that the tithe-holder's quantity being limited, he cannot depress the price of corn below its former rate; whereas the supply by importation, if unlimited, might depress it much lower, and force much of the inferior soils out of cultivation.

Different views in regard to rent and tithe have been taken by writers on political economy. But on one point they are nearly unanimous, that each writer's own system is attended with evidence equal to that of mathematical demonstration. We have endeavoured to trace what appears most probable, with all the care we can, though we deliver our opinion with considerable diffidence, as consequences may arise from different modes of polity, or from supervening circumstances, which it is very difficult to foresee.

On the whole, notwithstanding very respectable authority on the other hand*, we incline to the opinion that, in most cases, tithe falls chiefly, if not entirely, on the proprietor.

As the revenue of the tithe-holder is deteriorated when land is thrown out of culture, his interest will induce him not to exact rigorously tithe from sterile land, but to compound for it

* Ricardo on Political Economy, chap. ix.

on moderate terms. In like manner, in the imaginary case above supposed, he would compound easily for the tithe on wheat-land, to prevent it from being converted into barley-land.

The foregoing reasoning proceeds on the supposition that tithe is drawn in kind, or at least is fixed annually upon an assumed valuation of the crop for the present year. If the tithe be compounded for at a fixed sum for a term of years, or during the life of the incumbent, it is clearly a part of the rent kept back from the landlord. This is also the case in Scotland, where tithes (there called teinds) are levied on a different system, and at a fixed rate, payable sometimes in grain, sometimes in money.

# CHAPTER XII.

## DISTRIBUTION OF WEALTH.

WEALTH is only desirable as a means of increasing human enjoyment; and the relative value of different quantities of wealth ought to be estimated by the degree in which they promote the happiness of the owners. This depends upon the mode of its distribution, as well as upon its absolute quantity.

An inquiry into this subject is apt to raise an alarm in the minds of a considerable portion of society. They dread the introduction of levelling principles, the invasion of property, and subversion of the present establishment of society. These fears, which the higher ranks are at all times ready to entertain, have been much increased by the evils which accompanied the French Revolution. Though redress of political grievances only was at first held forth by the promoters of that event, it soon led to the dissolution of property, and to atrocities of the most enormous kind. Whilst we hold that the preservation of social constitutions should be maintained with the strictest care, and even where defects are manifest, that remedies should be applied with extreme caution,—we cannot go the length, which some do, of condemning indiscriminately every proposed amendment in the present arrangements, from the dread of the evils which may attend innovations. While we consider discussion on these points as conducive to the true interest of society, we would not willingly offend the feelings, or incur the indignation of alarmists. We hold that a certain measure of inequality in the distribution of wealth is not only unavoidable, but is conducive to human welfare, both in regard to external enjoyment and moral improvement; and if, upon a fair inquiry, it should appear that a nearer approach to equality, than at present takes place in most civilized states, is desirable, we not only reprobate the attainment of this by a violent invasion of property, but we disapprove of any measure which would occasion a sudden alteration in the present state of things, or which is revolting to the feelings which habit has established in the minds of a respectable class of the community. We may not approve these feelings: we may wish them gradually extinguished; but while they subsist, they ought not to be rudely violated.

By the gifts of nature and returns of industry mankind are possessed of ampler stores than are requisite for mere subsistence. A portion is applied for procuring comforts, elegancies, and luxuries. All must be provided in necessaries; but we may conceive the overplus either equally distributed among the whole community, or accumulated in the hands of a few, or of any part less than the whole, and that in all variety of proportions.

In a small and simple community, there is little inequality of circumstances. In a large and flourishing state the inequality is commonly very great. If the income of a common labourer in Britain be accounted one, there are some whose incomes exceed one thousand; and in most other countries of Europe the inequality is equally striking. Oriental countries present examples of still greater inequality. In the flourishing times of the Roman commonwealth and empire, the fortunes of the rich were enormous.

Let us suppose a small portion taken from the income of a rich man who has a thousand, and added to that of a labourer. An addition of one-tenth would sensibly increase the enjoyments of the labourer, and the want of it would hardly be felt by the rich man. The loss, if he knew it, might give him uneasiness, but is merely imaginary. His house, his furniture, his table and equipage, would undergo no sensible alteration. An increase of happiness is, therefore, obtained by this transfer of property. Such, at least, is its immediate consequence. If this be repeated a second, a third, and a considerable number of times, the successive additions do not in the same degree increase the enjoyments of the poor man, and the loss comes to be sensibly felt by the rich man.

There is a limit beyond which equalization of property ceases to be desirable. A state of complete equality is unsuitable to human nature, and would detract from those energies, the exertion of which, under due regulation, promotes the improvement of our intellectual and active powers, and extends the sphere of our higher enjoyments.

Industry is excited by the hope of improving our circumstances. This hope is founded on the supposition of inequality, and supported by the expectation of a suitable reward, and secure possession of what is obtained. Hence exertions are produced, which add to the mass of general wealth, and by their invigorating influence operate in a still more essential manner to the increase of human happiness.

Without some inequality of situation the powers of the human mind could not be brought to a high pitch of improvement. The acquisition of knowledge and cultivation of genius require a share of leisure incompatible with absolute equality. It is requisite that some men be exempted from manual labour, in order that they may apply to those studies and pursuits which not only raise their own minds to superior excellence, but lead to improvements of general use to society. A certain measure of competence affords facilities in these pursuits. Knowledge is collected from books, or acquired by general conversation and travelling, or investigated by expensive experiments; all of which are beyond the reach of the poor man.

Some regard is also due to the enjoyments afforded by the elegant arts, and other sources of innocent gratification, which affluence confers, and the more refined state of social intercourse which prevails in the higher ranks of society, and extends its influence in some measure to the inferior ones.

There is also reason to believe that the variety of duties resulting from the distinction of stations contributes to the improvement of our moral nature. The man who, under the influence of virtuous principles, discharges properly the duties he owes to his superiors, equals, and inferiors, appears to hold a higher place in the scale of moral excellence than he who has only one class of duties to discharge. The obligations arising from a greater variety of connections may be considered as a school of moral discipline, under which virtue is exercised, and advanced to a higher degree of perfection.

It is, therefore, desirable, first to ascertain the degree of inequality of circumstances most conducive to human happiness; and then, if the actual inequality exceed that measure, to inquire into the practical and admissible means of approaching to it, without doing violence to property, or introducing other disorders into society.

In regard to the former, it is obviously impracticable to fix the measure with precision.

Some general principles, however, may be proposed which ascertain it within certain limits.

The wisdom of the prayer of Agur must be admitted even by those who do not acknowledge the authority of the book in which it is contained. The eligibility of the middle station of life is become almost proverbial, and is the conclusion which a candid inquiry can hardly fail to lead to; and that, either upon the religious and moral views on which Agur founds his preference, or in regard to mere physical enjoyments. That it is preferable to a state of poverty, none will be found to question: that it is preferable to a state of great affluence is a doctrine that will not be relished by the ambitious and worldly-minded. But the philosopher, who considers the temptations to indolence and dissipation which affluence affords, and which are so seldom effectually resisted, and that want of relish for social and innocent enjoyments which is the frequent effect of an unrestrained course of enjoyment, can hardly fail to concur in Agur's supplication.

This leads us to desire that as large a proportion of mankind as possible be placed in the middle station of life, neither very rich, nor very poor. Under this class several descriptions of men are comprehended: those who enjoy a moderate competency from landed or other property; the greater part of those engaged in commerce, or who gain a livelihood by following the liberal professions; many who are employed in manufactures, but who are occupied in superintending others rather than in manual labour. These persons are not idle, but their employments are not servile or incessant, and they have leisure and opportunities for intellectual improvement. Though something is deducted by the existence of this class from the quantity of manual labour performed, the loss is fully repaid by their exertion in superior occupations, from which all ranks derive advantage.

But all cannot and ought not to be in the middle station. Such equality, were it practicable, which it is not, in civilized society, would be subversive of social order and happiness.

Let us inquire into the measure of wealth which would fall to the share of each person if it were fully equalized. This is not so great as most persons, upon a transient view, would be apt to suppose. The rich are so few in number, compared with the whole community, that the distribution of their wealth would not raise the general circumstances above a moderate competency.

In a former chapter we stated the average expense of the labouring classes and their families at nine pounds each person, and that of the aggregate of all ranks at eighteen pounds. If this be nearly correct, a system of complete equality would only raise the labourer's income to the last-mentioned sum. If only one half of the wealth at present possessed by the higher ranks were transferred to the labourer, it would raise his income to thirteen pounds ten shillings, and this seems the utmost extent to which the levelling system could be extended, without introducing consequences utterly subversive of the welfare of society. Whether a transfer to this extent would leave sufficient distinction of circumstances to answer every useful purpose, is a point not easily determined.

We maintain, however, without hesitation, that an alteration in the present state of society in this country, which would add something to the condition of the labourer, if such a change were effected gradually and imperceptibly by the silent operation of natural causes, would tend, on the whole, to the increase of human happiness.

A benevolent man, whose duty or situation leads him to visit the cottages of the poor, and inspect the manner in which they live, will observe, with regret, that the family is often very inadequately provided with lodging, furniture, and clothing; that sometimes they have not a sufficiency of wholesome food and fuel; and that not unfrequently the labourer is obliged to work too hard, or too long, in order to obtain a supply of mere necessaries to his family.

These hardships, however, do not press equally at all times, or upon every description of labour, and very much depends on the sobriety and good management of the heads of the family.

When these qualities prevail in times of ordinary plenty, and when labour is in ordinary demand, the visitor will frequently find a comfortable cottage, sufficient to accommodate the family without exposing them to the risk of disease, or want of cleanliness, from being overcrowded; provided with the most useful articles of plain furniture, and, perhaps, a few ornamental ones; their clothes decent, and sufficient for every-day wear, though plain, with a better suit for Sunday. The husband, when he returns from his labour, then receives a cheerful reception from his wife and family, and after partaking of a frugal, but unstinted meal, relaxes himself in innocent conversation till the family retire to rest. This picture is not utopian; we have often witnessed it, and it is a state of comfort which may be brought within the reach of all the labouring classes, unless they deprive themselves of it by intemperance, or some other kind of misconduct.

The bulk of mankind must be employed for the greater part of their time in manual labour, but they ought not to be forced to such severe exertion as exhausts their strength prematurely; nor should their labour be so long continued as to leave no time for relaxation and intellectual improvement. In general ten hours' labour in the day, from six to six, with two hours of interval, is as much as they should undertake. Those engaged in the labours of agriculture usually work longer in time of harvest, as manufacturers do upon urgent occasions, and this may be compensated by extending the hours of relaxation when circumstances admit of it. When labour is unusually hard, the time of its continuance should be proportionally shortened.

That sacred institution which withdraws one day in seven from the ordinary employments of life, and assigns it to religious and moral improvement, and the innocent pleasures of social conversation, can never be too much admired and respected. When viewed merely as a human institution, it deserves a preference to any which the heathen world can lay claim to; and we ought carefully to guard against any practice that may infringe on the reverence with which it is regarded, and thereby open the way for its gradual neglect.

As the labouring classes must always be the most numerous, to promote their welfare is to promote human happiness at large. An apprehension is entertained by those who are not inclined to favour the labouring classes, that too liberal a reward of labour would lead to idleness and intemperance. The most effectual remedy against these evils is to give them such an education, and induce such moral habits, as may promote a relish for the moderate comforts of life. The education of the inferior ranks is an object of so much importance as to require a separate discussion, and will be considered in a subsequent chapter.

As an ordinary share of industry should not miss a suitable reward, so extraordinary diligence or abilities should procure a larger share of enjoyment, or prove the means of raising a man to a higher station in life.

The different ranks of society should not be separated, as they are in some countries, by strongly marked and insurmountable barriers. They should be blended by shades, almost imperceptible, and a transition to a higher station should be easily accessible to merit.

Some other circumstances connected with the welfare of the lower ranks deserve consideration.

The numerous class engaged in manufactures, or manual occupation, are either journeymen employed by masters who furnish materials, and sometimes tools, and pay them wages for their work, or free labourers who find employment for themselves. In a simple state of society almost all are free labourers. In a more advanced state, journeymen are the most numerous. Those manufactures which require an expensive apparatus, and much division of labour, cannot be carried on otherwise; but as we consider the situation of the free labourer to be more eligible than that of the journeyman, we wish the number of the former enlarged in such employments as admit of it.

A person chiefly employed in manufacture or manual trade may allot some portion of his time to agriculture. This generally extends no farther than the cultivation of a garden, or perhaps some work in harvest. It can be most conveniently undertaken by free labourers, though journeymen are not altogether excluded from it. We think it desirable in situations that admit of it. It is conducive to health, and the variety of employment contributes in some measure to mental improvement. In some places a small piece of ground may be rented, and a cow or two kept, which the wife may manage, besides discharging her other duties. We have generally observed that families, where this system was followed, lived more comfortably than their neighbours.

The proper size of farms has been a subject

of much discussion, and the prevailing opinion at present seems to be in favour of large farms. The arguments in support of this opinion are, that agriculture is conducted in a superior manner by persons possessed of considerable property, and the land brought to a higher state of fertility; and that the requisite operations can be carried on at less expense by means of the superior instruments which the opulent farmer employs, and the economical arrangements which an extensive and improved farm admits of. Another circumstance tends, we believe, to corroborate this opinion. A traveller is gratified with the ornate appearance of the fields, the neatness of the farm buildings, and the rich farmer's comfortable house, almost rivalling the mansion of the country gentleman, and is induced to think favourably of the system which presents to him such agreeable objects.

A distribution of all the country into farms of this kind would be attended with serious evils. The number of such farmers must be comparatively small. The more numerous class of the possessors of moderate farms, occupying a middle station in life, would disappear.

We incline to the opinion that a gradation in

the size of farms is most conducive to the general good. Some branches of manufacture cannot be carried on, in the improved state to which they are now brought, without complicated machinery and extensive premises: but this is not the case in farming operations, where the division of labour is more limited, and the requisite implements comprehended in a narrower compass. Ploughs, harrows, and other agricultural tools of the best construction can be employed on farms of a moderate extent, and even the threshing-mill, the most complicated machine which the farmer has occasion for, is now constructed on a variety of scales, suited to farms of all sizes.

Perhaps some such arrangement as the following would be most eligible.

Every gentleman should himself occupy a farm of moderate extent. From his superior means of information he is likely to adopt the most approved modes of agriculture, and bring them into general use in places where they were not known before. The allotment of part of his time to this employment is rational and laudable, and will tend, in some measure, to form a bond of connection between him and the farmer.

Very large farms, which cannot be superintended by one person, and are therefore left to the management of hired overseers, are not so desirable.

A farm of four or five hundred acres of arable land is as large as any ought to be. To conduct such a farm requires considerable capital, and the management will give sufficient employment to a man of ordinary activity. The profits should place him in comfortable circumstances, and even put the acquisition of wealth within his reach.

We should propose that one-fourth of the arable land be laid out in farms of this size, including that which is in the actual possession of the proprietors.

We would allot one-half of the arable land in farms of various sizes, less than the former, but not under one hundred acres. Such farms require the employment of several servants.

The remaining fourth of the arable land we would reserve for small farms, of such a size that the work may be chiefly done by the tenant and his family, perhaps with the assistance of a single servant, or of labour hired occasionally. Part of this division might be laid out in portions of a still smaller size, that did not give full employment to the possessor, who might carry on, besides, the occupation of a miller, carter, independent tradesman, or occasional day-labourer.

Several advantages arise from having part of the land divided into small possessions. To the occupiers of these, it is an object to raise poultry, and some other articles for sale which are below the attention of the wealthy farmer; and where the cottager occupies little land, he can pay more minute attention to every part of it.

The improvement of small pieces of barren land, chiefly by manual labour, is sometimes effected by cottagers in circumstances where it would never be undertaken by the large farmer. The following incident, which we have heard upon good authority, is illustrative of this. A number of gentlemen who had an interest in a barren common, having met for the purpose of dividing it, found that an individual had, without notice or permission, settled himself in a corner of it, built a cottage, and brought a few acres into cultivation. On this they were disposed to punish him severely for his intrusion, when one of them remarked that, in his opinion, so far from being an object of punishment, he had conferred an obligation on them, by shewing them what the land could be brought to, and ought to be rewarded. To this opinion they all acceded, and granted him the absolute right, or long lease of the ground he had improved, on moderate terms.

Such a distribution of land as is here proposed corresponds with that gradation in the various ranks of society which we consider as beneficial to mankind. The farmer of the higher rate approximates to the country gentleman, and in descending from him to the cottager, we do not meet with any marked line of separation. Every man may raise himself to a higher class, if he have talents for it, without being repelled as inadmissible.

We have heard an argument advanced against the continuance of cottagers in a part of the country from which they had been banished by the great farmer. It was said that the same men, being hired by the farmer, lived more comfortably as his servants, than they did before upon their small possessions. We are not satisfied with this account of the matter. They were, perhaps, as well fed and clothed as before. But the independence of the cottager raises his character to a state superior to that of the servant.

By the gentle gradation proposed in the size of farms, the improved modes of agriculture, at first introduced by the gentlemen and wealthy farmer, would be gradually diffused through all inferior ones.

The system of absentees and middlemen deserves the severest reprobation. The latter have no other interest than to rack the actual cultivators to the utmost of their power. The wretched state to which a great part of Ireland is reduced by the prevalence of this system, affords a lamentable but instructive lesson in regard to it.

So long as the quantity of wealth belonging to the community remains the same, we cannot add to the portion assigned to one class without deducting from that of another. If we increase the comforts of the inferior orders, at whose expense would we do so? We would not lessen the number, or restrict the comforts of those who hold the middle station of life. We know not a more respectable character than that of a country gentleman who generally resides on his estate, takes an interest in the welfare of his tenants, encourages agriculture by his countenance and example, and discharges, as occasion requires, the functions of a magistrate. Overgrown fortunes admit of reduction, and if this can be effected without violence or injustice, it would hardly detract from the enjoyment of any rank, and might lead to arrangements that would increase the general happiness of society. Such overgrown fortunes are often employed in maintaining idlers, or squandered at Newmarket or other places of still more infamous description.

Every political institution, the tendency of which is the further accumulation of fortunes already overgrown, should be rejected.

## CHAPTER XIII.

### EQUALIZATION OF WEALTH.

ADMITTING that a distribution of wealth, approaching nearer to equality than the present one, is desirable, it is still a matter of difficulty to point out the means of obtaining it without injustice.

The stability of property fairly acquired is no less necessary for the poor man's pittance than for the rich man's treasure. If it be unhinged, a door is opened for every crime and every calamity. Regard is also due to those feelings which the present constitution of society have nourished.

While the mass of general wealth remains the same, the circumstances of the lower ranks can only be improved by raising the wages of labour, or by conferring on them some share of property as generally as possible. It is the latter of these we are at present to consider.

It will throw light on this subject, to inquire

into the causes of the inequality in the circumstances of mankind. Some of these are entitled to our highest approbation; others are of a more dubious kind; and others clearly reprehensible. Yet though these last should have been resisted at the beginning, it may not be consistent with the peace of society to disturb property, however wrongfully acquired, at a distant period.

As a large share of the wealth which a man enjoys is obtained by the exertion of his active power, an inequality of circumstances must arise from the inequality of these powers. We do not all possess the same bodily strength, and the inequality of our mental endowments is still greater. In some cases the want of power, corporeal or mental, is so great as to incapacitate a man altogether from acquiring a livelihood. When poverty arises from this cause, the sufferer is not to blame, yet, except in extreme cases, he cannot receive relief from any political institution.

Another source of inequality is to be traced to the different conduct of men. Some accumulate wealth by industry and frugality, while others dissipate it by neglect or extravagance. Here the successful are well entitled to their gains, while the sufferers deserve the hardships they have brought upon themselves. So far as inequality of circumstances arises from this cause, we are fully sensible of its propriety.

A third source of inequality arises from fortune or accident. These terms are somewhat vague. In illustration many instances may be adduced, though it is impossible to enumerate them all. The fruits of one man's field may be blasted by an unavoidable disaster, while that of another man is unusually productive. The result of mercantile undertakings is still more precarious. A man's success in life depends, in a great measure, on his being placed in a station where his peculiar talents have scope for exertion, or are brought into view. This is sometimes the result of his prudence; but it frequently depends upon circumstances, as to which he is in a great measure, or altogether, passive. The number and weight of his competitors often decide his fortune. The business of life cannot be carried on without incurring risk, by reposing confidence in other men, and in a variety of other ways. One man escapes the danger, another suffers by it to the full extent.

Another source of inequality is injustice, when

the powerful invade the property of the weak, or the crafty obtain that of the simple. Although these crimes be the objects of the highest reprobation; yet it is impossible, even in the best constituted societies, entirely to prevent them, and in disorderly times they prevail to a great extent.

A man of a benevolent but enthusiastic turn of mind may be desirous of calling in the interposition of power to correct these inequalities, and relieve the unfortunate industrious at the expense of the undeservedly successful. A little reflection, however, may convince him that this cannot be done without subverting the rights of property, on which the existence of society depends, and introducing worse evils than those which it was intended to remedy.

Institutions which tend, in some measure, to lessen the causes which lead to an inequality of fortune deserve every encouragement. The modern expedients of insuring against the dangers of the sea, and destruction by fire, and of equalizing the diversity in the circumstances of families occasioned by the diversity of the length of life, have proved highly beneficial.

A principal source of the inequality of circumstances arises from the wealth accumulated by former generations, and transmitted to a part of the present by inheritance or otherwise, in all variety of proportions. This is subject to regulation by the laws of the community, which are different in different countries. Some of them favour accumulation of property, and others tend to its dispersion.

The right of every one to enjoy the fruits of his own labour affords the clearest foundation of property, and this extends in a great measure to the property of land, as much of the value of land arises from culture and improvement. The right of property in land is now fully established in every civilized country, subject to the laws which must be inviolably observed till they be altered by the legislature of the community.

The industrious man may be better fed, better clothed, and better lodged than his neighbours. He may reserve a part of his gains for increasing his enjoyments at an after period, or supporting him under the infirmities of age. But has he a right to transmit what remains unconsumed to his children and friends; or does his property revert at his death to the general fund, open to every occupier, or common to all?

Some lawyers have affirmed, that the transmission of property from the dead to the living is merely an ordinance of positive law, and ascribe the title which children generally exercise over the property of their deceased father to the circumstance of their being generally the first occupiers.

"Naturally speaking," says a lawyer of the highest character, "the moment a man ceases to be, he ceases to have any dominion; else, if he have a right to dispose of his acquisitions beyond his life, he would have a right to direct their disposal for a million of ages after him, which would be highly absurd and inconvenient. All property, therefore, must cease upon death, considering men as absolute individuals, and unconnected with civil society. But as, under civilized governments, which are calculated for the peace of mankind, such a constitution would be productive of endless disturbance, the universal law of almost every nation (which is a kind of necessary law of nature) has either given the dying person a power of continuing his possession by will; or, in case he neglects to dispose of it, or is not permitted to make any disposition at all, the municipal law of the country then steps in, and declares who shall be the successor, representative, or heir of the deceased, that is, who shall have a right to enter upon this vacant possession, to prevent that confusion which its becoming again common would occasion. The right of inheritance, or descent to the children or relations of the deceased—is certainly a wise and effectual, but clearly a political establishment. A man's children, or nearest relations, are usually about him on his death-bed, and are the earliest witnesses of his decease. They become, therefore, generally, the next immediate occupants, till at length, in process of time, this frequent usage ripens into general law *."

We cannot agree to this doctrine. There is a sense of property congenial to the human mind, which extends beyond the life of the individual, and entitles him to transmit what he has acquired by his labour, and not consumed, to his children, or those whom he loves and esteems. The man who builds a house, or plants a vineyard, feels a right to lodge in that house, and use the fruits of that vineyard. He also feels a right to exercise the only act of property that can take place after his death,—to appoint the person who shall then

* Blackstone's Commentaries, book ii. chap. i.

possess and use them. The laws of society may subject the exercise of this right, as well as of any other, to such regulations as are conducive to the general good. They cannot be deemed to create it, although they may modify and limit it.

The right of disposing property, especially landed property, by will, has, in many countries, been posterior to the laws of descent, and in some countries has never been fully recognized. Yet it is naturally prior to it. What a man has gained by his industry is so completely his own, that he may use it, or convey, during his life, the right of using it to any person he pleases, and there is no reason why he should be more restricted in the appointment of its disposal after his death. From natural affection, he will generally prefer his own children, or, when these are wanting, his nearest relations. If he neglect to make a positive destination, the law supplies the omission, from a presumption of his will, founded on those natural sentiments.

In no civilized country does the property of the deceased revert into a common fund. But the regulations of different countries in regard to the permission or prevention of the disposal of property by will, and of the disposal of property where wills are not permitted, or not made, are extremely various. In the laws of antiquity, we meet with no distinction between succession in heritable and moveable property. In all modern codes, that distinction forms an important part. It derives its origin from feudal principles. So long as the feudal system continued in vigour, the securing of a vassal fit for military service being considered as essential, the law of primogeniture was inforced, and alienation of land by testament not permitted. At that time personal property was comparatively of less value, and the law paid little attention to it. The value of this kind of property has now become, in mercantile countries, greater than that of the land; but the laws which direct its succession are different.

The diversity in the rules of succession, in cases of intestacy, or where wills are not permitted, consist chiefly in admitting or rejecting the right of primogeniture, and the preference of males to females. There is also some difference in the rules by which the succession, when it devolves on collaterals, is regulated.

A man may be permitted to dispose of the whole of his property by will, or he may be limited to the disposal of a certain part, the residue necessarily descending to his children. His right of disposing of it may be limited to the appointment of the next possessor; or he may be permitted to appoint a succession of heirs who are in existence; or he may have the more extensive power of appointing a series of heirs, yet unborn, to the end of time.

We find all these varieties in the laws of different nations, and none of them, except the last, can be said to be contrary to the law of nature. The preference of one system to another is a matter of political wisdom, and should be given to that which tends most to promote the general welfare.

At Athens the sons succeeded equally to the inheritance of the father. At Rome, the sons and daughters succeeded equally. Disposal of property by will was not permitted in the earliest times, but was introduced afterwards, and even something similar to modern entails, by which the line of succession could be directed for several generations.

In the time of the Roman republic the plebeian party frequently attempted to introduce an agrarian law, for limiting the extent of land which any person could hold, and they sometimes obtained a partial and temporary success.

By the laws of England at present, a man, unless specially restricted by family settlements, may dispose of all his property, real or personal, if he observe the proper forms. In case of intestacy, the law of primogeniture takes place among males in heritable property; but when the succession falls to females, they all share equally. In personal property, the children, male or female, succeed equally. In some districts there are local rules of succession, different from the general law of the country.

In Scotland, the landholder, if not specially restricted, may not only settle the inheritance on whomever he pleases, but may determine the line of succession by a deed of entail, in all succeeding time. The rules of succession in heritage, when there is no will, are nearly the same as in England. In moveables his power is more limited. The children have an indefeasible right to one-third when there is a widow, and to one-half when there is none. This is called their *legitim*, and is equally divided among them, without distinction of sex: but, if the deceased also leave heritage, the heir has no share of the moveable property, unless he choose to throw the heritage and moveables into a common fund, and take an equal share of the whole with the other children. If there be no will, the whole moveable property is divided equally among the children, and, failing them, among the nearest relatives.

By the law of France, established during the revolution, a person who has one child is only permitted to dispose of one-half of his property by will, and the child inherits the other half as a matter of right. If he has two children he can only dispose of one-third by will, and if more than two of one-fourth, the remainder being equally divided among the children. In cases of intestacy, the property is equally divided among all the children, without regard to sex or seniority.

Different opinions will be entertained concerning the preference due to one or other of these systems, or others that may be supposed better than any of them ; and these will depend, in a considerable measure, upon the preference given to the aristocratical or democratical constitution of society.

Few, however, it is believed, will approve of the system of Scotch entails. They are, in every point of view, indefensible. Their tendency is to accumulate property to a very large extent: for an entailed estate can sustain no diminution; but may be augmented by frequent accessions, as every new purchase may be, and often is, added to the former entail. This evil is already of considerable magnitude, and is daily increasing. It is believed about one-third of the land in Scotland is already entailed, and that chiefly in large portions. It proves a severe restraint on the circulation of property, and threatens to stop it altogether. Many other arguments may be adduced against it;—the losses it occasions to creditors; the infringement on parental authority; the temptations to which it exposes inexperienced youth, from the consciousness of premature independence; the destitute state in which it often leaves the younger children of a family, and the discouragement it throws in the way of agricultural improvements. The motive which leads to it, a desire of perpetuating families, is not founded on any rational or commendable principle. It is the offspring of aristocratic pride, and is inconsistent with the transitory nature of human possessions and enjoyments. Upon the whole, there are ample reasons for censuring this part of our law, and wishing it may be speedily and completely abolished.

By an act passed a good many years ago, the holders of entailed estates in Scotland were authorized to grant leases of a certain duration; and by a late act they are entitled to burthen the estate with annuities to widows, and provisions to younger children to a certain extent. These alterations in the law lessen the evil of entails; but there still remains enough to make their entire abolition desirable.

A practice of the same nature, but still more pernicious, has been admitted, the assignment of the rents of an estate to trustees for a term of years, in order to accumulate, and be applied for the purchase of more land, or some other capricious purpose.

One argument in favour of entails is drawn from the aristocratic part of our constitution, and must be admitted to have some weight. The members of one branch of our legislature are hereditary, and it is fit that every person who exercises the functions of a legislator should possess a fortune that may render him independent. For this purpose, either the character of the legislator should fall with the dissipation of the estate (of which our records present one example), or an estate should be secured to accompany the right of legislation. This might be permitted, to every requisite extent, without any considerable encroachment on the state of general property, by limiting the quantity allowed to be entailed to what was sufficient to answer the purpose for which it is at all permitted.

We incline to the opinion, that every man should have the complete disposal of his property, heritable or moveable, but without any power of substitution; the person or persons who succeed him having an equal right to its free disposal. We do not mean to exclude him from the right of burthening his heir or heirs with what provisions or annuities he pleases.

It is not likely that society would receive any detriment from the power which this system would give to parents. They might, indeed, disinherit their children, and leave them destitute! But the natural affection of parents, even those of harsh character, is so strong that the instances of the exercise of that power would be very rare, except when the misconduct of the children was extreme. The welfare of families, as well as the public welfare, requires that parental authority be supported, and a salutary check given to that profligacy and extravagance which is the frequent consequence of early independence.

A right to the disposal of property at pleasure has been considered as beneficial to society, from the encouragement it gives to industry. If a man knows that the wealth which he acquires is to fall at his death in a different direction from what he wishes, his exertions, it is said, are likely to be more languid. We do not, however, see much weight in this argument, or suppose it necessary that a man should have the power of directing the succession of his acquisitions in an endless, or even in a long train, in order to excite his industry. We have seldom observed that those were less bent upon accumulating wealth, who neither knew nor cared who was to succeed to it; and are of opinion that the power of disposing of it in the first instance is fully sufficient to furnish every necessary stimulus to industry, and that no man ever relaxed in his exertions because it was not in his power to settle his wealth on a series of unborn heirs for all succeeding generations.

Holding that the disposal of property at the death of the owner should be always free, but always limited to the first instance, with the exception above-mentioned of the case of hereditary legislators, the next object of inquiry regards the most eligible mode of legal destination in cases of intestacy.

The law of primogeniture, especially if joined with a power of entailing, has a tendency to accumulate property; the law of equal distribution has a tendency to disperse it. If these laws be insurmountable, their effects in either way will be very extensive, and, at last, very pernicious. If they may be set aside by the will of the proprietor, and only regulate succession in cases of intestacy, their effect is still considerable, for many die without making a will; and besides, the general rule has an effect on the prevailing sentiments; so that even when a special settlement is made, it will most frequently be in some conformity to what the law would have directed if it had been wanting.

That such is the case appears from the experience of what happens in England. The disposal of property, heritable and moveable, is there, in general, unrestrained; yet landed gentlemen, almost uniformly, leave their estate to their eldest son, and often leave the younger children slenderly provided for. Merchants, on the other hand, commonly make a more equal distribution of their wealth among their children, unless they have invested it in land, in which case they may imbibe the spirit of the hereditary land-holder.

The enactment of an equal division of heritage among the children, in cases of intestacy, would be too violent a change in our present law, and too offensive to our prevailing sentiments. But a limited legal provision to the younger children would be a beneficial alteration in our law. By the late act relating to entails in Scotland, the holder is entitled to charge the estate with one year's rent, if he has one child besides the heir, with two year's rent if he has two children, and with three year's rent if he has three or more. It might be well if some such allowance were granted in all cases of intestacy, where there was not a sufficiency of moveable property to afford a like provision to the younger children. It would not occasion any sudden dispersion of property, or be attended with any other hurtful consequence.

The case of a younger brother, when left unprovided for, is worse than that of a man in inferior station who has no property. Being bred in his father's family, he has acquired habits of luxury, and is unfit for manual labour. The army and navy can only receive a limited number, and there are few other professions, consistent with the station he holds in society, that can be prosecuted with advantage by a person destitute of patrimony. It is desirable he should have some share of the paternal inheritance, not to supersede the necessity of exertion, but to enable him to exert his faculties with a reasonable prospect of success.

The revolutionary law of succession in France is said to have been extremely effective, and to have broken down much of the property into minute portions, to the ruin of many distinguished families, and general injury of society.

This division of the land into small portions is not entirely in consequence of the operation of the law of succession. At the revolution, many of the great proprietors were forced to leave the country, and the properties of the emigrants being seized by the revolutionary government, were disposed of, generally, in small allotments.

According to the statements of the Duc de Gaete*, the number of taxable proprietors in France, in the year 1816, was 4,833,000, and the number of persons in their families was 14,479,800, or about three to a family at an average (which we think too low), paying in property-taxes 282,935,928 franks, which being taken at 20 per cent. gives the annual value of their property 1,414,979,640 franks. Of these proprietors 3,665,300 pay only $12\frac{88}{100}$ franks at an average, and altogether 47,178,649 franks, answering to an annual value of 235,893,245

* The numbers in this statement are taken from the Edinburgh Review, No. lxxx.; as we have not Gaete's publication at hand, our opinions are, in some points, different from those of the able writers of that journal, and we have assigned our reasons.

franks, and the average annual value of each property is only $64\frac{4}{10}$ franks, or about 51*s.* of our money. These proprietors are day-labourers, with a cottage and garden belonging to themselves. The number of persons in their families is about eleven millions. The proportion of property allotted to this class is about one-sixth of the whole.

The number of proprietors in the superior classes is 1,167,700; the number of persons in their families, estimated as above, is 3,503,100; the amount of their taxation is 235,757,279 franks, or $201\frac{899}{1000}$ franks each at an average; therefore the annual value of their property is 1,178,786,395 franks, or $1009\frac{1}{2}$ franks, equal to about 40*l.* sterling to each at an average.

The whole statement is as follows:—

| No. of Proprietors. | Amount of Taxation. | Average Taxation. | Total Annual Value. | Average Income. | |
|---|---|---|---|---|---|
| | Franks. | Franks. | Franks. | Franks. | £. s. d. |
| 3,665,300 | 47,178,649 | 12.85 | 235,893.245 | 64 | 2 11 0 |
| 928,000 | 86,043,089 | 92.78 | 430,215.445 | 464 | 17 11 0 |
| 212,636 | 90,411,706 | 425.45 | 452,058.530 | 2,127 | 85 0 0 |
| 18,848 | 27,653,016 | 1,468. | 138,265.080 | 7,340 | 293 11 0 |
| 8,216 | 31,649,469 | 3,864.50 | 158,247.340 | 19,272 | 771 0 0 |
| 4,833,000 | 282,935,928 | | 1,414,679.640 | | |

Much as we reprobate the violence which has led to the present distribution of property in France, that distribution, as exhibited in this statement, considered in itself, does not appear to us so pernicious as it has been represented.

The eleven millions of the lowest class of proprietors, families included, constitute the mass of the labouring part of the community. Their small possessions do not supersede the necessity of their labour, nor indispose them for it, while the benefit they derive from them gives a considerable addition to their comfort. The application of one-sixth part of the rent, to ameliorate the situation of so large and useful a part of the community, we think, well bestowed; and the remaining five-sixths afford a sufficient fund for the higher classes, and for giving room to that gradation of circumstances which is essential to the welfare of society. If the class of cottage proprietors were abolished, and their possessions distributed proportionally among the other classes, this would only add one-fifth part to the income of each proprietor.

We see no reason for preventing, by any restrictive enactment, the division of property into parts, however minute. The peasant who has one acre and a cottage, may dispose of half his acre to another peasant, who is able to build another cottage, without doing any harm to the public.

The two next classes constitute what would be called yeomanry in England. The number of persons in these classes, reckoning three to a family, is about three millions and a half, and the value of their property is rather more than three-fifths of the whole. These are chiefly employed in cultivating their own possessions, though some of them will also engage in other labour.

The two highest classes constitute the gentry; and we, who are accustomed to overgrown fortunes, would consider them as gentry of an inferior order. There are two reasons, however, which should give us a more favourable view of their circumstances than that which the numbers in the statement at first suggest. The rentals being taken for the purpose of taxation, are probably considerably below the real value, and the power of money in the purchase of every commodity, and consequently the real value of a like nominal sum, is greater in France than in this country. The number of proprietors in these classes is about 27,000, and of persons in their families, exclusive of servants, estimated at five to a family, is 135,000, and the amount of their property is only about one-fifth of the whole.

The number of proprietors and families engaged in agriculture is said to be nearly one-half of the population; and, if to this be added the labourers who have no property, the whole number of agricultural labourers is said to amount to two-thirds of the population.

This is a great deal too much, and, if accurate, exhibits a deplorable state of the country. But we apprehend there must be some mistake in the statement. It is incredible that, in so fertile a country as France, the labour of two persons should be required to raise food for three. The numerous class of cottage proprietors are chiefly maintained by their labour. But they are not all engaged in agricultural labour. Many of them, it may be presumed, follow other occupations.

We consider the allotment of a large portion of the land to overgrown estates as an evil of great magnitude. It absorbs a large part of the wealth of the community for the gratification of the luxury of a few. It may be reasonably doubted whether it promotes their enjoyment, and there is still more reason to apprehend that its moral effects are unfavourable. The gentleman of modern fortune has a personal intercourse with his tenants. The great proprietor keeps aloof from them, and transacts his business with them by the intervention of agents or middlemen. He is apt to consider them as an inferior order of beings, in whose welfare he takes no farther interest than the increase of his rental is concerned. Such a separation of ranks is not favourable to the moral condition of either.

We are not disposed to favour legislative restrictions on the disposal of property: but if they be at all admissible, we think they should be directed, not to prohibit the division of property, but to prevent its too great accumulation.

Perhaps a law, framed to the following effect, would be liable to little objection.

Let a determined portion, and a pretty high one, either of landed or moveable property, be fixed on as the greatest that ought to receive any favour from the legislature; which portion we shall call the *permanent maximum*. At the same time let no man be restrained from acquiring as much as he can, by industry, or even by fortunate accident, and from transmitting his fortune to his family: but if he has more sons than one, he must not leave a larger share to the eldest, or any other, than the *permanent maximum,* providing his estate can be reduced within that limit by division among them. If otherwise, after leaving each son the *permanent maximum,* he may bestow the surplus on the eldest, or any other son at pleasure. In defect of sons, no nephew or other collateral relation should succeed to more than the *permanent maximum,* providing there be others in the same degree of consanguinity, and no larger share shall in any case be settled on a stranger. To render these regulations effectual, the person to whom the inheritance would fall next, might be entitled to take possession, on settling the *permanent maximum* on the person before him in succession. We omit, for the sake of brevity, some regulations that might be necessary to complete this system. We apprehend that this, or some similar system for the gradual reduction of overgrown estates or enormous wealth of any kind, would be beneficial to society. But Solon, the Athenian lawgiver, declares that he did not propose to his fellow-citizens the best laws which could be framed, but the best which they were capable of receiving; and every wise legislator will do the same. Whatever is offensive to prevailing sentiments and manners, if had recourse to at all, should be introduced gradually and cautiously.

The summary of our sentiments on this subject is as follows:

That entails on a perpetual succession of heirs should be completely abolished.

That, generally, every person should have the entire disposal of his property, of whatever kind at his death.

That this should be limited to the first appointment, and not extend to that of a succession of heirs, except in peculiar circumstances.

That he be permitted to charge his heir or heirs with annuities to persons in existence, or perhaps one step further.

That the laws of succession to heritable property, in cases of intestacy, be more favourable to the younger branches of a family than they are at present.

That there should be no impediment to the division of property into parts, however small.

That, as far as may be done without violence to prevailing feelings, measures may be adopted for discouraging the growth of very great estates, or great wealth of any kind, and operating the gradual reduction of such as are already overgrown.

# CHAPTER XIV.

## OF PROPERTY.

We have already found occasion to make some remarks on the foundation of property. We now propose to enter into a more full discussion of that important subject.

When we take a view of the various subjects to which individuals or communities claim a right, in the modern state of society, we shall find that, in some cases, the right is established on the firmest principles, and is most beneficial to society. In others the right is of a weaker kind, yet on the whole beneficial, and ought to be supported. In others, it is of a reprehensible kind, and should never have been admitted, but being established, must not now be rudely invaded, as the consequences of doing so would be more detrimental to society than any evils resulting from its continuance. In others, the claim is so clearly unjustifiable, that no continuance of property founded on it ought to be tolerated.

Most of the articles which contribute to human support and enjoyment, and which constitute wealth, derive their chief value from human industry, but the material is always obtained from land, and, in countries where all the land is appropriated, the industrious man, if he has no land of his own, must procure his materials by a fair agreement with the landed proprietor. When thus possessed of the material, he may convert it into any form, and apply it to his own accommodation, or transfer it at his pleasure. It is in every respect his absolute property.

It is the right to property in land which presents any difficulties. In regard to this, two subjects of inquiry, somewhat analogous, present themselves to our consideration. The right which certain tribes assume to the possession of extensive tracts of country, to the exclusion of the rest of mankind, and the right which individuals have to the undisturbed possession of the land which they occupy.

The first of these was prior in point of time. In the earliest ages, when the number of mankind bore no proportion to the extent of land which lay before them, there was no room for appropriation of any kind. When mankind became more numerous, and embraced the pastoral state, an imperfect appropriation took place. Tribe separated from tribe, but the members of the same tribe fed their flocks at large upon their common property. "Abraham said unto Lot, Let there be no strife, I pray thee, between me and thee, between my herdsmen and thy herdsmen, for we are brethren. Is not the whole land before thee? Separate thyself, I pray thee, from me: if thou wilt, take the left hand, I will go to the right; or if thou depart to the right hand, then I will go to the left."

When the number of the human race became so great, that the natural produce of the soil was insufficient for their maintenance, and recourse was had to agriculture, appropriation of land, in the strictest sense, became necessary.

No man would undertake the laborious employment of agriculture, unless his right to reap the crop which he had sown was acknowledged and secured, nor does his right to the land which he has tilled terminate when the crop is removed. Land, by being cultivated, is, in general, rendered fitter for future culture. Woods are cleared;

stones removed; inequalities levelled, fences raised; superfluous water drained off; and sometimes a beneficial supply of water introduced. The expense of these operations is not repaid by a single crop, nor is it reasonable that the man by whose labour they have been accomplished, should be deprived of a title to enjoy what he has rendered valuable, and to transmit it to his posterity.

After a country is fully settled, from the casual variety in the progress of population, the posterity of some of the original cultivators may not have land sufficient for their subsistence; while others have more than they require, or are able to cultivate. The former apply to the latter for a new and more equal division. The latter may well reply, "The present division, however unequal now, is the result of the natural course of things. Our fathers, by much labour, brought the land which we now possess to its present state of fertility and value. It was their's by the clearest of all titles, and is now our's, as succeeding to their rights. In order, therefore, to supply your necessities, you must either labour for us, and we will give you a suitable reward, or we will give you land to cultivate for yourselves, on your agreeing to pay us a reasonable consideration for its produce."

If the argument be carried further, the only reply of the claimants would be founded upon the original value of the land, previous to any labour or improvement. "We acknowledge that the superinduced value of the lands is the effect of the industry of your progenitors, and now belongs to you, as standing in their right; but, previous to these improvements, the lands were of some value, and your father's had no right to them in their natural state, superior to our's. You ought, therefore, to resign such a share as we have occasion for, upon our paying to you a consideration equivalent to the additional value which culture has bestowed on them."

An admission of such a claim would be productive of endless disorders in society. The natural and superinduced value of the soil are so intimately blended, that the precise proportions of each never can be satisfactorily fixed, and therefore whoever occupies and improves a piece of land, which none had a prior claim to, must be supported in holding it as his own.

The business of agriculture, as well as every other, is attended with hazard. The returns may not, and sometimes do not, repay the expense bestowed on them. It is, therefore, reasonable that those who run the risk should enjoy the profit, when the undertaking proves successful.

The right to property in land, where occupation is followed by improvement, rests upon strong principles of natural equity. It is corroborated by no less urgent reasons of expediency. Without its clear recognition there could be little improvement. The produce, and consequently the population, even of the most fertile regions, would be confined within narrow limits. Without it the possession of land would be an object of universal contention, and mankind, instead of applying to the beneficial occupations of peaceful industry, would be engaged in constant scenes of rapine and violence. This was the case in some parts of our own country, and other countries in Europe, some centuries ago.

Property in land thus acquired may be transmitted to the posterity of the original occupier, or devised in any manner agreeable to his wishes, or transferred by gift, or for a valuable consideration. In these cases the heir, devisee, donee, or purchaser, succeeds to the title of him from whom his title is derived.

Land is continually changing its ownership, by death, or more rapid means, and the titles of the various proprietors may be considered as so many links in a chain, by which they are connected with the original occupier and improver.

In process of time the original occupier is forgotten; and, if the present proprietor can shew an uninterrupted possession for a certain length of time, the former part of the chain is preserved, and his title cannot be questioned upon the grounds of the uncertainty of the original acquisition, now buried in oblivion. This right, by prescription, is acknowledged in every civilized country, though under different modifications.

The tenures of modern Europe are derived from feudal principles, and must be referred to the right, such as it is, of conquest. The leaders of the tribes who subverted the Roman Empire assumed, nominally, the possession of the whole of the conquered country, but were under the necessity of allotting large tracts of land to their subordinate officers, who again parcelled them out to those of inferior rank, and so on to the lowest gradation. Lands were at first held of the sovereign, or intermediate superior, chiefly for military services, which were afterwards commuted for pecuniary rents. The substance of the feudal system has gradually worn away in most countries, though much of its form still remains.

We know, in general, that the progenitors of the present proprietors expelled the former inhabitants from their possessions by violence; but we cannot now trace the posterity, either of the dispossessed proprietor, or of the invader. The rights of the present proprietors can only be resolved into occupancy and prescription.

We have said, perhaps, more than was necessary on the right of property in land where occupation was coupled with improvement. We next proceed to the consideration of the case where occupation is followed by no improvement.

If we review the grounds upon which property has here been made to rest, we shall find that they lose considerably of their strength when no improvement has taken place. Yet even here the right of property may be classed among those which are upon the whole beneficial to society.

There are so many gradations in improvement, and also in occupation, that it would be difficult to fix that precise amount of either by which property could be said to be adequately acquired.

The occupier who improves at all, however languidly, cannot be ejected to make room for a more active improver; neither is immediate improvement necessary. The man who has assumed a tract of land by a slight act of occupancy, and begun to improve, must be allowed a length of time to complete his improvement.

The circumstances attending the emigration of colonies from civilized countries, carrying along with them the arts of the parent country, and some portion of its wealth, chiefly claim our attention.

We shudder at the recollection of the atrocities which have been committed by such emigrants upon the natives of the countries in which they settled, whom they accounted savages. We shall turn our eyes to more agreeable scenes, where the country resorted to was formerly uninhabited, or where possession of a certain tract has been obtained by a fair compact with the natives.

The settlements of the colonies of North America, while under the dominion of Britain, and the still more extensive settlements which have been established since their separation, furnish examples of this on an extensive scale. Our late settlements in Southern Africa are of a somewhat similar kind.

In all these, whether they have remained under subjection to the parent country, or whether they have established an independent government of their own, permission has not been given to every individual to occupy what land he chose; but the whole region being considered as public property, tracts of land have been granted to the settlers, generally upon payment of a moderate price to the community, and sometimes subject to a quit-rent; such grants being limited in extent, and the occupants often bound to a course of gradual improvement. It would be an effectual bar to colonization if no more land could be secured in property to a settler than he could improve the first year.

Such is the most eligible way of extending

population and the arts of civilized life to those parts of the earth which they have not hitherto reached. Every such colony has a right to prevent the intrusion of other colonists into the countries where they have settled. To constitute this right, however, there must be some degree of actual possession. The titles claimed upon virtual acts of occupancy, such as the erection of a flag, or the like, are too slender to bear examination. It may, however, be a proper rule for preventing disputes among nations addicted to naval enterprize, that the property of uninhabited countries should be ascribed to those by whom they are first discovered and taken possession of, and the slightest ceremony may be agreed upon as an act of occupation. This, however, stands on the same footing as the established customs relating to ambassadors, and other particulars that occur in the transactions of nations with each other, which derive their validity from compact, express or implied, and not from the law of nature.

Having considered the right of property in land founded on occupation followed by improvement, or by occupation with the view to improvement, we next proceed to the consideration of certain things to which a title is in many countries acquired by occupancy alone, though they be unsusceptible of improvement, and their appropriation be upon the whole rather prejudicial than useful to the public. It would be better that no such property had ever been admitted, though it would be unwarrantable now to abolish it. When a man has honestly acquired any species of wealth, he seeks to secure it for himself and his posterity by purchasing something from which he and they will derive permanent benefit. He may purchase land; but if, instead of doing so, he purchase any thing else that is commonly bought and sold, and the right to which is supported by the laws of the country, it would be unjust to deprive him of it by challenging, upon abstract principles, the validity of his right to that which he possesses. After all, such property is rather to be tolerated than encouraged. Its further progress ought to be checked, and if the amount of it already established can be diminished by fair and peaceable means, it is desirable to do so.

A right to fish, either on the open sea or in

rivers, approaches to this class, though the former is sometimes, and the latter almost universally appropriated. So is a right to sail in navigable rivers, and to the use of harbours. These last generally require the aid of art to render them commodious; but as the expense may be defrayed by the public, and reimbursed by a suitable toll levied on those who partake of the benefit, there seems to be no reason for allowing them to afford a revenue to private proprietors. We do not deal in this manner with highways. The general good requires that roads be carried through appropriated ground; but we do not allow the proprietor to derive an emolument from this at the expense of the public. We give him a reasonable price for the ground which the road occupies, and impose a toll upon travellers, adequate to the gradual extinction of this price and the expense of forming the road and keeping it in repair, and no more. Though the authority of local acts of parliament be required for this purpose, these are now granted so much of course, that this may be considered as the established law of the land. Why we should not act in the same manner in regard to ferries is not immediately apparent.

The right of catching and killing animals *feræ naturæ* is of a like kind, though there may be good reasons for restraining certain classes of men from exercising it, or for bestowing it exclusively on the proprietor of the lands where the animals are found. In some parts of the country this right has been assigned for a pecuniary consideration, and has become an object of considerable value.

Some other established rights encroach still more upon natural freedom, and are entitled to less favourable regard. Of this kind are monopolies unsupported by any claim to invention. These are infringements on the right, which belongs to every man, of exercising his industry in whatever manner he pleases. This was an evil of considerable magnitude in England so late as the reign of Elizabeth, but is now almost entirely done away. The exclusive right of printing the Scriptures is an instance in which it still subsists.

Sinecure offices, and all offices which are bought and sold, and afford a sinecure profit to the holder, stand in this unfavourable predicament. The emoluments of these offices, in whatever manner they are paid, are ultimately a charge on the community. If the offices be useful, the public has a right to be served, on payment of a suitable compensation for the discharge of the duty, due allowance being made for the abilities it requires, and every other circumstance that may enhance its value; but if the person who exercises the office procures it for payment of a sum of money, or of an annual rent, this amounts to demonstration that the emoluments are more than adequate for the services performed. Besides the burthen thus imposed on the public, other important evils arise from this mode of conferring offices. It exposes them to the risk of being filled by improper persons. If the seller be allowed to choose, he will generally prefer the person who offers the highest price. Even when the consent of a superior is necessary to ratify the transaction, the seller, having the time in his power, will always have considerable influence in getting it settled in the way that suits his private interest.

In a neighbouring country, previous to the late revolution, the seats of justice were in general saleable. In this country the inferior commissions in the army are usually obtained by purchase. This system was introduced in the last century, and upon the whole has gained ground, notwithstanding regulations on the part of government to restrict it, which are much evaded. In the navy it has never obtained a footing, and every friend to our naval power would deprecate its introduction.

It would be hard to deprive an officer who had purchased, of the privilege of selling; but the system may be gradually done away by limiting the permission to that case alone. Measures to that effect have been embraced by our present Commander-in-chief, and deserve much praise; but it will require strict vigilance and long perseverance to give them full effect.

The Scottish aristocracy, previous to the rebellion in 1745, enjoyed hereditary jurisdictions in their respective demesnes very inconsistent with the genuine principles of liberty. These were abolished by the legislature, after the suppression of that rebellion, upon payment of a pecuniary consideration, less than they demanded, but more, perhaps, than they ought in strictness to have received.

A revenue arising from a tax levied on the public for the benefit of a particular family is a property of a very exceptionable nature. Of this kind is a tax on coals imported into the city of London.

The holders of monopolies, sinecures, and saleable offices, are not *in optima fide*, in regard to these kinds of property; yet their case is favourable when compared with those who claim a property in the persons of their fellow-creatures. The recognition of slavery is so gross a violation of humanity, of justice, of the clearest and most valuable natural rights, that no law or custom can sanction it, nor can any reasons of expedience be deemed sufficient to defend it. In ancient times, when slavery was in full force in Europe, the labours of agriculture and mechanic trades were chiefly performed by slaves, and a proposal of general manumission would have been considered as inexpedient, in consequence of the stop it would have occasioned to these necessary employments. Since slavery has, in many countries, disappeared, rather by the influence of religion and manners than the force of positive laws, the useful arts have been advanced to a much higher degree of perfection, through the exertion of freemen, animated by the prospect of reaping the reward of their own industry.

In Scotland, till lately, labourers employed in coal-mines and salt-works were bondsmen. This remnant of slavery is now abolished without any detriment to the proprietors. In some countries of Europe a certain degree of slavery still takes place among the peasants, who are *adscripti glebæ*, as was the general case some centuries ago. This species of servitude is relaxing, and has been discouraged by several intelligent princes, and voluntarily resigned by many liberal-minded proprietors. It will probably, in no long time, be completely done away.

But while Europe has thus happily got nearly free of slavery at home, she still countenances that wretched institution in her American colonies. Slavery prevails there to a very great extent, and is in some respects more severe than any that prevailed in former ages. To the execrable African slave-trade we may in a great measure ascribe the state of barbarism of one entire quarter of the globe. It does honour to Britain, that she has taken the lead in the abolition of that infamous traffic, and not only renounced it on her own behalf, and prohibited the exercise of it by all her subjects, under the heaviest penalties, but used her endeavours to procure the concurrence of other powers to the same effect, though hitherto with very little success.

While we decidedly condemn the institution of slavery as unjust and inexpedient, we would not provoke the precipitate overthrow of a fabric which has acquired so great magnitude. This might be attended with evils of a serious kind, even to the slaves themselves, which ought to be guarded against by such preliminary measures as prudence may suggest; while we pursue a cautious but decided course that may, at first, ameliorate the condition of that unhappy class of men, and afterwards lead to a full abolition of slavery, with all its concomitant evils. When this can be accomplished, although a pecuniary compensation to those who lose, or suppose themselves to lose, by the change, may be rather a measure of prudence than of strict justice, yet no good man would hesitate to contribute thereto, providing that by doing so he could accelerate an object in which the interest of humanity is so deeply concerned.

On the whole, the foundation of property

may be comprehended under the following aphorisms:—

1st. The share of wealth which arises from the labour of the present generation belongs, by the clearest of all titles, to the respective labourers.

2d. The share of wealth arising from the labour of former generations belongs to the posterity of those who produced it, or to those whom they have appointed their successors.

3d. The wealth acquired from land, being obtained in a great measure by culture and improvement, and its original and acquired value being intimately and inseparably blended, belongs to the original occupiers and improvers, and their representatives.

4th. As it is requisite, for the peace of society, that all land be appropriated, occupation, even when not followed by improvement, must be sustained as conferring a title.

5th. As the original proprietors are forgotten in the lapse of ages, possession for a certain length of time must be admitted as affording a presumptive right.

6th. The appropriation of things which may be enjoyed by all, as the right of fishing, and the like, is not necessary, yet may be supported by reasons of expediency, and when it has been admitted it ought to remain secure.

7th. Right of monopolies, offices, and the like, are a species of property *in mala fide*, and ought to be resisted, and abolished by peaceable means, but not without granting some indemnification to those who held them under the sanction of the laws of the society.

8th. The property which consists of slaves is *in pessima fide*, and ought to be abolished as soon as can be done without incurring greater evils. If any indemnification be given to the proprietors, it is rather a sacrifice to prudence and expedience, than a claim strictly due to justice.

9th. Property of every kind may be lawfully conveyed among the living by sale or donation, and the purchaser or donee succeeds to the full right of the former proprietor.

# CHAPTER XV.

## EDUCATION OF THE LOWER RANKS.

Religion is, beyond comparison, the most important part of education. When properly taught, it includes every moral and social duty; and, among others, industry, temperance, and economy. The communication of religious instruction is more peculiarly the duty of its ministers, and heavy is the responsibility of those who neglect it altogether, or perform it remissly. Notwithstanding the exertions of the most active minister of religion, the religious education of a family depends chiefly upon the parents. A pious parent in a Christian country can hardly be without sufficient knowledge to enable him to discharge this duty. His instructions and example will, in most instances, make a deep impression on his children, and the requisite time will hardly interfere with his other occupations, especially if Sunday be spent as it ought to be.

It is, however, what may be called the secular part of education that the political economist has chiefly occasion to consider.

An opinion has been entertained, and by many publicly avowed, that all attempts to raise the character of the lower ranks by education are improper, as tending to indispose them for that labour which their station in life subjects them to. They have been considered as machines, and the quantity of work that could be extracted from them as the only object to be attended to; and the improvement of their rational nature and moral qualities, unless so far as subservient to their mechanical use, ought, it has been thought, to be disregarded. Few, we hope, now entertain these illiberal opinions, and such as do are generally ashamed to avow them.

It is now generally admitted, that the inferior parts of education may be bestowed upon all without unfitting them for the occupations of a humble station; that a man is not unqualified for the plough or the loom, though he can read and write; and that these acquirements, to a certain degree, are useful and gratifying to himself, as well as advantageous to his neighbours.

But where ought the education of the lower ranks to stop? The objections to carrying it too far are, that it would occupy too much time, and would induce a turn of mind that indisposes the laborious ranks for the employments by which they must gain their bread; and of consequence impair, instead of promote, their happiness.

The narrowest opinion is, that they ought to be taught no more than is requisite for enabling them to perform properly what belongs to their own sphere. The more liberal opinion, which we embrace, is, that whatever contributes to improve their intellectual powers, or afford them sources of enjoyment, should be put within their reach, providing it do not lead to the bad consequences above-mentioned.

The great merit of the system of education for the poor in Scotland is generally acknowledged. In every parish a school is established, and in large parishes more than one, where reading, writing, and arithmetic are taught, and the scholars instructed in the principles of religion. Part of the schoolmaster's income is paid by the public, and the fees paid by the scholars are very moderate, and in some places the fees of poor scholars are paid from a charitable fund. These schools are regularly visited by a committee of parochial clergy appointed by their respective presbyteries, to whom a report of their condition is made, and these reports are afterwards arranged, and transmitted to the general Assembly, or supreme Ecclesiastical court in Scotland. The books read at these schools are chiefly the Scriptures and catechisms, sometimes a collection of extracts from good authors, in prose or verse. The masters are in general diligent, unexceptionable in their moral conduct, and sufficiently qualified for the discharge of their office; and not a few of them possess attainments superior to what is required in their situation. Few parents neglect to send their children to these schools, and few of the lower ranks in Scotland are unable to read and write, as those who cannot are every where held in little respect.

This system is good, and generally well conducted. It might, however, admit of improvement. The course of reading might be further extended in behalf of those scholars who can remain longer than others at school, and to all of them some knowledge of geography, natural and civil history, and the most useful parts of some other sciences, might be communicated. We do not think it proper to keep those who are to gain their bread by labour long at school. Habits of industry must be acquired in early life. But arrangements might be made by which a youth, who, after having been some time at school, was engaged in labour, might spend some portion of his time for a year or two afterwards in acquiring farther knowledge. We disapprove of teaching the learned languages at common parish schools, as being unsuitable to the classes for whom they are intended, and taking up the master's time, who has enough to do besides. Without derogating in the slightest degree from the value of classical literature, we apprehend that the establishment of grammar-schools in towns and large villages would be sufficient for all that ought to prosecute it.

The system of Sunday schools has of late been encouraged with truly Christian zeal. We deem them highly useful to those who can afford no more; but they ought not to supersede the more complete education which day schools confer, in cases where it can be afforded.

The income of the parish and other schoolmasters is generally too low, and they well deserve to have it increased.

A man who has acquired a little knowledge

at school, may have a desire to acquire more, and allot part of the time exempt from labour to that purpose. This takes place frequently, though not universally.

In a few parishes a common library is established by a part of the inhabitants, the expense being defrayed by a payment from each member at entry, together with a small annual contribution. It is to be wished that those were more general. They may be under the superintendence of the minister of the parish, who should select the books, consisting of religious and moral works; history, natural and civil; books relating to agriculture and other arts; poetry and miscellanies; but avoiding treatises of a controversial tendency, whether theological or political.

In several towns of this country institutions have of late been established in which courses of lectures on natural philosophy and chemistry, illustrated by experiments, are delivered in a manner adapted to the apprehension of those who have not much previous science. These lectures are chiefly attended by mechanics, who are admitted upon payment of a very moderate fee. They have been well attended, and are likely to prove very useful.

In reply to those who reprobate all attempts to raise the character of the poor by education, as tending to indispose them to labour, or as being altogether impracticable, we would appeal to those instances in which the effects of education have been most successful. We could point out some among them, who, though they have not become more wealthy than their neighbours, have yet attained a superiority of intelligence, which qualifies them to become agreeable companions to any order of society. This, indeed, is not very common, but as education is improved, it might be expected to become more general. We have never observed that persons of this character were less diligent than others in their ordinary occupations, and they are seldom or never addicted to intemperance.

# CHAPTER XVI.

## EFFECT OF NUMBERS IN A STATE.

BEFORE proceeding to the consideration of the consequences resulting from foreign commerce, it may be useful to take a view of the different measures of comfort and enjoyment which arise from the union of mankind in small or numerous communities. We have had occasion to touch on this topic incidentally already, and now propose to enter on a fuller detail of the effects of numbers on the condition of society, apart, as far as may be, from collateral considerations, though we may not be able to do this without some repetition.

In order to treat this subject with perspicuity, we shall consider societies of men, as they increase in number, to be constituted in several progressive states, which we shall distinguish by the letters A. B. C., &c.

It is hardly necessary to premise, that we do not consider these states as limited to the precise number and condition mentioned. They are not separated from each other by any broad or visible line of distinction. Each of them contains an indefinite number of gradations, blending into each other, and approaching on one hand to the highest grade of the class immediately lower, and on the other to the lowest grade of the class immediately higher.

A. We begin with considering the case of a very small community, and, as it is unnecessary for our present purpose to delineate one which has rarely existed, and which affords no instruction, we shall first take a view of the state of a few settlers, in a country of considerable fertility, who have some knowledge of agriculture, and the more common mechanic arts, and who possess the most common tools and some materials for present use. We shall also suppose that there is, adjoining to their settlement, an extensive tract of unoccupied country, by which they are enabled to extend their boundaries, as their numbers increase, without opposition. We suppose them (with an exception or two after-mentioned) to have no commercial dealings with any other nation: but we do not exclude them from such intercourse as may allow of emigration, and the introduction of useful arts. At first, the settlement may consist of about twenty families; such as is represented in the second part of the tale of Robinson Crusoe. For their immediate supply of food, they would collect any spontaneous fruits or esculent herbs which the country afforded; but, as these are likely to be insufficient for their maintenance through the year, they would as soon as possible have recourse to agriculture. As they have no labouring cattle, the cultivation of the land would be performed by the spade, and every man would cultivate a portion sufficient for his maintenance, and that of his family; but, as there is no way of disposing of a surplus produce, no more corn would be raised than they required. They might vary their food occasionally, by catching wild animals and by fishing, and would construct weapons and other implements required for these purposes.

One of their first employments would be to erect dwellings suited to the climate, of wood, or other materials which the country supplied, and provide them with the most useful articles of household furniture. As their families increased, they would enlarge the extent of their cultivated ground. All their time would not be required for the labours of agriculture, and a part of it would be occupied in rendering their houses and furniture more convenient, and in fabricating clothing from such materials as they could command.

It is likely that three or four families would have their habitations contiguous, for the sake of society and mutual assistance; but the community (supposed to amount to twenty families) would be distributed in several hamlets, so that each person might be near to the land which he cultivated. Whatever portion of land a man cultivated would become his property, and also what he inclosed for keeping domestic animals, when these were obtained.

As it would be desirable each should have a sufficient extent of contiguous land to be brought into culture when the increase of his family required it, the hamlets would be at such a distance as to give scope for this extension. To accomplish this, some conventional arrangement would be required among all the members of the society; and, if they had abundance of land, this would be accomplished without difficulty.

The hamlets would not be so far distant as to prevent all the settlers from meeting frequently.

If the Christian religion were known, they would convene at some central place on Sunday for divine worship, when one of the most respectable of the society would preside. A house sufficient to contain the whole community at these meetings, and on other occasions, would be built.

In this small community there is little occasion for division of labour, yet it might not be entirely wanting. Some of its members would have superior natural ingenuity, or mechanic skill. One of them would, most probably, have been bred a carpenter, another a blacksmith, another a mason or a shoemaker. Each of these would furnish what is required from his particular craft to the whole community, receiving in return such recompense in labour or otherwise as the other members could give. There would be no use for money of any kind. There would be few grounds for dissension, and any difference which might arise would be decided by the community. We have supposed no enemies; but if a risk of invasion was apprehended, it would lead to the training of every adult male to military exercise, and the use of weapons.

Such a community might enjoy a full allowance of the necessaries, and a considerable share of the comforts of life, though few of its luxuries. There would be little distinction of station. The children of each family would receive such education as the parents could give them at home, and would be put to labour when they became fit for it.

The occupation of mining is scarcely compatible with so narrow a society, yet without iron they could do little. We must, therefore, allow them, after their original stock is exhausted, to import that article from some other place, till their numbers be so much increased as to put the operations of the forge within their reach. The other metals they may dispense with till they arrive at that stage.

B.—As in a small society, possessing an extensive tract of land, there would be little impediment to early marriage, from the fear of want of food, or from the demands of luxury, their numbers would increase rapidly, and the increase might be accelerated by emigration. Let us suppose them increased to a thousand families, or five thousand persons, a number answering to one of our larger parishes.

The most important change in their condition would be a further progress in the division of labour. Not only the occupations of the carpenter, the blacksmith, the mason, and the shoemaker, but those of the butcher, the tanner, and the tailor, would be exercised by different persons, and these tradesmen would allot their whole time, or nearly so, to their respective occupations, and receive their food from the agricultural part of the community, in recompense for their services: whereas, in the smaller society, they only exercised their trades in the intervals of agricultural labour.

Several trades would now be introduced which were not practised before. In enumerating the few employments which might in some measure be separated in a very small community, we did not mention that of the weaver. We considered his loom as too complex a machine for that period. So long as it was not used, the materials for clothing would consist chiefly of the skins of animals, or the bark of trees. If any thing resembling cloth was made from the wool of their sheep, it would be fabricated by their females, in the most inartificial manner. They would scarcely use a machine more complex than the distaff or the knitting-needle. Now the introduction of the spinning-wheel and the loom give an important accession to their clothing. The machines used by them would be inferior to what we now employ, and the work performed by them would be plain and without variety; yet with these defects they would furnish a much more comfortable raiment than they had before. Wool would be the first material for their webs. Flax and cotton, if suited to the climate, would be cultivated and manufactured afterwards.

The corn-mill is another valuable machine that may be now introduced. Formerly their corn was prepared for food by pounding it in a mortar, or some such inartificial manner. The hand-mill would be the first step of improvement, and would be succeeded by the mill driven by water.

The ground requisite for the maintenance of a thousand families, and their flocks and herds, would be of considerable extent; but in a fertile country would not reach to a distance that prevented them from meeting once a week, in some central place, and their former habits would induce them to do so. A church sufficient to contain the number which usually assembled would be built. Respect for the character of the person who presided at divine worship and dispensed the ordinances of religion, and a sense of the importance of his functions, might induce the community to exempt him from other labour, and assign him a suitable maintenance. The business of a schoolmaster would also become a separate employment. At first the duties of the clergyman and the schoolmaster might be discharged by the same person. When, from the increase of numbers, these duties became too much for one man, the employments would be separated.

The increase of numbers would occasion the erection of new hamlets, reaching gradually to a greater distance from the original one, in every accessible direction: but the elder branches of each family would generally remain in the first hamlet; and the younger branches, when foris-familiated, would establish new ones in the remote parts of the settlement. The church and school would have their place in the first hamlet, and most of those who exercised mechanical employments would remain in the same vicinity. Hence a village would arise, which, besides those employed in cultivating the adjoining ground, would be inhabited by the clergyman, the schoolmaster, the miller, the carpenter, the mason, the blacksmith, the weaver, the tanner, the shoemaker, the butcher, and the baker, and by as many of each of these professions as the demands of the community required.

The separation of employments, however, would not be complete. In parts remote from the village, the inhabitants, though chiefly employed in agriculture, would occasionally do the work of the carpenter, the mason, and the blacksmith; and the operations of baking, brewing and dress-making would be performed in the family, chiefly by the females. This junction of employments takes place, partially, in communities pretty far advanced, at a distance from towns. It has not yet entirely ceased in some remote districts of Scotland, though it is fast wearing away.

For the smaller society we supposed the operations of agriculture performed by manual labour, as that appeared sufficient in their circumstances, and all that was attainable. We may now expect them to procure some labouring cattle by importation or otherwise. Though a few of these only were obtained at first, they would, by proper care, increase rapidly, and supersede manual labour in such agricultural operations as they could be employed in. The plough, from its superior efficacy, would confine the spade to the operations of the garden. These animals, being also employed for carriages and riding, would facilitate communication between different parts of the settlement.

Some other accessions may take place at this stage of society, or when it becomes a little more numerous. There are now some commodities to exchange, and the retail shopkeeper may become a useful member for their distribution. His shop, therefore, finds a place in the village. There is not yet much occasion for a circulating medium, yet money might find its way. Previous to the introduction of the precious metals, the value of commodities would be estimated by reference to a bushel of corn, or some other commodity selected for that purpose.

In a very small community there is not much inequality of circumstances. But this insinuates itself, and expands with the increase of numbers. Some men consume, almost immediately, all that they earn, while others lay up for futurity. There is not the same variety of ways for investing savings, in the stage of society we are now considering, as in a more advanced one, yet they are not entirely wanting. The increase of flocks and herds is one of the readiest. The mechanic may acquire more complete machinery, and all may acquire better houses and furniture, or lay up a share of materials for private use.

At the beginning of the settlement, land had no exchangeable value, as every man had access to as much as he could cultivate. Now, though he may still have a sufficiency of land by removing to a distance, there are many circumstances which render a residence near the centre of the settlement desirable, and a person who has acquired property of any kind may be willing to give a part, in order to a temporary or permanent possession of land in the most eligible part of the settlement. Hence land thus situated acquires an exchangeable value. It becomes a subject for sale, or may be let for an annual rent.

A medical man would now be required, and would find employment. As this small community could not contain an establishment fit to give him the requisite education, he must be brought from some country in a state of further advancement. He will exercise jointly the several branches of the profession,—medicine, surgery, pharmacy. If he have some knowledge of natural history, especially geology and mineralogy, he will prove a most useful member of the community.

It would be well, if, at this period, we could keep clear of the alehouse; but it is not unlikely it may intrude itself into some corner of the village.

Every enlargement that renders society more complex is apt to occasion differences in regard to property, and though it might be hoped there would be few or no heinous crimes, yet offences deserving punishment might sometimes be committed. When the community becomes too numerous to assemble collectively, it would delegate one or more of its most respectable members to exercise the functions of a magistrate, probably for a year, or other limited time, to be succeeded by others elected in the same manner. The duties of these magistrates would be within the reach of men of sound understanding and probity. As there is no complex system of laws, no special education would be required, and there would be no occasion for the separate profession of a lawyer. The excellent mode of trial by jury is likely to be had recourse to.

C.—The community, continuing to increase, will, in progress of time, amount to one hundred thousand persons, and occupy an extent of territory answering to one of our counties. The division of labour will now be carried farther. The occupations of the blacksmith, the farrier, the nailer, the cutler, the coppersmith, the tinman, and the plumber, will be exercised by different persons. So will those of the house-carpenter, the joiner, the cartwright, the sawyer, and the turner. Other employments will be subdivided in the same manner.

Another distinction will now take place, that of master and journeyman. In a small community, every mechanic is an independent workman: but now, the machinery being more complex, and many employments being carried on with more advantage on a large scale, they can only be carried on by persons who possess the requisite capital, and other tradesmen are obliged to engage as journeymen with such masters.

The want of capital is not the only circum

stance that induces tradesmen to engage as journeymen. They have generally more certainty of obtaining constant employment by doing so. An independent blacksmith or carpenter might be frequently out of work. By engaging with a master in extensive business, he is generally sure of constant employment for a considerable time, and he prefers this certainty though he gives his labour for something less. Still, however, there will be a considerable number of independent workmen in occupations of a simpler kind.

One of the most valuable improvements which may take place in this stage of society, is the forging of metals. The operations of mining, smelting, and forming the various articles for which metals furnish the materials, and constructing the requisite apparatus, could not be undertaken till the society became considerably numerous. The operations of the glass-house, and the potter's kiln, may also now be introduced.

Men have now learned to penetrate into the depths of the earth in search of hidden treasure. They will meet with fossil coal, if there be any in the country.

Agriculture, in a small society, is limited to

the cultivation of plants required for food. It will now become more varied, and applied to whatever plants contribute in any way to human comfort. Fruits of various kinds will be raised in the gardens, vineyards will be planted, flax, cotton, tobacco, sugar, and coffee will be cultivated as the climate suits, and afford the inhabitants a variety of materials for clothing and luxury.

The water-mill, formerly only used for grinding corn, will now be applied to a variety of purposes. We can hardly yet reach the steam-engine.

The extent of land which the community now occupies will occasion the erection of new villages in different places; and the original village, increasing gradually, will assume the character of a town. The more ordinary mechanical employments will be carried on in every village, but those of a nicer or more intricate kind will be confined to the town, or some appropriate situation. An easy communication between the town and country, that the wares of the former may be exchanged for the produce of the latter, will be an object of general importance. Highways will be formed, bridges built, and in due time a post-office will be established. A printing-press will be set to work, and a newspaper circulated.

The extension of wealth will lead to the introduction of several new professions. The jeweller, the watchmaker, the bookseller, the milliner will find employment. Perhaps some of the wealthiest may set up a wheel carriage. The coachmaker will be ready to lend his services.

As the church in the town becomes insufficient for the enlarged community, and too distant from the remote parts of the settlement, other churches will be built in the principal villages. Hence the division of the territory into parishes. Whether they assume the episcopalian or presbyterian form of church government, the ministers of the different parishes will be connected by some common bond of discipline and government. Schools will be opened in the villages, and a school of a superior kind in the town.

D.—In process of time the inhabitants increase to a million, forming a little kingdom or commonwealth. The division of labour, inequality of circumstances, and the introduction of a variety of employments subservient to luxury, which had made considerable progress in the former stage, will now be advanced to a higher pitch. Steam-engines and machinery of the most complicated kind will be had recourse to; navigable canals and railways constructed; and the civil engineer added to the list of professional men. The former villages will be enlarged into towns, and the former town will become a capital.

The government, whether monarchical, republican, or mixed, will become more complicated. Local magistrates with limited powers will be established in different parts of the country, subject to the control of a superior court in the capital. The profession of a lawyer becomes a separate one.

The important but equivocal measure of a separation between the civil and military states, may now be considered as inevitable.

In the former stages the profession of the elegant arts, and those subservient to luxury, if exercised at all, would remain in a feeble condition. Now they will meet with liberal encouragement, and this will lead to improvement and display of talent. The painter, the sculptor, the engraver, and the architect, will acquire distinction; so will the musician and the actor.

A theatre, and other places of public amusement, will be opened in the capital, and the performers will occasionally visit the smaller towns, till they be supplied by others of their own.

An university will be established, where instructions will be given in the several faculties of theology, law, medicine, philosophy, and classical literature, minutely subdivided into their respective branches.

**E.**—The state, if the territory be sufficiently extensive, will at last become a great nation, perhaps containing ten millions of inhabitants. It is foreign from our present design to enter into the consideration of the rank which such a nation is likely to assume among others; of its treaties, its naval and military exertions, or even its commercial intercourse with them. We inquire into the internal effects of so great an increase of numbers,—what alterations this would produce on the character and enjoyments of the different classes of the society.

All the results mentioned under the last head would extend in this to a higher degree. Mechanical improvements in every branch would have so ample a range as scarcely to leave any thing more to desire.

Inequality of wealth and distinction of station,

which had been gradually expanding with the enlargement of society, will now become excessive. It is to be feared that the vices which accompany luxury would prevail among the higher ranks, and that crimes would multiply among the lower ones.

The metropolis now becomes a large city. It is the seat of government, and the place where the superior courts of judicature are held. This fixes the residence of many to it. It is resorted to by the wealthy of every description, most of whom spend a part, and some of them the whole of their time in it, for the sake of the gratifications it affords. It is an expensive place, and the wages of labour are high; therefore it is not the seat of much manufacture, but it is filled by numbers, whose employments are subservient to luxury. It requires a large supply of provisions and other articles from the country, some of which are drawn from remote parts, and as it has not an equivalent to give in return, unless it be a place of foreign commerce, these are paid from the revenue of the wealthy inhabitants, from whatever source derived.

It is the chief seat of liberal arts, the works of which are exhibited in its galleries and museums. The manners of polished society are carried to the highest pitch of refinement, and the opportunities of improving conversation, and easy access to books, lead to a diffusion of general knowledge, which, though perhaps not of the profoundest kind, is both useful and agreeable.

The provincial towns assume the character of cities. Some of them become extensive places of manufacture, different branches of which are established in them, as convenience or accident directs. Hence an extensive intercourse between different parts of the country, and improvements in the highways, the railways, the canals, the carriages, the posts. Some of the cities become the seats of learning—others, the occasional residence of the idle and the valetudinary.

# CHAPTER XVII.

## OF COMMERCE.

THE wealth of a country may be greatly increased or diminished by its intercourse with other countries. The intercourse of nation with nation is either amicable or hostile. We are at present to inquire into the effects of commerce upon the public welfare, both in regard to the wealth, and the moral state of society.

Commerce, according to some, is a transfer of property in which the gain of one party arises from the loss of another, and in which the more artful is enriched at the expense of his improvident neighbour. Did wealth consist in gold or silver, this opinion would be just. For the quantity of these metals which flows into one country must be withdrawn from another.

A system founded upon this principle long prevailed, and regulated the commercial laws and treaties of nations. The sentiments which were held as incontrovertible about a century ago, will appear from the following extract, which we have selected on account of its brevity.

" Give me leave to say that neither you, nor all your clan of wits can put together so useful and commodious a treatise for the welfare of your fellow-subjects, as that which an eminent merchant of this city has lately written. It is called general maxims of trade, particularly applied to the commerce between Great Britain and France.

" I. That trade which exports manufactures made of the produce of the country is undoubtedly good, such as sending abroad our Yorkshire cloths, Colchester baize, Exeter serge, Norwich stuffs, &c., which being made up of British wool, as much as these exports amount to, so much is the clear gain of the nation.

" II. That trade which helps off the consumption of our superfluities is also advantageous, as the export was of allum, copper, leather, tin, lead, coals, &c. So much as the exported superfluities amount to, so much also is the clear national profit.

" III. The importation of foreign materials to be manufactured at home, especially if the goods, after being manufactured, are mostly sent abroad, is also without doubt very beneficial, as, for instance, Spanish wool, which for that reason is exempted from paying any duties.

"IV. The importation of foreign materials to be manufactured by us, although the manufactured goods may be chiefly consumed by us, may be also beneficial, especially when the said materials are procured in exchange for our commodities, as raw silk, gogram, yarn, and other goods from Turkey.

"V. Foreign materials wrought up here into such goods as would otherwise be imported ready manufactured, is a means of saving money to the nation: such is the importation of hemp, flax, and raw silk. It is, therefore, to be wondered at that these commodities are not exempt from all duties, as well as Spanish wool.

"VI. A trade may be called good, which exchanges manufactures for manufactures, and commodities for commodities. Germany takes as much of our woollen and other goods as we do of their linen. By means of which numbers of people are employed on both sides to their mutual advantage.

"VII. An importation of goods, bought partly for money, and partly for goods, may be of national advantage, if the greater part of the commodities, thus imported, are again exported, as in the case of East India goods; and in general all imports of goods which are re-exported are beneficial to a nation.

"VIII. The carrying of goods from one foreign country to another is a profitable article in trade. Our ships are often thus employed in Portugal, Italy, and the Levant, and sometimes in the East Indies.

"IX. When there is a necessity to import goods which the nation cannot do without, although such goods are chiefly purchased with money, it cannot be accounted a bad trade, as our trade to Norway and other parts, from which are imported our naval stores and materials for building."

"But a trade is disadvantageous to a nation,

"I. When it brings in things of mere luxury and pleasure, which are entirely, or for the most part, consumed among us; and such I reckon the wine trade to be, especially when the wine is purchased for money, and not in exchange for commodities.

"II. Much worse is that trade which brings in a commodity that is not only consumed among us, but hinders the consumption of a like quantity of our own. As is the importation of brandy, which hinders the spending of our extracts of malt and molasses; therefore very properly charged with excessive duties.

"III. That trade is eminently bad which supplies the same goods we manufacture ourselves, especially if we can make enough of them for our own consumption; and I take this to be the case of our silk manufacture, which, with great labour and industry, is brought to perfection in London, Canterbury, and other places.

"IV. The importation, on easy terms, of such manufactures as are already introduced into a country must be of bad consequence, and check their progress, as would undoubtedly be the case of the linen and paper manufactures of Britain (which are of late much improved), if these commodities were allowed to be brought in without paying very high duties*."

These maxims exhibit the spirit of the mercantile system which prevailed at that period, and was so firmly rooted in the public mind, that any reasoning in opposition to it would have been rejected with disdain. They contain some incontrovertible truths, with a large mixture of error, and a portion of spleen against a nation considered as our natural enemy.

The principle on which these maxims are

* Guardian, No. 170.

founded is, that we should export as much, and import as little as we can, in order that there may be a large favourable balance, applied to the increase of our public wealth.

Our celebrated nagivation act, and other commercial laws, were founded on these principles; and, being opposed by similar laws from other nations, gave rise to a commercial war, which sometimes broke forth into open war, and always tended to the obstruction of beneficial commerce.

As this system has been ably refuted by Dr. Smith and others, and is now not only generally discarded by the philosopher, but even the legislatures of commercial nations have embraced more liberal views, and relaxed much of their cumbersome restrictions, it seems unnecessary at present to enter into a detailed discussion of its merits.

In general we may observe, that exportation is only made for the sake of importation. Were we to export without importing, we should throw our commodities away. If we export a greater value than we import, we throw them partially away. If the *value in use* of our exports and imports be equal, the advantage of commerce would be problematic; and it is only beneficial when the commodities we import afford us a greater share of the necessaries and enjoyments of life than those which we give in exchange for them. When this is the case, the value of our imports, as exhibited in our custom-house books, would exceed that of our exports, if both were fairly appreciated.

A recollection of the now acknowledged weakness of a system, long held to be incontrovertible, should lead us to listen with candour to a discussion on other topics, in regard to which the public mind can hardly yet bear opposition to the prevailing opinions, though founded, perhaps, on no better basis than those now abandoned.

Were the opinion of the reciprocity of gain and loss in commerce well-founded, a philanthropist would not be disposed to hold commerce in high esteem, though so conducted as to prove beneficial to his own nation. If it only enriches one nation by impoverishing another, without adding to the mass of human enjoyment, it deserves no encouragement from him, whose aim it is to promote the general good of his fellow-creatures. Yet, even in this view, it would be too rigid to blame the merchants who engaged in it, or the statesmen who promoted it.

Every man and every state is actuated by a desire of advancing their own welfare; and, if they pursue this intention without deceit or violence, they cannot be blamed. Speculations in regard to the general good are involved in much obscurity, and there is reason to believe that it cannot be more effectually promoted than by the concurring efforts of individuals and communities, each acting to promote its own.

It is a pleasant theme to vindicate commerce upon liberal principles, and hold it forth as promoting the general welfare of mankind. Such is its natural tendency, and such in general will be its consequences, when its direction is not prevented by artificial restraints or excitement. It can never be considerably or permanently beneficial to one nation, unless it be also beneficial to those with whom it trades; and the affluence of nations around us is so far from interfering with our own, that it lays the foundation of a more extensive commerce, and furnishes the means of carrying general wealth to the utmost pitch which the circumstances of human nature admit of.

The only solid foundation of commerce between nations is the diversity of their commodities; each bestowing what the other wants, and thereby increasing their mutual comforts. This diversity arises from two sources; the natural difference of their climates, and the difference of the progress of the inhabitants in useful arts.

The diversity of produce is the most extensive and permanent source of commerce. Some necessary and many desirable articles can only be produced in certain climates, or at least are produced in these with so much greater facility, that it is expedient other nations should be supplied from them. By collecting from every country the commodities which it furnishes, something is added to the real enjoyment of life, and much to the gratifications on which habit and fashion have stamped a value. A modern Englishman cannot breakfast comfortably without the infusion of a Chinese herb, served up in a vessel from the same country, seasoned with the juice of a West Indian reed refined in the metropolis, and stirred with an implement obtained from the mines of Potosi.

Although some climates are more liberally supplied than others by the hand of nature, there are few that have not some articles to give in exchange for those they want. The coldest inhabited countries are often well supplied with wood and useful metals, and their seas abound with fish, particularly those kinds from which animal oil is obtained. When we enter the temperate zones, we meet with a country adapted for raising corn and pasturing oxen, sheep, and other cattle. At a certain latitude, the vine and the olive, and many kinds of delicious fruits, arrive at perfection. A little more warmth is required for raising cotton, and rearing the insect from whose labour silk is obtained. The warmest climates supply us with sugar, coffee, and spices. The cultivation of the tea-plant, though it does not require a very warm climate, has been hitherto confined to the eastern parts of Asia. The exchange of these, and a few other commodities, constitutes the greater part of modern commerce.

The other source of commerce is the diversity of skill which different nations have acquired in particular arts. Each nation gives in exchange those articles of which it has brought the manufacture to the greatest perfection. In process of time, other nations may acquire that skill in which they are at present deficient, and then commerce, so far as it arises from this source, will be discontinued.

The interchange of the works of mechanic art gives the utmost range to the division of labour. We have already remarked the progress and utility of that practice. In a large nation, it has sufficient scope by internal trade, in many articles; but there are some in which it is capable of being carried so far that the domestic market is insufficient, and a free commerce with the civilized world is requisite for its expansion. The English manufacture of hardware affords a remarkable instance of the perfection to which art can be carried, and the cheapness with which it can be executed on a large scale, when the extent of the market is very great.

In these ways the mutual advantages of commercial nations are promoted. The produce of the one, exchanged for the produce of the other, and the manufactures of the one for the manufactures of the other, afford to both a greater share of all that nature and art can supply. Perhaps one nation is so far superior in industry and skill, that their commerce is limited to an exchange of manufactures for produce. This may be beneficial to both nations; but in different ways. The industrious nation receives, as a reward for its labour, a larger share of the bounties of nature. The more indolent or unskilful partake of the benefit of those arts which they are unable, when in that state, to exercise.

An admission of these principles will tend to remove some prejudices which prevail very generally on this subject.

The activity of a trading town presents a scene that makes a forcible and pleasing impression on the imagination; a large body of shipping in constant motion, arriving from and departing for every quarter of the world; quays and warehouses filled with the productions of every climate, and every thing valuable that art can prepare; multitudes of men in different ranks of life, all active, many thriving; those who conduct the operations enjoying affluence and accumulating wealth; the diffusion of merchandise through the country by an hundred channels, and the spirit of industry excited wherever its influence reaches. The impression produced by these scenes is corroborated by the information which history affords, that mercantile nations have generally attained a high degree of wealth and population, of strength and energy. On the whole, we are led to entertain a high regard for commerce, and to believe that too much cannot be done for its encouragement.

The benefits, however, which commerce bestows, extensive as they are, flow from its free exertion. It does not bear restraint or direction. It does not even agree with encouragement. Its operations must be the result of the united efforts of men voluntarily striving to promote their respective interests. If extraneous inducements be held forth, they divert it from its proper purpose, and mar its beneficial tendency; and it is not those points which strike the imagination most that constitute its excellence. These are effects flowing from, and indicating a system highly beneficial; but if separated from their proper source, they lose all their value.

It will throw light on this subject to recur to the consideration of the state of commerce in the infancy of society, and the advantages which resulted from it. As communities increase in numbers and advance in arts, or open an intercourse with other communities, their transactions become more complicated; but still they are animated by the same motives, and their utility is to be estimated by the same principles.

A. cultivates a fertile corn farm. B. possesses a tract of land fit for pasture, and his herds afford him cheese and butter in abundance. C. plants an orchard in a favourable exposure. At the end of the season they meet and exchange their commodities, and each has an ample store of corn, cheese, and fruit. They might have raised corn and pastured cattle, each on his own land, but had they done so, their soil being less proper for the one or the other, their supply would have been less abundant; and if A. and B. had no ground fit for an orchard, they must have fared without fruit, if their intercourse with C. had not supplied them.

D. pastures a flock of sheep, and their wool is wrought by his household and villagers into cloth fit for winter garments. E. cultivates a field of flax, and his villagers occupy themselves in the manufacture of linen. The several villagers soon discover that they will be more comfortably clothed the whole year round, when they possess garments of both kinds, and they exchange their manufactures for their mutual convenience.

It is not, however, impracticable to raise the different materials in the same farm, and manufacture both kinds in the same village. This, however, is done to disadvantage, partly because the soil is less adapted to the one purpose or the other, and partly because the inhabitants are less skilful in preparing and manufacturing the material to which they have not been accustomed.

One of these inconveniences is insurmountable, and the other not easily surmounted. They will therefore confine themselves each to the manufacture of that material which suits their soil, and which they understand best, providing they have access to exchange their commodities.

But if a superior should impose a tax upon the goods thus exchanged, this must discourage the commerce, and may put a stop to it. The villagers, accustomed to the joint use of linen and woollen garments, will raise materials for both, and manufacture them the best way they can. Their labour is employed to disadvantage; but the loss which this occasions may be less than the burthen imposed on their intercourse. This is a misapplication of labour, produced by a measure designed for the profit of the superior, who oppresses the villagers, and loses his aim.

In order to convey the goods between the villages a highway may be wanted. Perhaps they are separated by rugged mountains, and the making of the highway is a work of much difficulty. The expense it requires will be balanced against the advantages expected from it. The villagers may, perhaps, act a wiser part, in making the most, each of their own industry, rather than opening a communication that costs so dear. The labour of the undertaking may be more than the additional labour, which would procure among themselves every advantage, expected from its accomplishment.

A benevolent superior, from a desire of encouraging trade, makes the highway for them. Still, if the expense exceed the utility, there is a misapplication of labour. The same quantity of labour put in motion by the same means, but applied to a different purpose, would have been more productive in adding to the stock of wealth. This is an instance of an ill-judged, though well-meant, encouragement, producing a similar effect as the imposition of an oppressive burthen.

The road being completed, waggons are employed to convey the goods between the villages, warehouses are built for their reception, and factors are required to conduct the business. A traveller, who passed through the country some years before, visits it again, and is gratified with the appearance of opulence and activity which these objects present. But the road, the waggons, and the warehouses, do not, in themselves, add to the enjoyment of the villagers, nor does the gain of the waggoner or warehouseman constitute any acquisition to their wealth. These are all burthens on the villagers, tending to lessen the fund from which their subsistence and accommodation is derived. These burthens, indeed, are, or ought to be, liberally re-paid by the accommodations afforded.

If this intercourse be neither compelled nor incited by extraneous motives, it cannot be doubted that it is profitable. The villagers will not make the highway, employ the waggons, or build the warehouses, unless they derive an adequate benefit from them. A superior, who designs to establish a market, may threaten his dependents with his displeasure, unless they frequent it; he may offer premiums, he may promote horse-races, and thus draw the villagers together from motives of profit or amusement. But when their resort to the market is owing to these motives, its advantages are at least equivocal.

This illustration, however familiar, is instructive. It sets the advantages of commerce in their true light, and removes the glare produced by some of the objects that attend it. What is true of the highways and waggons, is no less true of the quays, the shipping, and all the splendid objects and bustle of a mercantile town. The expense of all these is a burthen upon industry. If they be executed by compulsion, they may well be accounted pernicious. If rewards be held forth to encourage them, there is reason to doubt their utility; but, if they be the natural consequences of a free commercial intercourse, we may be assured that they contribute to the wealth of the community.

If all commodities could be raised, and all kinds of manufacture carried on in every country with equal advantage, all commerce would cease. We should lose our trading towns, with their quays and warehouses; our shipping would disappear; our merchants, and all their numerous dependents, would be dispersed for want of employment; the appearance of activity which arises from trade would be no longer displayed, yet the community would be richer. All the labour expended upon the shipping, warehouses, and other appendages of trade, would be applied directly to the production of articles which contribute to human welfare.

To encourage commerce by any kind of bounty is a measure of extreme delicacy, and very doubtful tendency. The sums which have been expended in this way by trading nations is very great: for, besides direct bounties, which have been granted liberally, we may refer to this head the establishment of foreign settlements, the support of garrisons for their defence, and of a navy for the protection of their trade. The expense of all these should be defrayed from the profits of commerce, and there is no other way of putting the advantage of commerce to the test, than by loading it with all the expenses which it gives occasion to. If it will not bear them all, and afford a profit besides to the merchant, it cannot be beneficial to the public. It will greatly swell this charge if we include that of all the wars waged for controversies which the pretence of infractions on commerce gives rise to.

It would be going too far, however, to reprobate bounties as, in every instance, prejudicial. If we could stop at the proper bounds, there are some cases in which they might be properly granted. Prudence may restrain individuals from engaging in projects, where the event is doubtful, and where bad success would ruin them. Public encouragement may, therefore, be needed to set new enterprizes a-going, and let them have a fair trial. If they succeed, the encouragement should be withdrawn; and the wealth which they introduce may not only replace to the public what it has contributed to their establishment in their infancy, but also what has been expended by it on other projects which have never succeeded.

When encouragement of this kind is given, there is great occasion for discretion in the choice of objects. If government give way to such applications at all, they are harassed with applications from every quarter. Much art is used in misrepresenting, and a minister, who cannot be a competent judge on every subject, is exposed to deception, and induced to grant encouragement to projects which do not require it, or do not deserve it. A bounty should always be limited in point of time. The utmost that should be done is to afford the undertaking a fair trial, after which, if it will not go on without the aid of a bounty, it ought to be relinquished.

Trade supported by a bounty may increase by degrees, and acquire a considerable magnitude: the bounty, of consequence, becomes a considerable burthen on the community. Specious arguments, however, for its continuance are drawn from the success which has attended it. The shipping, the seamen employed in the trade, the capital engaged in it, the industry it has put into motion by giving vent to manufactures or otherwise, the wealth it has introduced, are all displayed in strong colours; and the continuance of the bounty urged by those who are interested in the trade. The just inference from these premises is, that the trade has already had an ample trial under the encouragement of a bounty, and, if its profits be not delusive, it is well able to subsist without one if they be, the country has already paid too dearly. Yet, the less the bounty is needed, the more difficult it is to withdraw it. The wealthier the merchants concerned in it have become, their voice is the louder, their influence the more powerful, and the magnitude of the object at stake lays hold on the public imagination. Great caution is, therefore, requisite in the admission of a measure which is very difficult to discontinue when it becomes improper.

We have thus endeavoured to state the direct advantages of trade in increasing wealth. It enlarges the comforts of life by introducing the productions of other climes. It supplies us with those articles in the preparation of which other nations excel us on cheaper terms, and it encourages those in which we excel them by opening a more extensive market, and giving room for a more complete division of labour. The shipping, and all the other apparatus employed in carrying it on, and the risks necessarily incurred, are a burthen on the community. The gain or loss arising from trade is the excess of the one of these above the other. When trade is left to itself, if it go on, it must be profitable to the public; for unless it were profitable to the merchants, they would leave it off; and the gain of individuals is an increase to the public wealth. If it be upheld by bounties, in whatever form, the general effects are questionable.

We have next to direct our attention to a very important consequence of trade, distinct from its tendency to the accumulation of wealth, namely, the moral effects produced on the human character by extending the intercourse of mankind with one another.

To resume our former mode of illustration. Let us suppose the lord of a manor establishes a market, and draws the neighbouring inhabitants to frequent it by means of premiums, horse-races, and the like. Those who resort to it carry their commodities along with them for the purpose of traffick, and derive some advantage from their sale, though not sufficient to defray the expense, and recompense the loss of time which attendance on the market requires. They would not have gone there, had it not been for the premiums and the horse-races. Villages convene from every quarter, and some come from a considerable distance. New objects are presented to their view; the circle of their acquaintance is enlarged, and their spirits enlivened by the scenes which the market presents; and, in the course of their conversation, each communicates what he knows, and they return home better informed than they came. By frequenting such meetings they become more acute. The objects which they meet inspire new desires, and stimulate exertion. In order to gratify these desires, they are induced to prosecute their former employments more assiduously, or to strike out new branches of industry.

The attentive reader will already perceive that we have as yet only drawn the favourable side of the picture. The habits of idleness and intemperance which such meetings lead to are too common to escape observation, and render the general estimation in which they should be held extremely doubtful.

Effects of a like kind take place in a higher degree from the intercourse of nations with each other. The arrangements of foreign trade require more varied knowledge, and call forth more exertion of mind than domestic transactions. A merchant must know what commodities will suit the demands of every country, and what they can give in return; what the one will sell for, and what the other may be bought for. The sciences of geography and natural history are chiefly founded upon the discoveries which commerce has led to. The arts of ship-building and navigation have chiefly arisen from it. Every useful discovery, in whatever nation made, has been rapidly communicated through the civilized world. An acquaintance with the various manners and characters of different nations has enlarged our knowledge of human nature, and induced a general liberality of sentiment and manners.

Moralists assign a peculiar character as connected with the different professions which mankind embrace in civilized society; and, though there be many exceptions, that character generally pervades the profession in some degree. The character of a merchant contains many estimable points; diligence, activity, accuracy, sobriety. The important virtue of honesty may also be ascribed to him. Experience has established the maxim, that a fair character obtained by uniform rectitude is the surest way to wealth. Hence the merchant's education and habits lead him to be an honest man. The minute and constant attention which a merchant must give to gain and loss seems calculated to induce some degree of avarice; yet many merchants are distinguished for liberality. An extensive merchant is generally a well-informed man, and superior to vulgar prejudices.

In a commercial country the number of merchants is so great, and the rank which many of them hold in society so high, that their character and manners have considerable influence on those of the whole community.

A modern merchant, for the most part, has a fixed residence in some sea-port town, from which he despatches ships laden with his cargoes, and carries on his correspondence with merchants established in a similar manner, in various other countries. In ancient times the merchant went along with his cargo; his character and that of the voyager were considered as inseparably connected.

> Mercator contra, navem jactantibus austris.
>
> HORAT.

The peculiar character of the mercantile voyager is, in some respects, different from that of the resident merchant. His situation requires a more enterprising spirit, and more personal courage: perhaps it presents inducements to artful practices not consistent with that strict integrity which generally characterises the established merchant.

The tendency of commerce, as it is conducted between civilized nations, is, in many respects, favourable to the improvement of the human character; and nothing that can be adduced on the opposite side is sufficient to counterbalance its beneficial influence. We are not so confident that this can be affirmed in regard to the commerce which takes place between a country advanced in arts, and one which is in a simple, or, as we term it, a savage state.

We may draw a pleasant picture of the mutual advantages which such a commerce might afford; —the communication of useful arts and induction of civilized manners, on the one side, and the acquisition of useful commodities and disposal of spare ones, on the other, accompanied with an addition to the knowledge of nature, and of mankind. When we consult history, we find that this picture has been seldom realized, and that one of very different features generally presents itself.

The power which art and intelligence confer is so great, that a handful of colonists from a civilized nation is sufficient to subdue a tribe of rude natives, and a consciousness of this superiority has generally kindled the passions of avarice and ambition, and supplanted every principle of justice and humanity. Accordingly we find that wherever the nations of Europe have established settlements in countries in a comparative state of rudeness, the natives have been subjected or exterminated, sometimes with circumstances of shocking treachery and barbarity.

It gives some relief to the painful feelings which these facts excite, to find that the voyages of discovery undertaken during the last and present reign have been conducted in a very different spirit, and measures embraced for communicating the benefits of civilization to the countries visited by our navigators; and that these attempts have been, in a considerable degree, successful.

Among the advantages of commerce, the supply of manufactures to foreign nations is generally estimated to hold a principal place. This gives a means of investing capital, and furnishes employment to a numerous population, and diffuses a spirit of industry through the community. These advantages, in no case to be slightly valued, may, in particular states of society, be very important: they are remarkably so at present in Britain; yet even with us internal commerce is a superior object. Home consumption affords a more ample source of employment than foreign trade, and a more certain one. It may be carried so far in a large and industrious nation as to render it, in a great measure, independent of foreign commerce.

The commerce of Britain at present is, perhaps, the most extensive that any age or nation has ever attained, and cannot fail to have the most powerful influence on the public welfare. The following statements, taken from the official returns for the years ending 5th January, 1826, 1827, and 1828, will give a view of the present state of our trade, and assist us in forming a judgment of the advantages derived from it.

PRODUCE and MANUFACTURES of the United Kingdom, exported from Great Britain to all Parts, except Ireland, in the Years ending 5th January, 1826, 1827, and 1828, at the official and declared Values.

| | Official Value. | | | Declared Value. | | |
|---|---|---|---|---|---|---|
| RAW PRODUCE. | Year ending 5th Jan. 1826. | 5th Jan. 1827. | 5th Jan. 1828. | 5th Jan. 1826. | 5th Jan. 1827. | 5th Jan. 1828. |
| | £. | £. | £. | £. | £. | £. |
| Coal | 265,669 | 298,069 | 314,202 | 132,811 | 143,692 | 154,042 |
| Salt | 278,225 | 202,343 | 245,918 | 154,577 | 113,203 | 121,039 |
| Fish | 178,429 | 178,613 | 187,252 | 202,280 | 194,545 | 182,084 |
| Tin, unwrought | 119,518 | 159,691 | 180,768 | 148,302 | 171,034 | 187,887 |
| Beef and Pork | 73,400 | 59,556 | 57,645 | 136,591 | 106,828 | 87,394 |
| Butter and Cheese | 62,643 | 55,091 | 53,830 | 189,899 | 149,760 | 145,848 |
| Bacon and Hams | 22,391 | 20,535 | 29,021 | 27,424 | 24,494 | 32,494 |
| Corn, Meal, and Flour | 11,651 | 19,362 | 27,577 | 35,492 | 53,839 | 70,915 |
| Hops | 1,807 | 6,297 | 8,883 | 3,439 | 4,901 | 7,172 |
| Seeds | 6,068 | 5,534 | 6,260 | 6,256 | 5,513 | 5,886 |
| Bread and Biscuit | 12,960 | 5,391 | 5,549 | 17,243 | 7,654 | 8,068 |
| Alum | 4,089 | 3,064 | 3,306 | 2,891 | 1,972 | 2,290 |
| | 1,036,850 | 1,013,546 | 1,120,205 | 1,057,205 | 977,435 | 1,005,129 |
| MANUFACTURES FOR CLOTHING. | | | | | | |
| Cotton Manufactures | 26,597,574 | 21,445,742 | 29,203,138 | 15,046,902 | 10,522,407 | 13,956,825 |
| Cotton Yarn | 2,897,706 | 3,748,526 | 3,979,759 | 3,206,729 | 3,491,268 | 3,545,568 |
| Woollen Manufactures | 5,929,342 | 5,041,568 | 5,979,701 | 6,194,926 | 4,982,908 | 5,277,861 |
| Linen Manufactures | 2,709,772 | 2,056,558 | 2,808,081 | 2,130,697 | 1,487,662 | 1,895,186 |
| Apparel | 457,136 | 367,920 | 389,390 | 457,136 | 367,920 | 389,390 |
| Mats | 236,443 | 167,778 | 159,485 | 294,795 | 206,204 | 192,405 |
| Silk Manufactures | 150,815 | 106,648 | 173,334 | 296,662 | 168,383 | 236,092 |
| Haberdashery and Millinery | 30,511 | 33,832 | 62,216 | 400,557 | 349,949 | 499,534 |
| Umbrellas | 35,620 | 23,741 | 38,010 | 35,620 | 23,741 | 38,010 |
| | 39,044,919 | 32,992,313 | 42,793,114 | 28,064,024 | 21,600,442 | 26,030,971 |

PRODUCE and MANUFACTURES of the United Kingdom, &c.—*continued.*

| | Official Value. | | | Declared Value. | | |
|---|---|---|---|---|---|---|
| MANUFACTURES FROM METALS. | Year ending 5th Jan. 1826. | 5th Jan. 1827. | 5th Jan. 1828. | 5th Jan. 1826. | 5th Jan. 1827. | 5th Jan. 1828. |
| | £. | £. | £. | £. | £. | £. |
| Iron and Steel, wrought & unwrought | 1,106,606 | 1,329,569 | 1,581,413 | 1,048,063 | 1,105,618 | 1,214,948 |
| Hardware and Cutlery . . . . | 629,958 | 563,147 | 713,523 | 1,391,112 | 1,169,105 | 1,390,428 |
| Brass and Copper manufactures. . | 405,158 | 524,626 | 776,895 | 485,118 | 571,149 | 786,803 |
| Arms and Ammunition . . . . | 375,256 | 383,019 | 261,686 | 526,266 | 620,600 | 406,312 |
| Plate, Jewellery, and Watches . . | 210,323 | 153,163 | 168,003 | 215,083 | 156,196 | 169,449 |
| Pewter Wares, and Tin Plates . . | 206.546 | 241,017 | 299,799 | 208,408 | 242,991 | 301,753 |
| Lead and Shot . . . . . . | 91,100 | 107,651 | 141,094 | 214,906 | 239,542 | 256,181 |
| | 3,024,947 | 3,302,192 | 3,942,413 | 4,088,956 | 4,105,201 | 4,525,874 |
| MANUFACTURES OF WOOD, LEATHER, &c. | | | | | | |
| Machinery and Millwork . . . | 212,416 | 228,504 | 201,551 | 212,416 | 228,504 | 201,551 |
| Stationery . . . . . . . . | 181,151 | 182,240 | 193,046 | 181,151 | 182,240 | 193,046 |
| Leather, wrought and unwrought . | 130,195 | 91,810 | 102,115 | 323,945 | 260,957 | 280,265 |
| Sadlery . . . . . . . . . | 108,200 | 101,730 | 88,434 | 108,200 | 101,730 | 88,434 |
| Glass . . . . . . . . . | 128,779 | 111,408 | 146,109 | 593,266 | 430,121 | 527,110 |
| Cordage . . . . . . . . . | 100,727 | 68,618 | 63,013 | 205,483 | 144,541 | 127,832 |
| Earthenware. . . . . . . . | 95,179 | 78,922 | 91,711 | 405,098 | 345,794 | 437,812 |
| Cabinet and Upholstery Wares . . | 74,659 | 67,136 | 56,407 | 74,659 | 67,136 | 56,407 |
| Musical Instruments . . . . | 68,170 | 70,891 | 68,393 | 68,170 | 70,891 | 68,393 |
| Mathematical Instruments . . . | 31.333 | 36,791 | 32,339 | 31,333 | 36,791 | 32,339 |
| Books . . . . . . . . . | 30,352 | 18,482 | 17,025 | 135,088 | 111,517 | 106,925 |
| | 1,161,161 | 1,056,532 | 1,060,143 | 2,338,809 | 1,980,222 | 2,120,114 |

## PRODUCE and MANUFACTURES of the United Kingdom, &c.—*continued.*

| | Official Value. | | | Declared Value. | | |
|---|---|---|---|---|---|---|
| MISCELLANEOUS ARTICLES. | Year ending 5th Jan. 1826. | 5th Jan. 1827. | 5th Jan. 1828. | 5th Jan. 1826. | 5th Jan. 1827. | 5th Jan. 1828. |
| | £. | £. | £. | £. | £. | £. |
| Sugar, refined | 897,590 | 917,130 | 1,117,329 | 779,194 | 704,463 | 963,430 |
| Soap and Candles | 177,096 | 131,429 | 223,597 | 185,542 | 140,544 | 227,695 |
| Painters' Colours | 129,307 | 109,562 | 124,983 | 129,307 | 109,562 | 124,983 |
| Saltpetre | 51,493 | 58,174 | 42,088 | 21,825 | 23,016 | 17,942 |
| Beer and Ale | 49,345 | 45,448 | 55,504 | 184,312 | 172,575 | 212,390 |
| Horses | 15,565 | 12,020 | 15,642 | 72,099 | 47,419 | 62,131 |
| Whalebone | 13,744 | 17,167 | 20,102 | 23,168 | 37,486 | 45,316 |
| Train Oil | 8,454 | 9,111 | 16,434 | 12,656 | 10,852 | 18,464 |
| Tobacco and Snuff | 1,631 | 1,267 | 1,581 | 18,141 | 11,928 | 14,981 |
| | 1,344,225 | 1,301,308 | 1,617,260 | 1,426,240 | 1,257,845 | 1,687,332 |
| SUMMARY. | | | | | | |
| Raw produce | 1,036,850 | 1,013,546 | 1,120,205 | 1,057,205 | 977,435 | 1,005,129 |
| Manufactures for Clothings | 39,044,919 | 32,992,313 | 42,793,114 | 28,064,024 | 21,600,442 | 26,030,871 |
| Manufactures from Metals | 3,024,947 | 3,302,192 | 3,942,413 | 4,088,956 | 4,105,201 | 4,525,874 |
| Manufactures of Wood, Leather, &c. | 1,161,161 | 1,056,532 | 1,060,143 | 2,338,809 | 1,980,222 | 2,120,114 |
| Miscellaneous Articles | 1,344,225 | 1,301,308 | 1,617,260 | 1,426,240 | 1,257,845 | 1,687,332 |
| Articles not specified | 840,892 | 666,945 | 743,286 | 1,102,070 | 926,357 | 1,027,003 |
| Shillings and Pence | 27 | 18 | 27 | 26 | 26 | 16 |
| | 46,453,021 | 40,332,854 | 51,276,448 | 38,077,330 | 30,847,528 | 36,396,339 |

**FOREIGN and COLONIAL MERCHANDIZE exported from Britain to Foreign Parts, in the years ending 5th January 1826, 1827, and 1828, at the Official Valuation*.**

| Articles obtained chiefly from American Colonies. | 5th January, 1826. | 5th January, 1827. | 5th January, 1828. |
|---|---|---|---|
| | £. | £. | £. |
| Coffee | 1,708,621 | 1,987,589 | 1,841,048 |
| Cotton Wool | 1,160,201 | 1,663,393 | 1,517,946 |
| Sugar | 605,751 | 751,837 | 645,255 |
| Rum | 437,975 | 416,775 | 486,479 |
| Cochineal | 106,844 | 86,669 | 164,098 |
| Logwood | 95,798 | 82,008 | 99,761 |
| Cocoa | 55,293 | 62,255 | 113,194 |
| Tobacco | 54,848 | 191,466 | 240,736 |
| Cod Fish of Newfoundland | 48,847 | 36,636 | 34,902 |
| Pimento | 39,616 | 43,602 | 60,921 |
| £ | 4,313,794 | 5,322,230 | 5,204,340 |
| **Articles chiefly obtained from the East Indies.** | | | |
| Cotton Manufactures | 818,634 | 591,562 | 673,371 |
| Indigo | 741,953 | 836,675 | 591,405 |
| Pepper | 180,787 | 288,647 | 221,533 |
| Silk Manufactures | 144,538 | 105,205 | 221,614 |
| Saltpetre | 113,254 | 111,802 | 111,542 |
| Cinnamon | 100,106 | 86,101 | 89,923 |
| Tea | 67,531 | 42,123 | 38,249 |
| Spices, viz.—Cassia, Cloves, Mace, and Nutmegs | 57,852 | 137,382 | 91,876 |
| Rice | 52,895 | 40,391 | 52,310 |
| £ | 2,277,550 | 2,239,888 | 2,094,825 |

* The values are taken from the Finance Accounts, 5th January 1828, in which those of the two former years are repeated. The value given in the Accounts for 5th January 1826 and 1827, are not all exactly the same, but the differences are not considerable.

| Miscellaneous Articles. | 5th Jan. 1826. | 5th Jan. 1827. | 5th Jan. 1828. |
|---|---|---|---|
| | £. | £. | £. |
| Spelter | 305,614 | 409,156 | 346,428 |
| Wine | 190,340 | 186,817 | 268,041 |
| Brandy | 175,326 | 115,050 | 176,052 |
| Silk, raw and thrown | 139,400 | 228,296 | 38,430 |
| Hides | 136,202 | 103,554 | 33,820 |
| Iron in Bars | 87,724 | 29,527 | 44,988 |
| Geneva | 85,739 | 55,923 | 69,871 |
| Corn and Flour | 77,257 | 41,408 | 119,350 |
| Lead, Pig | 54,823 | 27,700 | 34,233 |
| Wool | 46,662 | 61,111 | 53,359 |
| Woollen Manufactures | 46,562 | 11,607 | 9,628 |
| Skins and Furs | 43,412 | 45,303 | 50,472 |
| Raisins | 39,494 | 40,961 | 23,283 |
| Ashes | 36,129 | 26,578 | 35,252 |
| Copper, wrought & unwrought | 29,935 | 131,640 | 79,713 |
| Cotton Manufactures of Europe | 29,915 | 31,673 | 14,722 |
| Cortex Peruvianus | 22,878 | 19,881 | 26,017 |
| Flax | 16,087 | 18,991 | 13,390 |
| Olive Oil | 15,855 | 48,825 | 27,488 |
| Fustic | 9,541 | 14,253 | 6,826 |
| Silk Manufactures of Europe | 9,219 | 21,661 | 19,993 |
| Barilla | 5,360 | 2,855 | 374 |
| Hemp | 3,871 | 2,564 | 26,160 |
| Currants | 3,542 | 17,606 | 6,753 |
| Annotto | 3,309 | 3,896 | 6,935 |
| Linen | 2,459 | 24,778 | 19,095 |
| Train Oil | 1,080 | 2,473 | 2,730 |
| Amt. of Miscellaneous Articles | 1,617,735 | 1,724,087 | 1,553,398 |
| Articles chiefly obtained from American Colonies | 4,313,794 | 5,322,230 | 5,204,340 |
| Articles chiefly obtained from East Indies | 2,277,550 | 2,239,888 | 2,094,825 |
| Articles not specified | 946,201 | 780,274 | 953,661 |
| Shillings and Pence | 25 | 23 | 23 |
| Total Foreign and Colonial Merchandize exported | 9,155,305 | 10,066,502 | 9,806,247 |
| Produce and Manufactures of United Kingdoms exported from Britain | 46,453,021 | 40,332,854 | 51,276,448 |
| Total Exports from Britain, except to Ireland | 55,608,326 | 50,399,356 | 61,082,695 |
| Exports from Ireland | 711,856 | 642,666 | 967,312 |
| £ | 56,320,182 | 51,042,022 | 61,050,007 |
| Produce and Manufactures of United Kingdoms exported from Ireland | 697,667 | 632,882 | 942,832 |
| Foreign & Colonial Merchandize exported from Ireland | 14,189 | 9,783 | 24,480 |
| £ | 711,856 | 642,666 | 967,312 |

IMPORTS into Britain from all Places, except Ireland, in the Years (ending 5th Jan.) 1826, 1827, and 1828, at the Official Value.

| | 5th Jan. 1826. | 5th Jan. 1827. | 5th Jan. 1828. |
|---|---|---|---|
| USEFUL PROVISIONS. | £. | £. | £. |
| Corn, Grain, Meal, and Flour | 1,128,341 | 2,117,390 | 1,994,214 |
| Butter | 398,080 | 273,326 | 291,579 |
| Cheese | 331,660 | 258,977 | 272,625 |
| Fish of Newfoundland | 62,184 | 48,615 | 26,942 |
| Smalls | 10,770 | 4,115 | 10,074 |
| Rice | 61,283 | 87,702 | 143,691 |
| | 1,992,318 | 2,790,125 | 2,739,125 |
| LUXURIES. | | | |
| Sugar | 5,055,655 | 5,602,844 | 5,328,114 |
| Coffee | 3,237,980 | 2,569,245 | 2,945,023 |
| Tea | 2,934,571 | 2,984,040 | 3,974,523 |
| Wine | 1,178,930 | 786,440 | 867,545 |
| Spirits—Rum | 342,893 | 416,447 | 497,207 |
| Brandy | 246,709 | 199,534 | 236,788 |
| Geneva | 30,869 | 18,243 | 19,100 |
| Amount of Spirits | 620,471 | 634,224 | 753,095 |
| Spices—Pepper | 92,013 | 234,976 | 151,641 |
| Cinnamon | 85,128 | 31,297 | 253,488 |
| Mace | 45,227 | 74,359 | 14,246 |
| Pimento | 40,223 | 40,302 | 57,891 |
| Cassia | 39,674 | 40,067 | 31,194 |
| Nutmegs | 36,694 | 67,740 | 14,971 |
| Cloves | 23,038 | 70,087 | 63,346 |
| Amount of Spices | 361,997 | 558,828 | 586,777 |
| Fruits—Currants | 131,803 | 89,166 | 151,766 |
| Raisins | 121,831 | 139,591 | 88,109 |
| Lemons and Oranges | 56,036 | 69,158 | 66,259 |
| Almonds | 15,566 | 14,487 | 28,126 |
| Figs | 14,741 | 13,985 | 13,910 |
| Juniper Berries | 7,256 | 12,300 | 21,865 |
| Amount of Fruits | 347,233 | 338,687 | 370,035 |
| Molasses | 236,116 | 192,598 | 261,447 |
| Cocoa | 72,369 | 49,961 | 103,264 |
| Total Luxuries | 14,045,322 | 13,716,867 | 15,189,923 |

ARTICLES re-exported.

| | 5th Jan. 1826. | 5th Jan. 1827. | 5th Jan. 1828. |
|---|---|---|---|
| | £. | £. | £. |
| Corn | 77,257 | 41,408 | 119,350 |
| Butter | | | |
| Cheese | | | |
| Fish of Newfoundland | 48,847 | 36,636 | 34,902 |
| Smalls | | | |
| Rice | 52,895 | 40,391 | 52,310 |
| | 178,999 | 118,435 | 206,562 |
| Sugar | 605,751 | 751,837 | 645,255 |
| Coffee | 1,708,621 | 1,987,589 | 1,841,048 |
| Tea | 67,531 | 42,123 | 38,249 |
| Wine | 190,340 | 186,817 | 268,041 |
| Spirits—Rum | 437,975 | 416,775 | 486,479 |
| Brandy | 175,326 | 115,050 | 176,052 |
| Geneva | 85,739 | 55,923 | 69,871 |
| Spices—Pepper | 180,787 | 288,647 | 221,533 |
| Cinnamon | 100,106 | 86,101 | 89,923 |
| Mace | 15,261 | 48,524 | 30,179 |
| Pimento | 39,616 | 43,602 | 60,921 |
| Cassia | 27,806 | 34,778 | 42,769 |
| Nutmegs | 11,566 | 25,863 | 11,501 |
| Cloves | 3,219 | 28,217 | 10,429 |
| Fruits—Currants | 3,542 | 17,606 | 6,753 |
| Raisins | 39,494 | 40,961 | 23,283 |
| Lemons and Oranges | | | |
| Almonds | | | |
| Figs | | | |
| Juniper Berries | | | |
| Molasses | | | |
| Cocoa | 55,293 | 62,255 | 113,194 |
| | 3,747,973 | 4,232,668 | 4,135,480 |

IMPORTS into Britain, &c.—*continued.*

| | 5th Jan. 1826. | 5th Jan. 1827. | 5th Jan. 1828. |
|---|---|---|---|
| MATERIALS FOR MANUFACTURE. | £. | £. | £. |
| Cotton Wool | 7,405,618 | 5,726,997 | 8,963,688 |
| Flax | 2,078,844 | 1,346,802 | 1,786,304 |
| Sheep's Wool | 1,436,606 | 478,419 | 883,785 |
| Raw Silk | 1,437,336 | 1,060.344 | 1,524,568 |
| Hemp | 491,024 | 396,054 | 463,240 |
| Rags for Paper | 41,355 | 22,965 | 31,407 |
| | 12,890,783 | 9,031,581 | 13,652,992 |
| ARTICLES ACCESSORY TO MANUFACTURE. | | | |
| Dye Stuffs, viz.—Indigo | 895,959 | 1,084,749 | 801,393 |
| Madder | 572,316 | 330,391 | 451,086 |
| Logwood | 245,112 | 114,768 | 124,501 |
| Cochineal | 242,738 | 156,625 | 255,871 |
| Fustic | 51,835 | 32,844 | 35,896 |
| Shumach | 30,534 | 14,585 | 23,878 |
| Annotto | 25,578 | 10,824 | 40,211 |
| Amount Dye Stuffs | 2,064,072 | 1,744,786 | 1,732,836 |
| Ashes, Pearl and Pot | 313,958 | 275,582 | 168,747 |
| Barilla | 65,910 | 83,353 | 159,296 |
| | 2,443,940 | 2,103,721 | 2,060,879 |
| ARTICLES PARTIALLY MANUFACTURED. | | | |
| Thrown Silk | 928,245 | 212,146 | 555,490 |
| Linen Yarn | 326,130 | 142,565 | 181,343 |
| | 1,254,375 | 354,711 | 737,033 |
| ARTICLES FULLY MANUFACTURED. | | | |
| Cotton Manufactures of India | 371.994 | 449,796 | 273,097 |
| Cotton Manufactures of Europe | 40,663 | 40,090 | 39,100 |
| Silk Manufactures of India | 147,883 | 275,525 | 176,209 |
| Silk Manufactures of Europe | 42,763 | 170,399 | 379,665 |
| Woollen Manufactures | 61,175 | 27,839 | 42,659 |
| Linen | 34,827 | 88,783 | 67,695 |
| | 699,305 | 1,052,432 | 978,425 |
| METALS. | | | |
| Spelter | 577,792 | 241,984 | 299,986 |
| Quicksilver | 380,096 | 38,284 | 176,652 |
| Iron, in Bars | 226,526 | 126,620 | 180,439 |
| Lead, Pig | 92,459 | 13,700 | 32,456 |
| Copper, unwrought | 46,743 | 66,152 | 40,904 |
| | 1,323,616 | 486,740 | 730,437 |

## ARTICLES re-exported—*continued.*

| | 5th Jan. 1826. | 5th Jan. 1827. | 5th Jan. 1828. |
|---|---|---|---|
| MATERIALS FOR MANUFACTURE. | £. | £. | £. |
| Cotton Wool . . . . . . . . | 1,160,201 | 1,663,393 | 1,517,946 |
| Flax . . . . . . . . . . . | 16,087 | 18,991 | 13,390 |
| Sheep's Wool . . . . . . | 46,662 | 61,111 | 53,359 |
| Raw Silk . . . . . . . . . | | | |
| Hemp. . . . . . . . . . . | 3,871 | 2,564 | 26,160 |
| Rags for Paper . . . . . . | | | |
| | 1,226,821 | 1,746,059 | 1,610,855 |
| ARTICLES ACCESSORY TO MANUFACTURE. | | | |
| Dye Stuffs, viz.—Indigo. . . | 741,953 | 836,675 | 591,405 |
| Madder . . | | | |
| Logwood. . | 95,798 | 82,008 | 99,761 |
| Cochineal . | 106,844 | 86,669 | 164,098 |
| Fustic. . . | 9,541 | 14,253 | 6,825 |
| Shumach . | | | |
| Annotto . . | 3,309 | 3,896 | 6,935 |
| Amount Dye Stuffs . . | 957,445 | 1,023,501 | 869,024 |
| Ashes, Pearl and Pot. . . . | 36,129 | 26,578 | 35,252 |
| Barilla . . . . . . . . . | 5,360 | 2,855 | 374 |
| | 998,934 | 1,052,934 | 904,650 |
| ARTICLES PARTIALLY MANUFACTURED. | | | |
| Thrown Silk . . . . . . . . | 139,400 | 228,296 | 38,430 |
| Linen Yarn. . . . . . . . | | | |
| ARTICLES FULLY MANUFACTURED. | | | |
| Cotton Manufactures of India | 818,634 | 591,562 | 673,371 |
| Cotton Manufactures of Europe | 29,915 | 31,673 | 14,722 |
| Silk Manufactures of India . | 144,538 | 105,205 | 221,614 |
| Silk Manufactures of Europe. | 9,219 | 21,661 | 19,993 |
| Woollen Manufactures . . . | 46,562 | 11,607 | 9,628 |
| Linen . . . . . . . . . . | 2,459 | 24,778 | 19,095 |
| | 1,051,327 | 786,486 | 958,423 |
| METALS. | | | |
| Spelter . . . . . . . . . . | 305,614 | 409,156 | 346,428 |
| Quicksilver . . . . . . . . | | | |
| Iron, in Bars . . . . . . . . | 87,724 | 29,527 | 44,988 |
| Lead, Pig . . . . . . . . . | 54,823 | 27,700 | 34,233 |
| Copper, unwrought . . . . | 29,935 | 131,640 | 79,713 |
| | 478,096 | 598,023 | 505,362 |

IMPORTS into Britain, &c.—*continued.*

| | 5th Jan. 1826. | 5th Jan. 1827. | 5th Jan. 1828. |
|---|---|---|---|
| MISCELLANEOUS ARTICLES. | £. | £. | £. |
| Tallow | 1,180,205 | 866,973 | 1,249,800 |
| Wood, various kinds | 978,708 | 738,413 | 658,376 |
| Mahogany | 145,079 | 184,265 | 175,903 |
| Hides | 876,362 | 558,507 | 423,789 |
| Oils | 639,110 | 640,634 | 742,718 |
| Seeds | 444,673 | 347,207 | 407,558 |
| Tobacco | 371,575 | 242,468 | 308,645 |
| Skins and Furs | 336,109 | 242,709 | 314,093 |
| Bark, oak and cork tree | 198,649 | 105,725 | 158,335 |
| Gums | 156,048 | 117,964 | 98,965 |
| Turpentine | 139,210 | 81,315 | 144,781 |
| | 5,465,728 | 4,126,180 | 4,682,963 |
| DRUGS, viz. | | | |
| Cortex Peruvianus | 35,794 | 15,566 | 48,211 |
| Rhubarb | 33,046 | 70,007 | 57,609 |
| Isinglass | 19,522 | 21,797 | 22,467 |
| Liquorice | 9,645 | 32,600 | 41,121 |
| Bark, Quercitron | 7,454 | 3,061 | 2,847 |
| Jalap | 7,330 | 6,458 | 7,782 |
| Borax | 6,758 | 62,774 | 7,203 |
| Camphire | 4,046 | 1,310 | 4,616 |
| | 123,595 | 213,573 | 191,856 |
| Brimstone | 100,193 | 119,431 | 102,705 |
| Pitch and Tar | 91,322 | 116,177 | 139,107 |
| Whale Fins | 66,617 | 64,754 | 119,162 |
| Saltpetre | 58,582 | 78,701 | 121,117 |
| Cork | 41,837 | 33,247 | 45,282 |
| Bristles | 37,745 | 21,793 | 43,271 |
| Elephants' Teeth | 36,202 | 26,906 | 20,204 |
| Bees'-wax | 27,937 | 19,528 | 38,068 |
| | 6,049,758 | 4,820,290 | 5,603,735 |

ARTICLES re-exported—*continued.*

| Miscellaneous Articles. | 5th Jan. 1826. | 5th Jan. 1827. | 5th Jan. 1828. |
|---|---|---|---|
| | £. | £. | £. |
| Tallow | | | |
| Wood, various kinds | | | |
| Mahogany | | | |
| Hides | 136,202 | 103,554 | 33,820 |
| Oils | 16,936 | 51,299 | 30,213 |
| Seeds | | | |
| Tobacco | 54,848 | 191,466 | 240,736 |
| Skins and Furs | 43,412 | 45,303 | 50,472 |
| Bark, oak and cork tree | | | |
| Gums | | | |
| Turpentine | | | |
| Drugs, viz. | | | |
| Cortex Peruvianus | 22,878 | 19,881 | 26,017 |
| Rhubarb | | | |
| Isinglass | | | |
| Liquorice | | | |
| Bark, Quercitron | | | |
| Jalap | | | |
| Borax | | | |
| Camphire | | | |
| Brimstone | | | |
| Pitch and Tar | | | |
| Whale Fins | | | |
| Saltpetre | 113,254 | 111,802 | 111,542 |
| Cork | | | |
| Bristles | | | |
| Elephants' Teeth | | | |
| Bees'-wax | | | |
| | 387,530 | 523,305 | 492,800 |

## ABSTRACT OF IMPORTS.

| Abstract of Imports. | 5th Jan. 1826. | 5th Jan. 1827. | 5th Jan. 1828. |
|---|---|---|---|
| | £. | £. | £. |
| Useful Provisions . . . . . | 1,992,318 | 2,790,125 | 2,739,125 |
| Luxuries . . . . . . . . | 14,045,322 | 13,716,867 | 15,189,923 |
| Materials for Manufacture. . | 12,890,783 | 9,031,581 | 13,652,992 |
| Articles accessory to Manufactures . . . . . . . | 2,443,940 | 2,103,721 | 2,060,879 |
| Articles partially manufactured | 1,254,375 | 354,711 | 737,033 |
| Articles fully manufactured . | 699,305 | 1,052,432 | 978,425 |
| Metals . . . . . . . . . . | 1,323,616 | 486,740 | 730,437 |
| Miscellaneous Articles . . . | 6,049,758 | 4,820,290 | 5,503,735 |
| Articles not specified. . . . | 1,961,497 | 1,682,448 | 1,875,156 |
| Shillings and Pence . . . . | 40 | 36 | 42 |
| Total Imports into Britain, except from Ireland . . . | 42,660,954 | 36,038,951 | 43,467,747 |
| Imports into Ireland . . . . | 1,547,853 | 1,647,162 | 1,420,027 |
| Total Imports into United Kingdoms. . . . . . . | 44,208,807 | 37,686,113 | 44,887,774 |
| Of which re-exported. . . . | 9,169,494 | 10,076,286 | 9,830,728 |
| Used in the United Kingdoms | 35,039,313 | 27,609,827 | 35,057,046 |
| Imports from Ireland to Britain | 6,544,575 | | |

## ABSTRACT OF ARTICLES RE-EXPORTED.

| Articles Re-exported. | 5th Jan. 1826. | 5th Jan. 1827. | 5th Jan. 1828. |
|---|---|---|---|
| | £. | £. | £. |
| Useful Provisions . . . . . | 178,999 | 118,435 | 206,562 |
| Luxuries. . . . . . . . . . | 3,747,973 | 4,232,668 | 4,135,480 |
| Materials for Manufacture . . | 1,226,821 | 1,746,059 | 1,610,855 |
| Articles accessory to Manufactures . . . . . . . . | 998,934 | 1,052,934 | 904,650 |
| Articles partially manufactured | 139,400 | 228,296 | 38,430 |
| Articles fully manufactured . | 1,051,327 | 786,486 | 958,423 |
| Metals . . . . . . . . . . | 478,096 | 598,023 | 505,362 |
| Miscellaneous Articles . . . | 387,530 | 523,305 | 492,800 |
| Articles not specified. . . . | 946,201 | 780,274 | 953,661 |
| Shillings and Pence . . . . | 24 | 22 | 24 |
| Amount of Articles re-exported from Britain . . . | 9,155,305 | 10,066,502 | 9,806,247 |
| Articles re-exported from Ireland . . . . . . . . . | 14,189 | 9,784 | 24,481 |
| Articles re-exported from United Kingdoms . . . | 9,169,494 | 10,076,286 | 9,830,728 |

It appears from these statements, that the quantity of raw produce exported is inconsiderable. The great mass of our exports consists of manufactured goods, the production of our industry, a considerable part of them from foreign materials. Of these, articles for clothing form the far greater part; cotton, woollen, linen, and silk manufactures, the first and last entirely, the others partially, from imported materials. Woollen manufactures were formerly the most considerable branch. Now those from cotton have risen to an immense magnitude; the amount of these exported exceeding all our other exports together. That of linen is less considerable than any of the former, and the quantity imported from Ireland into Britain (not included in the foregoing statements) is nearly equal to that exported to foreign countries. The next to these in amount are articles formed of iron, and other metals, the material of which was formerly for the greater part imported, but is now almost entirely supplied by our own forges. We also re-export a large quantity of colonial produce imported.

In return for these and some miscellaneous articles, we receive, besides materials for manufactures, a few necessary articles, which our own country does not supply, and a large amount of luxuries, of which sugar, coffee, tea, spirits, and wine, form the greater part. The consumption of the last is confined to the rich; that of the other pervades, in some degree, every rank of society. The quantity of foreign manufactures imported is very small.

The most striking circumstance that presents itself to our attention, upon reviewing the foregoing statements, is the great excess in the official value of the exports above the imports. We exported, in the first of these years, to the value of fifty-five millions, in the next fifty millions, and the last sixty-one millions. Our imports were valued at forty-two millions, thirty-six millions, and forty-three millions; and there was a similar excess in the estimated value of our exports above that of our imports, for a long course of years preceding. This leads us to inquire, in what manner, and for what purpose, we give away this surplus of exports. In time of war it is easily accounted for, by our foreign belligerent expenses, and the subsidies we pay to our allies. In time of peace the cause is not so obvious.

According to the doctrine of the old school, this excess of exportation is a desirable matter.

It gives us what was termed a favourable balance, and being supposed paid in the precious metals, by increasing the quantity of these, formed an addition to our national wealth. This doctrine now does not require refutation.

Without undertaking to develop the whole of this mystery, the following circumstances appear to have considerable weight, and to account, at least in part, for the great and permanent superiority of our exports.

Although our warlike operations have been discontinued, at least in Europe, for a good many years, we still keep a large military establishment in our colonies, and occasionally in other services. The other expenses of our numerous colonies are very great, and only a small part of them is defrayed by any revenue raised in the colonies. The expense of our establishment for convicted criminals in New South Wales forms a pretty large article. The expense of our embassies at foreign courts is considerable. Some of these may be paid in the first instance by money, or bills of exchange; but all of them must be ultimately paid by the export of commodities.

We may next reckon the sums remitted to British subjects resident abroad. Since the peace, the number of such absentees, now residing in France and other foreign countries, some of them transiently, many of them permanently, owing to the greater cheapness of living abroad, has been very considerable, and their expenditure is also supplied in the same manner, and a small part only of this is recompensed by the expenditure of foreigners in this country.

The amount of goods clandestinely imported is another countercharge against our exports. This was formerly very great, and though now, by the amendment and better execution of our laws against smuggling, it is much diminished, enough still remains to have a sensible influence.

Since the peace large sums have been furnished in Britain towards foreign loans, and for carrying on speculative undertakings in foreign countries.

The amount of British funded debt held by foreigners is not now very great, but whatever it be, the dividends remitted to foreign fundholders must be taken into account.

Lastly, we may notice, that, as Britain possesses no mines of the precious metals, an annual supply will be required to replace the waste of our coin, by wear and other accidents, though no addition be made to the quantity of our metallic circulating medium, and also to answer the other purposes to which these metals are applied. Gold and silver do not form any part of the imports exhibited in our official returns.

Such are the circumstances that occur to us at present, as accounting for the excess of our exports above our imports. We may have omitted some, and we suspect, after all, that there is something in the manner in which the values are estimated in the official accounts, that renders them not altogether a just standard for exhibiting the real state of our trade. We cannot overlook, that, in some articles of foreign and colonial merchandize, the quantity exported for a course of successive years is greater than that imported. It belongs to those who have the management of this branch of the revenue to explain that paradox. The articles to which this observation applies are—cotton and silk manufactures of India, saltpetre, pepper, cinnamon, rum, geneva.

The declared value of the produce and manufactures of the United Kingdom, exported from Britain in these years, is less than the official value, owing to the great excess of the latter in the article of cotton manufacture exported. If that article be set aside, the declared value of the other exports exceeds the official value, and on the years preceding 1821 the declared value of the whole exports exceeded the official value. The declared value of foreign and colonial merchandize re-exported is not given in the official statements.

*Note.*—By the returns made to Parliament up to the present time (1830), it is established, beyond all doubt, that the official value of most articles exported has, during every year, greatly exceeded the real or declared value for each of the last eight or ten years; and this difference will, to a great degree, account for the apparent excess which, in the preceding chapter, is supposed to have existed between the annual value of our exports over that of our imports.

# CHAPTER XVIII.

## POPULATION.

No branch of political economy has engaged more attention than that of population, and none is more deserving of it. The points which claim our attention are, How far a dense population is desirable? What are its limits, necessary or contingent? How far the constitution of human nature, when not under restraint, leads to an increase of number? What restraints naturally occur in different stages of society? Whether it be wise to stimulate population by artificial encouragement? Or whether, on the other hand, it be requisite to check its too rapid progress by artificial restraints? What are the results of an increasing, stationary, or diminishing population in regard to human happiness?

It appears clearly desirable, that every country should be peopled to an extent consistent with the comfortable subsistence of its inhabitants. The bountiful Author of Nature created this world, in order that it might be inhabited by mankind; and although the human race be sprung from a single pair, it was appointed that they should increase and multiply, and replenish the earth. Even apart from sacred history, there are sufficient proofs of the gradual increase of the human race, and its gradual dispersion over different regions of the earth.

As the natural fruits of the earth are only sufficient for a very narrow population, the requisite supply of food, as mankind multiply, must be obtained by human industry, and the quantity of food raised will be regulated by the number of consumers. More will not be raised than they require, for it would be useless; and if the quantity were much less, part of the human race must perish by hunger. There is, however, a considerable range between a full and a scanty subsistence, in which the quantity of food, compared with the number of mankind, may vibrate.

The labour of a certain portion of mankind (or what comes to the same thing, a certain proportion of the labour of the whole) is, in most cases, sufficient for providing food for the whole; and the remainder may be applied for procuring clothing, habitation, and other comforts. The proportion of mankind required to be employed in the production of food varies much, according to the fertility of the soil, the nature of the food, and the agricultural skill and industry of those who furnish it. Perhaps, in a fertile country, the labour of three men among twelve may be sufficient to supply food for themselves and nine other labourers, together with the requisite proportion of women and children, and the other nine may be employed in providing houses, furniture, clothes, and other accommodations. In a sterile country, the labour of nine may be required for obtaining food, and that of three only be applicable to other purposes. These are, perhaps, nearly, the limits within civilized society. Supposing their skill and industry equal, the former will be amply, and the latter scantily, supplied with the conveniences of life. In Britain, the number engaged in miscellaneous employments predominates. According to the census of 1821, the number of families employed in agriculture was 978,656. That of those employed in trade and manufacture 1,350,239. An additional quantity of food, when necessary, may be obtained by employing additional labour on the land already cultivated, or by bringing waste land into cultivation; but when this is had recourse to, though food may be raised for a greater number of men, the number of free hands whose labour is applicable to other purposes may be smaller. The land may produce a greater absolute quantity of food, but a less disposable quantity. Is this desirable?

The greater number of modern political economists answer this question in the negative. None more decidedly than Mr. Ricardo. "Provided the net income be the same, it is of no consequence whether the number of inhabitants be ten or twelve millions."—"Would it be any advantage to the country, that, to produce the same net revenue, seven millions of men rather than five should be employed? It would not enable us to add a man to our army, or a guinea to our taxes."

If a large army, or a large revenue, were the ultimate object, this would be sound doctrine. But if the welfare of mankind be the object, if the only legitimate use of the army be to defend the community, and the only proper application of the revenue to supply the necessary expenses of a government established for the protection and benefit of the people, whose happiness it is their duty to promote, we must answer the question in a different manner. The world was created that man might inhabit and enjoy it. Is it of no consequence whether the gift of nature be limited to a small, or extended to a great number of inhabitants?

We apprehend that this desirable extent of population cannot be marked by any precise line, though the general principle be clear. It is eligible that every country be peopled to an extent consistent with the comfortable subsistence of the inhabitants. When there is a great number of surplus hands, after serving the purposes of agriculture, some of them are likely to be employed in a way that may be accounted capricious, or in forming articles that add little, if anything, to human comfort. It would be better that these hands were employed in raising additional food, and thereby enabling the country to support an additional population. To employ the whole population in agriculture is impracticable ; to approach near to this is not desirable, neither is it so to enlarge the proportion of spare hands by confining cultivation to the most fertile soils on which food for a considerable number can be raised by the labour of a few. But it is impossible to ascertain the boundaries between comfort and caprice, or the measure of comfort that may be sacrificed for the sake of extending the benefit of what remains to a more numerous population.

The limits to population are partly assigned by the hand of nature, and partly depend on the political structure of society. The number of inhabitants on the earth cannot exceed what the food it may produce can maintain. It is also restricted by the means of the labouring classes finding employment. The former limit is absolutely and obviously insurmountable. It is not so clear that the other may not be surmounted by a different structure of society, although it generally comes in operation before the other. Those two great sources of restriction to population are not, however, necessarily or universally connected. In Ireland, where a redundant population at present prevails, it is not alleged that the soil is incapable of producing a sufficiency of that food which they chiefly subsist on, and the abundance of that cheap food is even assigned as the cause of the excess of population, and of misery consequent thereon. A famine may depopulate a country, and a succession of bad seasons may retard the progress of population, or even render it retrograde, although the accumulated capital of the country affording means of employment remain undiminished Something of this kind took place in Britain at the commencement of the eighteenth century. These restrictive causes being, in a great measure, independent of each other, ought to be considered separately, though they are generally blended by writers on political economy. At present we shall confine our attention to the natural limit. The political limit shall be the object of a subsequent discussion.

The prevailing opinion, till lately, was, that population ought to be encouraged, and political measures, with a view thereto, have been had recourse to, and some contempt bestowed upon a state of celibacy. No danger or inconvenience from excessive population was apprehended. About thirty years ago Mr. Malthus advanced a very different doctrine. The natural progress of population, according thereto, advances rapidly and presses upon the means of subsistence, and would soon overcome it, unless checked by moral restraint, vice, or misery. The former of these, by far the most desirable, is, therefore, an essential duty, and is the only means of avoiding the others.

Mr. Malthus enters into an elaborate and detailed research concerning the state of population in almost every country, ancient and modern, and points out the checks, preventive or positive, which have, in a greater or less degree, retarded the population in all. Of these, moral restraint operates but feebly, and the increase of its influence is a most desirable object. The other branches of the preventive check arise from the desire which men in a state of civilization have of maintaining and elevating their station in society, and enjoying the comforts which art and industry afford. The extent of its influence is regulated by the habits and manners of the age, and its effect is generally inferior to that of the positive checks to population. Of these war is the most prominent, and next to it are famine and pestilential diseases. In modern Europe the positive check is less prevalent, and the preventive more so than in times past. Abundant food occasions abundant population. Agriculture is the efficient cause of population,—not population of agriculture: yet population is oftener restricted by want of employment than by want of food. Population is most promoted when the industry of an old state operates on the fertile and unappropriated land of a new one.

The ultimate limit to population from want of food is not, as Dr. Wallace and other theorists suppose, a very distant event, and therefore, at present, deserving of little regard, but is a calamity likely to overtake us much sooner than these suppose. Population advances by geometrical progression. The increase of food, by more extensive and better cultivation, cannot be expected to advance faster than an arithmetical progression; and therefore the former must soon outstrip the other, supposing the period of doubling to be twenty-five years, which appears to be conformable to the rate of increase in the North American United States, and is within the bounds it would probably reach if all impediments were removed. The population of Britain being reckoned eleven millions at present, and the produce sufficient for the easy support of that number, at the end of twenty-five years the number of inhabitants would be twenty-two millions; and if the quantity of food be also doubled in that period, the means of subsistence would be equal to this increase. In the next twenty-five years the population would be forty-four millions, and the means of subsistence, receiving an increase equal to what it did in the former period, would be equal only to the support of thirty-three millions at the former rate, and would afford a very scanty fare to the existing number. At the next period the population would be eighty-eight millions, and the means of subsistence increasing at the former rate, would be only equal to the supply of half that number, and at the conclusion of the first century the population would be one hundred and seventy-six millions, and the means of subsistence only equal to the support of fifty-five millions, leaving a population of a hundred and twenty-one millions totally unprovided for.

It should be our object to promote the operation of such restraints as may proportion the population to the food, for we cannot proportion the food to the population. If the number of births be great, the number of deaths must be great in proportion. If we act consistently when we give encouragement to the former, we should at the same time use means to promote the latter. In order to keep up an extent of population as great as the country can maintain, it is far more eligible to increase the health and longevity of mankind, than to stimulate by encouragement a large number of births, accompanied by a proportional number of deaths as an inevitable consequence.

The danger of distress from excess of population being imminent, it is an imperious duty to retard, and, if possible, avert it, by those measures which produce the least degree of suffering. This can only be done by increasing the operation of the preventive checks. In opposition to this, the English poor-laws, by allowing maintenance at the public expense to the children of the labouring classes, when above a small number, give undue encouragement to early marriages. Mr. Malthus proposes a repeal of these laws in regard to all marriages contracted after a certain period, with the exception, perhaps, of families unusually large. He does not go so far as to debar any set of men from marriage, or even to prohibit marriage under a certain age, but he strongly insists on the propriety of inducing such habits, and inculcating such sentiments as may have a general influence on retarding the age of marriage till its prolificness be diminished to such a degree as to confine the increase of population within the bounds that an increase of food may be obtained for.

Mr. Malthus is unfavourable to the cottage system, and has a particular dislike to the potatoe. He deprecates the view of milk and potatoes, instead of wheat, becoming the common food of an Englishman. He is of opinion that when potatoes are the common food, as they are in Ireland, and every man who wishes to marry may obtain a piece of ground sufficient, when planted with that root, to support a family, the consequence must be an over-population, and attending wretchedness; and that the indolent and turbulent habits of the lower Irish can never be corrected, while the potatoe system enables them to increase beyond the regular demand for labour; that, when the common people of a country live principally on the dearest grain, as they do in England on wheat, they have great resources in a scarcity; and barley, oats, cheap soups, and especially potatoes, present themselves as less expensive means of nourishment; but when their habitual food is the lowest in the scale, they are absolutely without resource.

We have thus attempted to give a concise view of the doctrines advanced in Mr. Malthus's celebrated work, and, we trust, a just one. We are sure, at least, we have not willingly misrepresented them. In many of them we heartily concur, and we believe they are all dictated by the benevolent desire of averting misery and promoting the welfare of the most numerous classes of society. Some of his doctrines we think require modification, and in regard to some we are entirely at issue with him.

We have now briefly to state our sentiments on this important subject.

1. We hold that, agreeably to what is related in Scripture, mankind originated from a single pair, and have, in the course of some thousand years, multiplied and extended themselves till

they occupy, in more or less dense population, almost every region of the habitable earth. Profane history, however obscure and imperfect in regard to the earlier periods, concurs with Scripture in informing us of the gradual expansion of the human race, and in pointing out the middle part of Asia as the country from which it originated. We do not undertake to solve the obscure problem of the population of America. We believe it to have commenced from some migration from the old world, the particulars of which are now lost in unfathomable oblivion; not improbably from the eastern parts of Asia, to the countries on North America lying along the Pacific Ocean. We see no reason for admitting the supposition of a separate creation, and we have abundant proofs that the population of that portion of the earth commenced at a later period than that of the old continent.

2. The increase would go on in geometrical progression so long as circumstances remained the same, and that at a very rapid rate. If the longevity of mankind in the first ages be admitted, as recorded in Scripture, the increase would be more rapid than any which can now take place under the most favourable circum-

stances; and we find even this is very considerable. The rate of increase may vary a little from the nature of the climate, but more from the habits and manner of life of the inhabitants. The United States of North America, since the establishment of their independence, exhibit a favourable example of rapid population, the industry of an old state operating there on the fertile and unappropriated land of a new one. It appears, by comparing the censuses taken there, that the population has doubled in about 25 years. Perhaps, in stating this as the natural rate of increase, too little is allowed for emigration. According to the census of the American States, taken in 1800, the number of white inhabitants of all ages was 4,308,971. These would be reduced, by the ascertained rate of mortality in ten years, to 3,200,000, which is the remnant of the former stock that would be alive in 1810, all above ten years of age; but the number of white persons in the United States above the age of ten, in the year 1810, by the census taken that year, was 3,845,389, giving a surplus of 645,389, which can only be accounted for by emigration; and to this number we must add a number of emigrant children under ten, and the emigrants who died within the ten years, to complete the whole number of emigrants. The whole increase of population in these ten years was 1,556,122, of which nearly one half was added by emigration*. Mr. Malthus is of opinion that the rate of doubling in twenty-five years is maintained, even after checks to population, preventive or positive, have operated in a considerable degree, and that there is reason to believe mankind would double in fifteen years, if every check were removed. Perhaps, if we assume twenty years as the shortest period of doubling, consistent with the present state of the human constitution, we may not be far from the truth.

3. It is evident this rate of population could not go on long. The earth would be overpeopled in a few centuries beyond the physical possibility of subsistence. The interval between the time of the deluge, and of Jacob's removal into Egypt, according to the scripture chronology, is six hundred and forty years, or thirty-two periods of doubling. At this supposed rate the number of mankind originating from three pairs at the deluge would amount to about

* This statement is taken from Mr. David Booth's Dissertation on the Increase of Population, and the Means of Subsistence, published by Mr. Godwin.

twenty-five thousand millions when Jacob journeyed into Egypt,—a much greater number than the whole earth ever did or can support.

4. Accordingly checks have occurred in every age and nation that have much retarded this extreme rate of population, but very different in their nature, and in the extent of their operation in different ages and nations.

5. The ultimate and insurmountable check to the increase of mankind is the impracticability of procuring food, even at the lowest rate, for more than a limited number. The absolute want of food, however, has seldom been the actual check to population, and the earth has never been peopled to the extent it is capable of maintaining. A large portion of the earth is still uninhabited, or very thinly inhabited. In the most improved countries there is much imperfectly cultivated, and very little brought to the utmost pitch of fertility of which it is susceptible.

6. There is reason to believe that, with few exceptions, the number of mankind has increased in every age, and extended farther, though at a rate gradually diminishing from the increase of checks, resulting from the increase of numbers.

7. Mr. Malthus founds much upon the dif-

ferent nature of geometrical progression, by which, from the human constitution, there is a tendency for mankind to multiply, and the arithmetical progression by which he supposes an additional quantity of food may be procured. We do not think him altogether correct in this last position. The power of procuring additional food depends on the industry and skill of the cultivators, and the extent and fertility of unoccupied land, and may, in some cases, advance much beyond the arithmetical rate of an equal increase in an equal time.

We have no reason to believe that mankind ever existed in a state altogether venatory to any great extent, or for any considerable length of time. The only remains of that state now are to be found among the savage tribes of North American Indians, and these are now nearly extinct. The pastoral and nomadic state has been far more extensive and of longer duration, and still prevails in extensive regions of the earth. Cattle, in that state, furnish the chief food of mankind; and as the increase of cattle, as well as that of mankind, goes on in geometrical progression, and even doubles in a shorter period, there is no reason why the supply of food should not keep pace with the increase of mankind, however rapid, so long as there is a sufficient range of pasture land; and the ambulatory habits of men in that state would render their change of country, in quest of pasture, a matter of no hardship.

By degrees the agricultural system, at first from choice, rather than necessity, is blended with the pastoral, and in time obtains a superiority over it. The earth yields its produce to the agriculturist in consequence of cultivation, and so long as there is enough of fertile land to cultivate, that quantity of food produced will be in proportion to the number of cultivators, and go on, as they do, in geometrical progression. Indeed, when fertile unappropriated land becomes scarce, and recourse is held to more sterile soils, the case is extremely different.

8. The number of mankind has thus a tendency to increase, somewhat according to a geometrical progression, but at a rate which becomes slower as the population increases. The food which they can procure also advances at first by geometrical progression, but this is kept back by checks, still more operative than those which take place to retard the increase of mankind. Of these the most prominent is, the necessity of having recourse to the cultivation

of more sterile soils, after all the fertile ones are brought into full culture. As the utmost possible extent of population is limited by the quantity of food which the land, fertile or sterile, and all cultivated as well as possible, could maintain, so the utmost actual extent is limited by the increased labour requisite for the production of food from barren soils. If a tract of land, though capable of being brought to a state in which it will yield some food for mankind, requires the work of more labourers than can be maintained on what it can be made to produce, it is evident it never will be cultivated. Nor will cultivation even nearly reach that limit. The cultivators must have clothes, habitation, and other accommodations, as well as food. If they cannot obtain these from the produce of the land, they will cease to cultivate it, though no rent be demanded.

9. The extent of cultivation, in regard to barren soils, is therefore connected with the measure of accommodation and comfort which the labouring classes can obtain in the existing state of society. The agriculturist must obtain an equal share of these with the other classes, and as every friend to humanity wishes this as ample as circumstances will admit, it is not

desirable that land, below a certain degree of fertility, should be cultivated. If the disposable part of the produce will afford very few comforts to the agricultural labourer, the mass of the society must be in a state equally indigent. The same observation applies to the bestowing additional labour on more fertile soils, to bring them to a higher state of cultivation. The question recurs, does the additional produce repay the additional labour at an equal rate as other labour is remunerated? Improvements in agriculture, however, which lessen the requisite labour on soils of whatever quality, may render the cultivation of more sterile soils eligible, and is of advantage to society*.

* There is much land which cannot be brought into a state of cultivation without a heavy expense, but, when once brought in, may be retained so at a moderate expense, and give a return adequate thereto. Should such land be cultivated? If we consider this as a mere question of loss or gain, we would answer in the negative. The proprietor or farmer who improved it would be a loser, for we suppose the first expense greater than the value of the land after improvement. But, if we extend our view to the general good of the country, we must consider the cultivation as desirable. The loss is only in the first instance, the improvement of the country extends to future generations. But how shall such improvements be carried into execution? Some proprietors have a laudable pride in the cultivation of their estates, and will make exertions which, though not conformable to narrow prudence, confer an important advantage on the country. We have known considerable tracts of very rough ground, in the vicinity of a trading town, brought into a

10. Although we have taken a view somewhat different from Mr. Malthus, of the relative progress of population and food, we agree with him in the chief point, that the former must in time outstrip the latter. Whatever advances at a rate of geometrical progression, however low the rate, must in time amount to an indefinite number, and surpass the progress of what is limited by an insurmountable barrier. This point is incontestable.

11. The time in which the progress of population is likely to surpass the practicable increase of population is an important consideration. In this we are inclined to assume a middle rate between Dr. Wallace and Mr. Malthus. The former considers it as a very distant event, the latter as very near, or already at hand. We do not think it so remote as the former supposes, or so near as the latter apprehends. The utmost possible increase by procreation is limited by the human constitution. If we state at five in the hundred yearly, which is equivalent to a rate of doubling in about fifteen years, we surely take it high enough. An additional quantity of

high state of cultivation, by the more opulent citizens, each improving a small portion, at an expense, perhaps, never repaid, but extending a scene of fertility to some miles distance from the town to which it owed its improvement.

food, amounting to one-twentieth at most, will be what is wanted for the additional number of mouths produced in one year. Indeed, less will be sufficient, as young children do not require the average allowance. There does not seem to be much difficulty at present in Britain, and other countries in similar circumstances, of procuring that quantity by more extensive or better culture. Suppose that no more food was raised than before for one year, the consequence would only be that the people must be served with a sparer diet, to the extent of one-twentieth, foreign commerce being out of the question. This is no very heavy calamity, yet would be sufficient to raise the price of provisions so much as to give a stimulus to agriculture, and thereby produce a sufficiency to give an allowance in the following year as ample as before; and the increase of agricultural produce might thus keep pace with that of population for a considerable number of years.

12. We are led by these observations to modify Mr. Malthus's doctrine, that agriculture is the efficient cause of population, not population of agriculture. No more land will ever be cultivated than so much as there is a demand for the produce of. In a country, therefore, where the

agricultural system has commenced, but which is as yet thinly inhabited, much land of considerable fertility will remain uncultivated, but ready to yield a plentiful return, so soon as it is subjected to the labour of the agriculturist. In this state food being easily procured, mankind will multiply rapidly, and more land will be gradually brought into cultivation to supply their wants. So long as this continues, population is the efficient cause of agriculture, not agriculture of population. When there is no longer an extent of fertile land remaining uncultivated, and when there is a population sufficient to consume what the country in its present state produces, and no means of foreign supply, then population will be checked by the difficulty, and ultimately by the impossibility of procuring food, and can only be increased by more extensive or better agriculture. Then, according to Mr. Malthus, agriculture may be accounted the efficient cause of population.

13. Although a time must come when the increase of population will be checked by want of subsistence, if other checks be not interposed, yet so long as there are means of increasing the quantity of food in a country to meet the additional demand for a considerable number of years,

without any essential diminution of comfort, there is no occasion to have recourse to any political regulation for checking the progress of population. We see but little into what lies in the recesses of futurity, and should not adopt measures which impair present happiness, from the apprehension of remote consequences, which may never occur, being intercepted by other causes, at present beyond our view.

14. Admitting that the agriculture of Britain, or any other old country, were brought to such a pitch as to be unsusceptible of much further improvement, we might, nevertheless, give encouragement to population, providing the means of emigration were easily within reach. Such is the state of Britain at present in regard to America. That quarter of the world presents immense tracts of land uninhabited, or very thinly inhabited, and, though of considerable fertility, very little cultivated. The means of emigration to these countries is not very difficult, and they are not likely to be fully peopled for ages. They afford, therefore, a resource for removing a redundant population, likely to continue as long as human foresight can reach, subject, however, to the difficulty and expense which must always attend emigration. Australia

also affords an extensive field for emigration, although, on account of the distance, attended with greater difficulties. Government should afford every facility to emigration, and has done so of late; though at a former period, when different opinions were entertained, the general policy was rather to discourage it. Direct assistance in money to defray the expense of the passage, and the first wants of the emigrants, may also be given to a certain extent, though under requisite limitations. This has also been done. It has been proposed that the money thus advanced should be repaid by instalments, as the land allotted to the settlers was brought into cultivation, and a lien retained in the grant for that purpose. The validity of this security for repayment may be equivocal, but the supply of our manufactures to these settlers, before they had arrived at a state in which they could manufacfacture for themselves with advantage, would probably afford a sufficient compensation to the parent country for what aid they had afforded to the emigrants.

15. We fully agree with Mr. Malthus that no stimulus should be given to population by any direct political measure, and therefore that the encouragement given to early marriage among

the lower ranks by maintaining all the children above a certain number, and that not a large one, from the poors' rates, is improper ; and the poor-laws, so far as they establish such a claim, should, after due intimation, be repealed. This is the chief point which Mr. Malthus desires to establish, and it has our unqualified approbation. We do not approve of the poor-laws in general, especially that part of them which supplies part of the necessary wages of the labouring classes from that fund. This has the effect of confounding the views of charity and legal right, and of doing away the sense of degradation at receiving eleemosynary support, so natural to an unsophisticated mind, and so beneficial to society. If recourse to poors' rates be admitted, we think it should be limited to cases of age and sickness, or other severe distress, and of widows left with young families.

16. We do not, however, go so far as to impute any blame to charitable persons who may give pecuniary aid to some in the lower ranks whom they are inclined to favour, though it may, in some instances, induce them to marry earlier than they would otherwise do. Such acts of beneficence generally proceed from laudable motives, and are not likely to be so frequent as to

produce any hurtful effect on the mass of society. We would never inculcate any doctrine, the tendency of which was to harden the human heart against the demands of want and misery, to increase the separation between the opulent and the indigent, and induce a temper alike inconsistent with the spirit of the christian religion, and the dictates of humanity.

17. Admitting that no encouragement be given to early marriage by allowing a legal provision to the children, should we go any further? Should we prohibit, or at least discourage, such marriages by any positive enactment? We think not. If measures undertaken with a view to this could be rendered effectual, which would not be easily done, the increase of licentiousness would be almost the inevitable consequence; and this is too serious an evil, whether considered in a religious, moral, or political point of view, to be slightly regarded. Should a positive restriction, however, be judged necessary, perhaps something of the following kind might be the least exceptionable. Married women and widows are entitled, by the laws of this and other well governed states, to certain legal privileges. Might not these be refused, or restricted, when the woman, at the time of her marriage, was under

a specified age? This might have the effect, in frequent instances, of inducing young persons who had formed an attachment to each other, to defer their marriage till the woman had obtained the specified age. A breach of chastity between them before marriage to incur the same or a higher legal disqualification than a marriage before the limited time. If the morals of the parties be not previously depraved, their entertaining such views, and not a very distant prospect of obtaining the completion of their desires, seem to afford as favourable a ground of expectation of restraining licentiousness as any measure merely human can afford. We have, however, suggested this measure not as what we approve of, but as the least hurtful, if any of the kind be had recourse to. Our opinion is, that in these matters government should not interfere.

18. Though we do not approve of very early marriages, we are still more averse to very late ones. We believe the attachments formed in early life for the most part lead to the happiest unions, and our observations concur with those of Dr. Franklin, that the sentiments of the parties mould more into conformity with each other when young and flexible. The frequent instances of divorce among the higher ranks from

marriages contracted at a period of life when interest is the prevailing motive, afford a lamentable proof how little such marriages are desirable. Mr. Malthus observes, "That the expression, late marriages, refers to no particular age, but is entirely comparative. The marriages in England are later than in France, the natural consequence of that prudence and respectability generated by a better government. Two or three years in the average of marriage, by lengthening each generation, and tending, in a small degree, both to diminish the prolificness of marriages, and the number of born living to be married, may make a considerable difference in the rate of increase, and be adequate to allow for a considerably diminished mortality. But I would by no means talk of any limits. The only plain and intelligible measure with regard to marriage is the having a fair prospect of being able to maintain a family."—Vol. iii. pages 361-2. In these observations we fully concur.

19. There is no point in which we differ more from Mr. Malthus than in his abhorrence of the potatoe. If that, or any other species of food, were unfavourable to the health and vigour of the human frame, and especially if, by the reaction of the body on the mind, it had a prejudi-

cial influence on the noblest part of our nature, this would form a most imperious reason for discouraging the use of such food. But there seem no good grounds for entertaining such an opinion in regard to the potatoe. Dr. Smith asserts a contrary one, and we think the reasons he assigns for doing so are satisfactory; they concur with our own observations. In many districts of Scotland the potatoe furnishes a considerable portion of the food of the lower ranks, without any apparent injury to their health or welfare; nor is such a supposed injury, though Mr. Malthus insinuates something of this kind, the point on which he chiefly rests his argument. The purport of his reasoning is, that the facility of procuring food, afforded by the prolific nature of the potatoe, gives undue encouragement to early marriages, and, consequently, to redundant population, which, not being able to find employment, from a want of proportional capital, is reduced to a state of wretchedness. Such reasoning appears to lead to inadmissible consequences, and not to accord well with the principal doctrines which Mr. Malthus aims to establish. These require us, because we *cannot increase food beyond a certain measure*, to limit population to that measure. But if we can maintain a greater number by introducing a more productive kind of food, why not do so? If the same ground will support a much greater number of men when applied for raising potatoes than wheat, why not apply it accordingly? If we can find another plant still more productive than the potatoe, why not have recourse to it, and supersede the potatoe in its turn? Mr. Malthus's reasoning leads to this, that to suppress redundant population we should lessen the quantity of food, by raising a less productive kind, when we have a better one in our power. The same reasoning should induce us to lay aside wheat, and substitute for it some less productive plant, or lead us to consider it as desirable that the fertility of the earth were diminished, to save the risk of mankind increasing too fast, from the facility they find in procuring food for their children.

The argument adduced by Mr. Malthus, for the common people of a country living chiefly upon the dearest grain, appears to us untenable. "When they live principally on wheat, as they do in England, they have great resources in a scarcity, and barley, oats, rice, cheap soups, and potatoes, all present themselves as less expensive, yet at the same time wholesome means of nourishment; but when their habitual food is the lowest in the scale, they appear to be absolutely without resource, except in the bark of trees, like the poor Swedes, and a great portion of them must necessarily be starved."—Book iv. chap. xi.

The attainment of the substitutes here proposed seems impracticable. While wheat is the chief food used in the country, no more potatoes, or other food, will be raised than what is required for the subordinate consumption of these kinds of food, in aid of that which is chiefly depended on. In a bad season, the wheat fails. Suppose one-tenth of the food usually consisted of potatoes, there could not be more than that quantity expected in such a year, nor even so much as the usual quantity of barley and oats, as these crops are likely to suffer from the same inclemency of the weather which renders the wheat crop deficient. Supply, in such a distressing case, must, if practicable, be derived from other sources.

20. We are much more favourable to the cottage system, and the practice of cottagers keeping cows, than Mr. Malthus, and some other modern writers on political economy, and have assigned our reasons,—Chap. xii. p. 192. We are well pleased that Mr. Malthus partially retracts

(book iv. chap. xiii.) what he had advanced in a former chapter against that system, and thereby approaches nearer to our sentiments on the subject.

21. It is, we believe, an undoubted fact, that the human race advances more rapidly in population in its earlier stages, and that the rate of increase becomes slower with the progress of art and civilization. This arises from the difference of habits that accompany the change of the state of society, and is likely to operate still more powerfully as art and civilization are carried to a higher pitch, and, without having recourse to harsh measures, may be expected to restrain the progress of population within the necessary limits. Mr. Malthus admits this doctrine to a considerable extent, and states it thus: " Consequently, admitting the desirableness of the end (the diminished proportion of births), it is not necessary to risk the promulgation of any new opinions which may alarm the prejudices of the poor, and the effects of which we cannot with certainty foresee; but we have only to proceed in improving our civil polity, conferring the benefits of education upon all, and removing every obstacle to the general extension of all those privileges and advantages which

may be enjoyed in common; and we may be quite sure that the effect, to which I look forward, and which can alone render these advantages permanent, will follow.

" I acknowledge the truth and force of this argument, and have only to observe, that it is difficult to perceive that we should not proceed with more celerity and certainty towards the end in view, if the principal causes which tend to promote or retard it were generally known. In particular, I cannot help looking forward to a very decided improvement in the habits and temper of the lower classes, when their real situation has been clearly explained to them; and if this were done gradually and cautiously, and accompanied with proper moral and religious instructions, I should not expect any danger from it, &c."—Vol. iii. Appendix, p. 375.

# CHAPTER XIX.

## ARTIFICIAL STATE OF SOCIETY.

In the foregoing part of this treatise, and especially in chap. xv., we have delineated a state of society, which the principles of human nature and the means in the power of man naturally lead to, and in which he may enjoy a considerable measure of comfort and prosperity. The efficient cause of his obtaining the necessaries and conveniences of life is his industry and skill; and the motive for putting these in action, is his desire of obtaining such objects, at the same time that the exertions made to obtain them contribute to the more important end of intellectual improvement. The fruits of his labour are greatly increased by the use of tools and the division of employment, without some measure of which he could do little; but the most useful of the former are easily procured, and are possessed by the rudest tribes; and the first step in the latter, the division of the farmer from the artizan, and of this last into the separate employments of mason, carpenter, smith, weaver, and a few others, is easily attained, and even this step contributes, perhaps, more to the extension of comfort, than others which are more complex, and of later attainment. In this state, any increase in the quantity or efficacy of industry would increase the general quantity of commodities, and consequently the portion that should fall to the share of each member of the society. This state does not require an equality of wealth and station, though it does not accord with extreme inequality; neither does it exclude the advantages which commerce may bestow, by supplying better materials for clothing, and other purposes, than our own country affords, or even articles for direct consumption. But its principal foundation is the products of general industry, employed for the most part upon native commodities, prepared for the use of the inhabitants, and consumed by them.

When we take a survey of the different civilized countries of the earth, we seldom see this picture realized in any considerable degree, and never to its full extent. Those who advocate it are generally treated as enthusiastic visionaries. In countries where art has been longest established, and where wealth seems most to abound, we often find the great mass of the community placed in very uncomfortable circumstances, and unable to derive any considerable advantage from their industry. Capital, in this state, is held requisite to put industry in motion, and to find a market for the articles produced becomes a principal object. The operative part of the community, from the lowness of their circumstances, only consume a small part. The consumption of the rich and luxurious takes off so much more; but there is still a surplus of commodities which must be taken off by foreign commerce, and purchased by less skilful or less active nations, for anything they have to give in return. In countries highly commercial, such as Britain, the quantity of manufactured goods we can dispose of to other nations is considered as the basis of our prosperity, and even as necessary for our existence. This state of society may be accounted artificial. It proceeds from the natural state above described by gradual steps, but the extremes are marked by the most obvious and important distinctions.

Here, several points of the highest importance present themselves to our consideration. Is this artificial state of society desirable? Does it, on the whole, promote human happiness? Should we endeavour by artificial stimulus to accelerate its progress? or, should we rather use means to retard it? Is it practicable to do so? If practicable, is it expedient? Supposing it already extensively established, and followed with hurtful consequences, would it be practicable, or would it be wise to endeavour to retrace the steps by which it has advanced, and return to a state of greater simplicity? If the progress towards this highly artificial state be inevitable, and on the whole beneficial, by what means can we best prevent, or retard, or alleviate the evils which accompany it?

If the mass of accumulated wealth be the ultimate object, there is no doubt that the highly artificial state of society will furnish the largest state, and should be promoted by every effectual means, and such sentiments will always be entertained by the generality, after the system has made considerable progress. But to those who consider wealth as only desirable, so far as it is the means of promoting human welfare, the solution of the question will not appear so easy.

In the earliest stages of society every man may obtain land of tolerable fertility, without purchase or rent, and can raise a sufficiency of food by part of the labour which a man of ordinary industry exerts. The remainder of his labour is applied to procure him lodging, clothing, and other articles of convenience or comfort, either by his exercising mechanical employments himself, or by raising more provisions than he has occasion for, provided he have access to a market for disposing of what is superfluous. So long as this state continues, there is a certain portion of comfort which naturally falls to his share. But, when all the land is appropriated, the price of provisions which he then must purchase may be so high, and the returns he can receive for his labour so low, as to render his situation hard, or even destitute. Having no land to cultivate, he may suffer from want of food, though placed in the midst of a fertile cultivated country.

In consequence of the division of labour, the mass of labourers, being only trained to one kind of work, are unfit for any other, and when demand for that branch fails, they are reduced to severe distress. The man who has been bred to the loom, and has always wrought at it, perhaps at one branch of the weaving trade, is ill-qualified to build a cottage for himself, to supply it with furniture, or to make the tools requisite for the exercise of his own craft. Even in opulent countries, where trade and manufactures are in general flourishing, demand in particular branches frequently fails, and those who were engaged in them are little qualified, and always unwilling to turn to any other kind of employment. The sudden introduction of machinery, to perform, by other powers, what was formerly done by human labour, is another cause of throwing labourers out of employment. This has frequently led to the unhappy consequence of urging the discarded workmen to rise in mobs, to demolish machinery, and commit other outrages, for the suppression of which recourse to harsh measures becomes necessary. These evils are most likely to happen in manufactures which require extensive premises and complicated machinery, and where, consequently, a great number of workmen are collected together; and the distress occasioned by stagnation of demand is most likely to take place when the demand arises from foreign trade, which many causes, altogether beyond the power of the manufacturer to prevent, and which even Government cannot overcome, may put a stop to, or divert into a different channel.

Under the artificial system, capital being considered as necessary to put industry in motion, the number of labourers that may exist, and the wages and measure of comfort they may obtain, is held to depend on the amount of capital possessed by some portion of the community. Capital is said to be required for three purposes, —for supplying the labourer with materials, for maintaining him during the time that intervenes between the commencement of his labours and receiving its price, and for furnishing the requisite tools for the exercise of his craft.

The last of these is chiefly that which is frequently deficient. Nature, assisted by culture, affords, in most countries, at a certain season of the year, a supply of food sufficient, in ordinary cases, to maintain the inhabitants for the whole year; and thus, when the harvest is concluded, there is a store of food provided, and in possession of a part of the community, for the subsistence of the whole, till the ensuing harvest. The materials on which the labourer has to operate are chiefly those subservient to clothing, building, and furniture; and most countries afford a sufficiency of these, though great advantage may often be gained by importing more commodious articles in exchange for others that can be spared. In Britain, the chief materials for clothing are wool, flax, cotton, and silk. The two former partially, and the two latter entirely imported.

Yet, there is no doubt, the two former alone might afford us very comfortable clothing, and might be raised in sufficient quantities to supply all our wants of that kind. Wood and stone, the chief materials for building, are generally at hand.

In regard to tools, the case is widely different, though even as to these there is much diversity, according to the nature of the work, and the state to which art has advanced. The tools of the husbandman are not very complex. The spade is a cheap instrument, the plough and the harrow are not very expensive. In mechanic arts, the requisite tools are generally much more complex and expensive, though more so in some employments than others. The carpenter is rarely at a loss for a hammer or an axe; but to supply a modern carpenter's shop with all the tools required, for the execution of the nicer parts of his art, is no easy matter. The weaver's loom, even that adapted for plain work, is a complex instrument, and the machinery used in the nicer branches of that art much more so, and the expense of providing them forms a large portion of the necessary price of the manufactured commodity. The premises required for their commodious application cannot be erected without great expense, and all this must be incurred, and consequently capital provided, long before a return is expected. An extensive manufactory, even when most successful, never repays the expense of its erection for many years, and the undertaker lays his account with this, and regulates his measures accordingly.

Metals are an essential ingredient in the formation of tools, and are also required for many other important purposes. These, unless obtained by foreign commerce, which at present is out of the question, require the operations of mining and forging, both very expensive, and in which a great deal of capital must be invested, and labour exerted, long before any return can be drawn.

When a commodity is consumed at home, the tradesman who makes it may, and generally does, receive its price so soon as the article is completed and delivered to the consumer, or not long after; but when it is intended for foreign consumption, it is long before any return can be looked for. The immediate workman is not, in general, able to abide this delay. He sells his commodity to the exporting merchant, who must be possessed of the requisite capital, and must draw a suitable return from the price which the commodity bears abroad. If that fall below the requisite rate he ceases to purchase; the commodity stagnates; the workman is thrown idle; misery, and often lawless riot, are the fatal consequences.

The progress of art, and increasing efficacy of labour, in providing the commodities which men desire, cannot be prevented. The accumulation of capital is the necessary consequence of the desire which most men have to improve their circumstances; and an increase of skill results from experience and observation, and the superior ingenuity of some individuals. Any attempts to stop its progress would deserve severe reprobation; nor are any such likely to be undertaken: yet it is, perhaps, to be desired that the progress should be gradual.

The mass of commodities is increased by the superior efficacy of better directed human labour, and by the substitution of other powers to accomplish the work which was formerly done by that labour. The quantity of human labour requisite for the direction of these powers, and constructing the necessary machinery, is much less than was formerly employed for the direct execution of the work, and, consequently, the supply of commodities more ample, and the community more affluent; and, unless there be something very faulty in the constitution of the society, a portion of this wealth will flow through every rank.

The most eligible way of consuming the additional commodities produced by the improvements which have been introduced, is their more plentiful use by the mass of the community. One of the most remarkable improvements in art which has taken place in Britain within the last half century is that in the cotton manufactory, by the machinery invented by Arkwright and others. Though the manufactured article is exported to a great extent, the home consumption is still a superior object; and it is obvious that the natives, especially the female sex, are better clothed than they were before. There can be no reasonable doubt that there would be an equal improvement in their lodging, and other accommodations, providing the mechanic professions which supply these were susceptible of improvement in the same degree that has taken place in the cotton manufacture.

The consumption of a larger portion of commodities requires a change of habit in the consumers, and this change is only effected gradually. If the increased mass produced exceed the additional consumption, and the surplus be not taken off by foreign commerce, the evils above-mentioned must ensue. This consideration may lead to caution in the application of any artificial stimulus for the extension of production, before a correspondent increase in consumption can be rendered available. When production is pushed beyond the measure of consumption and demand, the evil cures itself by the glut of the market and loss incurred by the producers; but as this does not take place till much misery has been endured, it is better if it can be averted by a more gradual increase in production.

A reason, somewhat different, which may render gradual increase of production desirable, is taken from the natural and necessary limits of wealth and art. These are not susceptible of endless accumulation, though the precise extent to which they may be carried cannot be ascertained. There is, however, a limit, and the nearer this limit is approached, the progress will be slower. Now the happiness of an individual in civilized society does not depend so much on the extent of his wealth, as on its being in a state of progression. The man who from a moderate outset gradually improves his circumstances, and increases his means of comfort, will generally have more enjoyment than another, who, beginning with superior wealth, spends his life in a uniform luxurious train. The same observation applies to communities. That community which is advancing in wealth and art, may be accounted more prosperous than that which is already farther advanced, but has now ceased to make progress. This argument appears to us to have some weight. We are aware, however, that it will generally be thought far-fetched, and the apprehended evil too remote, to deserve consideration.

We cannot, however, think lightly of the check which is given to intellectual improvement, when division of labour is carried to a great extent, by confining the labourer, almost during his whole time, to the repetition of the same operation, with nothing to excite his energies. The far greater part of such workmen merely execute what they are taught and directed, and think of nothing more. Not one in a hundred makes any improvement in the machinery of his art, or the way of employing it. In regard to the few who make improvements, the mental exertion thereby brought into action is very beneficial to them, yet it is generally confined within the narrow bounds of the machinery of a particular craft. If the man who spends twelve or fifteen hours a day in the manufactory, repeating the same uniform operation, should spend an hour or two, after his work is over, in the ale-house, among his fellow workmen, who have passed the day in the same manner, this is a wretched resource for solacement; and a life spent in this way is far from promising to raise the human mind to that degree of intellectual and moral improvement of which it is susceptible, and to which it ought to be the object of civil institutions to advance it.

In a former part of this treatise we mentioned with favour the cottage system, under the belief that it was desirable the tradesman should employ some part of his time in the cultivation of a small patch of ground, or garden, where his situation rendered it practicable. This, if not a perfect remedy, seems one of the best palliatives for the serious evil above-mentioned.

We are aware of the difficulties which attend this branch of our inquiry, both in regard to the objects we should aim at, the means of attaining them, and the restrictions with which they should be guarded. On the whole we are inclined to adopt the following maxims.

Whatever increases the efficacy of human labour, or performs by other powers what was formerly done by that labour, tends to increase the mass of human enjoyments, and its ultimate consequence must be beneficial. Improvements in the weaving craft have the effect of affording us better clothing with the same labour ; and if all our wants of that kind be supplied by a smaller number of hands, there will be a greater number to provide conveniencies of other kinds: nor does there seem any limit to the enlargement of the mass of commodities, while improvements in art can supply them, till every desire of men be universally and fully gratified ; an event not likely to take place. We, therefore, consider every improvement in art which tends to increase production as desirable, and that the reasons adduced in opposition thereto from numbers being thereby thrown out of employment are not admissible when the ultimate result is regarded.

But though every improvement is beneficial in the long run, the rapid increase of production may not be attended with a simultaneous increase of consumption, and the evils resulting from this are too weighty to be disregarded. It is desirable that the mass of the community have the means, and then it will not be long before they have the desire of enjoying a larger share of comforts, and consequently increasing the general consumption. If production be enlarged beyond that measure, and the surplus not taken off by foreign commerce, the evils above-mentioned must follow.

We are far from thinking that, under any circumstances, the efficacy of improvements in art should be checked by any restrictive regulation, and, as far as we recollect, nothing of that kind has ever been attempted by any legislature. If attempted, we believe it would be ineffectual. The attempts made by the mob to check the use of machinery, by destroying the machines, have never succeeded.

But though we would never approve of any coercive measures to restrict production, the considerations above suggested may have sufficient weight to abate our zeal for its rapid promotion, and the application of direct encouragement for that purpose, especially when the consumption chiefly depends on a foreign and precarious commerce.

We are decidedly of opinion that those branches of industry are most beneficial, and deserve most encouragement, the productions of which are chiefly used at home, being applied to the comfort of the mass of the community.

For obtaining this end, the labouring classes must be able to purchase; they must receive good wages. Mr. Ricardo, we think, first advanced the doctrine, that the value of the article produced must be divided between the capitalist and the labourer. We cannot increase the share of the one without diminishing that of the other. We cannot raise the wages of labour without lowering the profits of capital, and *vice versâ*.

When a commodity is ready for use, it has a certain value, resulting from its application to the maintenance or comfort of man. A part of this value falls to the proprietor on whose land the material, which formed the basis of the commodity, was raised. This being satisfied, the remainder is divided between the capitalist who furnishes the machinery used in its preparation and the necessary advances, and the various labourers employed on it, from the farmer who raises the material, to the mechanic who completes the work. So far Mr. Ricardo's doctrine seems incontrovertible. The value of the commodity is a given quantity resulting from its utility. The portion of this value which you assign to the one you must take from the other.

It should be observed, however, that the mass of productions, the stock of wealth to be divided between the capitalists and labourers, is increased by the efficacy of capital. The accumulation of capital has a tendency to lower the rate of profit, and consequently to raise the wages of labour. The labourer is thus enabled to enlarge his comforts, and increase his consumption in two ways. His labour produces more, and a larger proportion of it falls to his share, in so much as a smaller share accrues to the capitalist by the fall of the rate of profit. At the same time the capitalist may not be a loser, for the increased consumption of the great body of the community will afford an extensive field for the investment of his capital, which could otherwise have been only sought for in the far more precarious resource of foreign commerce. For these reasons we consider high wages as desirable, and as affording the most solid basis to national prosperity.

It is impossible to fix with precision the proportion which wages and profits should bear to each other, and the actual proportion must, from obvious causes, be in a state of continual fluctuation.

The favour we are inclined to assign to high

wages will not be relished by those who consider the quantity of goods exported as the basis of national prosperity, and the paramount object to be pursued. Articles which are in general request through the civilized world will be purchased from that nation which can bring them to market at the lowest money price, and therefore low wages, being a principal ingredient in cheap production, are requisite for enabling us to supply the demands of foreigners by underselling others, and the more so if, in consequence of heavier taxes, or other causes, our manufactures be subject to burthens which bear lighter in other nations. We have been accustomed to boast that our superior skill in machinery, and our large capitals, give us a decided advantage, and will secure us a large share of the foreign market, notwithstanding our heavier burthens. The effect of these, however, has its limits, and it is unreasonable to expect we should always maintain the superiority we may at present possess.

But though we admit that low wages, by enabling us to bring wares to market at a cheaper price, is favourable to the trade of exportation, we remain of opinion that this advantage may be gained at too high a price, and that wages considerably high, whether considered as promoting the comfort of the most numerous part of the community, or enlarging the domestic market, by enabling them to purchase more liberally, are conducive to the general welfare.

Notwithstanding the vast extent to which foreign commerce is carried in Britain, and the immense capitals invested in it, we cannot consider it as the most solid or desirable source of national prosperity. Neither do we approve of that system which has been long carried on between the different states of Europe, which may be termed a commercial warfare. In the prosecution of this system each country endeavours, by restrictions, prohibitions, and other artificial means, to procure within itself the articles it has occasion to consume, and also to afford a supply to other nations. Such a system is certainly prejudicial to the civilized world at large, and we doubt if it be ultimately advantageous to any particular nation. Every nation possesses an advantage in manufacturing the materials which its own soil produces for its own supply, and it is expedient that every nation should supply itself with commodities, unless where substantial reasons induce an opposite conduct. These reasons are diversity of produce in different climates and soils, and superiority of mechanical skill. The former is a permanent source of commerce; at least it could only be superseded by such a change in national habits as would induce any state to be satisfied with the articles which its own country produces,—a change not likely to take place so long as a foreign supply is within its power. The other is a much more precarious source of commerce.

If the validity of the above reasoning be admitted, if the artificial state of society may be carried so far as to impair instead of promote human welfare, what measures ought to be deemed eligible in a nation where such a state has already taken place, and is firmly established?

We should certainly never recommend to endeavour to check it by any restrictive or coercive means. If such were attempted, we believe they would be ineffectual; and if they could produce any effect, it would be that of aggravating the evils they were intended to remedy. We are of opinion that the exertion and direction of human skill and industry should be free and uncontrolled, and that every attempt to restrain them, and almost every attempt to promote them, does harm.

If this be sound doctrine, an alteration in the state of society can only be induced through the medium of the habits and manners of the community. If we can improve these, besides the individual good, we shall ameliorate the general condition of society. Proper education, religious and moral instruction, good government, personal freedom, and absence of cumbersome restrictions, are conducive thereto. Stronger measures are more likely to do harm than good; and any violent change in the state of society is always productive of much present distress, and seldom leads to any permanent good. We are conscious that any hints we have offered on this important subject are very imperfect. But it is one step gained if we can point out the end we ought to aim at, and the general principles upon which the attainment of that end is most likely to be promoted.

# CHAPTER XX.

## PAPER CURRENCY.

AMONG the expedients which have been had recourse to in a state of society highly artificial, that of a circulating paper medium of commerce is one of the most remarkable. It has been the subject of much discussion among political economists. It has been much attended to by the legislature, and many statutes have been enacted for its establishment, regulation, or restraint. Its effects on the state of society, especially in regard to commerce, are considerable, though we think more good and more evil have been ascribed to it than it can justly lay claim to.

In Chapter VI. we advanced the doctrine, that money derived its value from its use and universal reception as a circulating medium, and an equivalent for every commodity; that the absolute quantity of gold and silver in circulating coin was of no consequence, as the money price of commodities would accommodate itself to the relative proportion of the precious metals and goods in circulation; that the use of these metals for other purposes was of little importance; and that their value, if their use as a circulating medium was discontinued, would greatly fall; and that any substitute for them, the reception of which was equally firm, would answer the purpose as well. But in order to secure this reception, it is requisite that the basis of the medium should be considered as possessing an intrinsic value, and that its estimation should not be confined to one country, but extend over the commercial world, so as to command from any country the commodities which it can furnish, and we require. Gold and silver possess these qualities in a superior degree.

The use of written obligations to supply the place of coin is a modern invention. Its commencement, at least in a regular manner, in Britain, may be dated from the establishment of the Bank of England in 1694. A chief object of Government in that establishment was the obtaining a loan to supply the exigencies of the state, and recourse has often since been had to it for the same purpose; but its effects in supplying a substitute for the precious metals is what at present chiefly claims our attention.

A Bank note is a written or printed obligation, by which that establishment is bound to pay to the bearer a specified sum, in the current coin, upon demand. So long as there is full confidence on the part of the public that the funds of the Bank are amply sufficient to discharge these obligations, and as it continues to do so readily, when demanded, these notes will be received in payment as readily as coin, because the holder can easily obtain coin for them, should he prefer it, which, in ordinary cases, he will have little inducement to do. Although these notes were not rendered a legal tender in payment of a debt by any positive enactment, their use was found so convenient, and the public confidence in their security so complete, that they soon were substituted for a considerable part of the coin which formerly constituted the only circulating medium. For a long time, as no notes were issued under five pounds, they did not supersede the use of coin for smaller sums. Many private companies were afterwards instituted, which issued notes in a similar manner. A monopoly was so far granted to the Bank of England, that no private company consisting of more than six partners was permitted to issue obligations of the nature of bank notes. This restriction, by confining the capital of private banks within narrow limits, lessened their security, and not a few of them have become insolvent. Yet, as the accommodation they afforded in the districts where they were established was deemed beneficial, the circulation of their notes in remote parts of the country has been, and is still considerable.

In the further discussion of this subject, two separate objects of inquiry present themselves:—

1st. What advantage or disadvantage attends the use of a circulating paper currency as a substitute, in any proportion, or in whole, for a metallic one, without regard to the general amount of the currency.

2d. The effects of a paper currency in increasing the amount of circulating medium, and in occasioning more sudden alterations in the amount than would otherwise take place.

On the first point it is argued that gold and silver are articles of great value, and the amount of them in circulation forms a considerable part of the national wealth. In countries which contain no mines of these metals, the original quantity required must be procured by giving other articles in exchange, thus parting with so much of our national wealth; and the annual waste by wear must also be supplied in the same manner. The whole amount of circulation in Britain is estimated at present to exceed sixty millions. If we could find an unexceptionable substitute for a considerable part of this in a material comparatively cheap, we might import useful commodities in return, and thus add to our national wealth.

It is also argued that payments of large sums are more easily made in paper. The weight of the metals renders their transportation from place to place a matter of labour, and even the telling them is a tedious employment, when the sum is very large. For these reasons we find that payments of large sums are generally made in paper, wherever the system of paper currency is established.

These considerations have considerable weight. There are, however, strong arguments in favour of metallic currency to set against them. The reception of a circulating medium depends, as we have noticed, on the opinion of its possessing an intrinsic value, and as a paper currency has no value in itself, its circulation can only be maintained by its convertibility into metallic currency. So long as this conversion is readily obtained when demanded, and no doubt entertained of its continuing to be so, the paper currency maintains an equal value with the metallic, and may be used in considerable proportion as a substitute for it, affording the above-mentioned conveniences, and not attended with any disadvantages, so far as internal commerce is concerned, and so long as the whole amount of circulating medium is not unduly increased.

But if the conversion of notes into coin be suspended or refused, whether by legal enactment or deficiency in the means of the Bank, the case is otherwise. Even the apprehension of such an event excites alarm, and occasions a run on the Bank, which is likely to bring on a stoppage of payment. When this happens, it is held forth on the part of the Bank that the stoppage is only temporary, and payments will soon be resumed. Statements are given out, to show that the Bank is possessed of sufficient funds to answer all demands, and that its creditors incur no risk of sustaining ultimate loss. Notwithstanding this, the value of its notes is depreciated, and the holders part with them for a lesser amount in coin than the sum which they bear, or, as it is sometimes expressed, the current value of coin and bullion rises above the mint value. This depreciation increases the longer the payment in coin or bullion is discontinued, and in length of time may fall to little or nothing. Such was the fate of the French assignats, and of other sorts of paper circulation in many countries, not founded of a solid and convertible description. The governments which issue, or countenance such paper circulation, use every means to support its credit; but all their endeavours to that effect have proved, and must prove ineffectual. It is nothing to tell the holder of paper that the funds of the Bank are sufficient to answer his demands. If these funds be beyond his reach, and likely to continue so, they might as well be in the coffers of the Grand Lama, or in the planet Saturn.

For about a century after the establishment of the Bank of England, the convertibility of their notes was uniformly maintained. Gold or silver was immediately given for every note when demanded. In the year 1797, when the demands of an expensive war had nearly withdrawn the precious metals from circulation, and emptied the coffers of the Bank, an important law was passed, prohibiting the payment of bank notes in metallic currency. At first it was held forth that this suspension would be of short duration; but the war continued much longer than was expected, and the suspension of payment did not terminate on the restoration of peace. It continued about twenty-four years. The resumption of payments in coin was not legalized till the year 1821, after several preparatory steps. Some public distress, which took place about this time, owing to other causes, was attributed by not a few to their resumption. According to this doctrine, the cessation of payments in specie ought to have been perpetual. A writer on political economy, about this time, has advanced the paradoxical opinion, "that the renewing the restriction act, and rendering it perpetual, could not have the least effect on the value of our paper currency, providing its quantity was not at the same time increased*."

The holders of this doctrine appear to confound the depreciation which the currency, of whatever kind, undergoes, in regard to its command of commodities by the increase of the total quantity in circulation, with the relative depreciation of paper compared with metallic currency. It is this last that is the present object of consideration, and it is an undoubted fact, that such a depreciation took place not long after the suspension of cash payments, and to a con-

* Supplement to Encyclopædia Britannica, article Money.—Vol. v. part ii. p. 515.

siderable extent. The holder of gold was able to obtain for it a sum in paper, considerably above its legal value, perhaps twenty-six shillings for a guinea, and this notwithstanding the fear of penalties attaching to such practices. It is with regret we find a resolution passed by Parliament, about this time, that there was no depreciation, when every person engaged in business knew the contrary.

Before the suspension of payments, so firmly was the credit of the Bank established, that the anticipation of such an event would have been considered as chimerical. It took place, however, attended with its inevitible consequence, notwithstanding endeavours on the part of Government to prevent them. The Bank seems now to have regained the public confidence, nearly to the same degree as before. But what has happened once may happen again, and there is little doubt that if any national exigence should require recourse to a measure similar to that of 1797, a like depreciation would take place.

It seems unnecessary to enlarge on the evils attending a depreciation of the currency, the injustice to creditors who must receive payment in a depreciated currency, and a like injustice to debtors who borrow during the depreciation, and are obliged to pay in a currency of full value after the depreciation is removed;—a convulsion is given to mercantile contracts and transactions by so violent a measure. There are abundant reasons for regretting that it was ever had recourse to, and for wishing it may never take place again.

There are other advantages in a metallic currency, to be placed against the inconveniences that are alleged to attend it. From its universal reception in all nations, it possesses a solid value which may afford essential aid in great national emergencies. Suppose the case of a famine, from a deficient crop in this country, while some other countries have a surplus which they can spare. We will not obtain it from them, unless we have something to give them in return which they value. We will, no doubt, endeavour to supply them with goods; but such may be the state of our commerce, that we have not a sufficiency of these to spare, or they do not want them. In such a case, the exportation of gold or silver affords a certain and effectual relief, and if we have none to offer, we must sustain the pressure of a heavy calamity.

The distresses of 1797 were chiefly occasioned by the exportation of a large amount of the precious metals to the continent, for the expenses of our troops abroad, and subsidies to states with which we were in alliance. Whatever opinion may be formed of the wars in which we were then, or at any other time, engaged, the possibility of a just and necessary war will not be questioned; and the command of a large amount of gold will give vigour to our military operations, and may determine the event of the war.

We proceed now to consider the effects of a paper currency, in increasing the amount of the circulating medium, and in occasioning more sudden alterations in its amount than would otherwise take place.

It is unnecessary to repeat what has been already observed of the evils resulting from a sudden and considerable alteration in the amount of the circulating currency, and such alteration is much more likely to take place when a great proportion of the currency consists of paper. The precious metals are not to be procured by nations which do not possess mines of them, except in exchange for substantial commodities, and even then will not be imported at the expense which they cost, except in such quantities as are required, in the existing commercial state of the country and present price of commodities. The material of paper currency is scarcely of any value, and it is profitable to the Bank to extend it as far as it can. The Bank receives interest for every note it can keep in circulation. There is, however, an effectual check on a redundant issue of notes, so long as the Bank is obliged to pay them in coin, when demanded. The price of commodities does not immediately rise in proportion to the increased circulation, and as nobody keeps money on hand which he has not use for, the superfluous bank notes regorge upon that establishment. The Bank, therefore, is obliged to contract its issues, and it is its interest to do so, as an attempt to extend them would increase their expense, and prove ineffectual.

When a suspension of payments is authorized by act of Parliament, the case is widely different. There is nothing to deter the Bank from issuing as many notes as it can, and abundant demands from borrowers are not likely to be wanting.

The results accruing to the community from the facility of obtaining credit afforded by the establishment of banks, public or private, is an important subject of consideration. There is no doubt it gives a stimulus both to agriculture and manufactures. A farmer is often prevented from the exertions he is disposed to make in bringing waste land into cultivation, or improving that already under culture, for want of capital. If there be a bank at hand ready to supply his wants, his exertions are brought into operation. Extensive effects of this kind in different parts of the country, and obviously owing to this cause, must have fallen under the notice of every person who has given attention to the state of the country. A like observation may be made on the state of manufactures. Many flourishing manufacturing establishments owe their origin to credit obtained from banks, without which, in the present state of the country, they could not have been brought into action.

It may, however, be questioned, whether the rapid progress of these improvements, though presenting a beneficial appearance, be always ultimately beneficial. All the undertakings of the agriculturist and manufacturer do not prove successful. Many of them are reduced to bankruptcy, and this is sometimes the lot of the most enterprizing and industrious. The bankruptcy of the banks which gave them credit follows of course.

We think that bad consequences are more likely to take place from an excessive stimulus to exertion in the department of manufacture than in that of agriculture. The farmer may not be repaid for the outlay on his improvements within the time his wants require. He becomes insolvent, and we are sorry for him; but his improvements remain, and are a permanent addition to the wealth of the country. It is otherwise with a manufacturing establishment. If the proprietors, for want of demand for their commodity, or from their not being able to produce it at the price it will fetch in the market, become insolvent, their establishment is then swept away, and leaves not a trace behind.

We have now endeavoured, as impartially as we can, to state the comparative merits of a metallic and a paper currency. Very different opinions have been advanced, and we think exaggerated ones, according as the interest, or supposed interest, of different classes seemed to incline. On the whole, our sentiments rather incline towards a metallic currency, at least for a considerable part of our circulation. If not always the most active, or the most convenient, it is the most solid instrument of commerce. Operations conducted by means of it may be slower, but they are surer.

While we give this opinion in favour of a metallic currency, we are far from thinking that where a paper currency has been introduced on an extensive scale, it should be suddenly, or at any time altogether, withdrawn. A sudden alteration in the amount of the currency always occasions distress. If considerable evils result from its sudden increase, others, still worse, result from its sudden diminution. Too great a facility in obtaining credit gives rise to improvident and unsuccessful schemes. The sudden withdrawing of this credit occasions general bankruptcy.

This is one, among many other points, in which governments are apt to overlegislate. Though, in a system now become so extensive, some restrictive regulations may be necessary, we think much should be left to the free choice of the community. On the one hand we would not render the receipt of bank notes, even those of the Bank of England, compulsory. On the other, we would not prohibit the circulation of the notes of a private bank among those who are willing to take them. Some security for the validity of such banks may, however, be required as a safeguard to the public from the evils resulting from their failure. We have already given our opinion in regard to a legislative prohibition of payments of bank notes in specie.

# CHAPTER XXI.

## OF THE CORN TRADE.

MANY who entertain the most liberal views of the advantages of a free commerce, and disapprove in general of prohibitions, cumbersome restrictions, regulating duties, and even bounties, consider the trade in corn as an exception to the system of free trade, and hold that effective restrictions in that branch are expedient, and even necessary. Though exceptions to general rules, established upon solid principles, are seldom defensible, yet in this case the arguments adduced are neither groundless, nor of slight importance.

Some of them are founded upon the present political state of Britain, compared with that of the other commercial states in Europe, particularly of those from whom we may receive a supply of corn. Britain is burthened with a large national debt, and consequent high taxation, a part of which is paid by labourers of all descriptions. This renders higher money wages necessary. Perhaps the habits of the English labourers are less frugal than those of foreigners, and this occasions a further rise of wages. Hence we cannot raise corn at so low a rate as foreigners can do; and even the expense of freight, and other charges attending importation does not counterbalance the advantage they possess, and they are able to undersell us in the corn market, unless prevented by prohibitions, or heavy duties. Hence the agricultural part of the community is depressed; and inferior soils, not being able to repay the expense of cultivation, though let for little or no rent, are thrown waste, and the landed interest reduced to a state of comparative poverty.

But the principal arguments in support of legislative interference in the corn trade are drawn from the absolute necessity of a supply of food. If the effect of such measures be to afford us additional security for obtaining the requisite supply, the imperious nature of the demand should supersede all inferior considerations.

It is argued, that when a nation depends for a considerable part of its food on other nations, if that supply should be stopped, either by a change of the political state of the nations who give it, or by war, this nation, being unprepared for such an event, may be exposed to the calamity of famine, or at least of a scarcity approaching to famine.

We are far from regarding lightly the weight of these arguments, and think that they ought to influence, to a certain extent, the legislative measures embraced in this important and difficult branch of political economy. On this the two parties of agriculturists and manufacturers have set themselves in array against each other, and both have advanced claims higher than circumstances warranted.

We are of opinion that every nation of considerable magnitude should draw the greater part of its food from its own resources. There is a considerable difference between the quantity of provisions actually consumed by a given number of inhabitants in times of ordinary plenty, and that which is absolutely necessary for their subsistence. We hold that this latter quantity should always be supplied from the national agriculture; and if restraints upon importation be necessary to keep it up to that pitch, such restraints should be imposed. Whether we should go beyond this, and give higher encouragement to the agriculturist, it is not so easy to determine, but it is not so imperatively necessary. This limits the quantity of foreign corn which may be admitted to the difference between the consumption of a plentiful and a scarce year; and it is believed that, except in years of uncommon scarcity, it never went beyond that.

Sir James Stewart delivers it as his opinion, that no annual produce of grain in Britain was ever so great as to supply its inhabitants fifteen months, *in that abundance in which they feed themselves in a year of plenty;* and that there never was a year of such scarcity, as that the lands of England did not produce above six months' subsistence, *such as the people are used to take in years of scarcity.*

The height of the wages in Britain arising from heavy taxes is, we believe, an indisputable fact, and however we may disapprove of the system that raised the national debt to its present enormous magnitude, and made these taxes requisite, the present state of matters must remain while that debt and these taxes exist, and can only be removed in the course of time by their gradual extinction. For this reason we think the British agriculturist entitled to such support, by legislative enactments, as may put him on an equal footing with the foreigner. This has been the object of the corn law lately enacted, by which the importation of foreign corn is permitted upon payment of a duty, varying by a scale, depending on the average price of corn in Britain. Whether the method now used for ascertaining the average be accurate, and whether the scale of duties be the proper one, experience must determine. It approaches much nearer to the free system, than that which prevailed for the twelve years preceding, during which period the price at which importation was permitted was fixed so high, that the actual price scarcely ever reached it; and consequently there was little or no importation, and the British agriculturist possessed the monopoly of the market.

Poland contains extensive tracts of fertile land, much more than sufficient to maintain its present population, and the extent kept under culture is regulated by the foreign demand. When Britain has occasion to import, it receives much of its supply from that country. An increase of population, or other causes, may curtail that supply, as well as that from other countries from which we now import when our own produce is insufficient; but as this, if ever it take place, is likely to happen gradually, it will give us warning, and time to look out for other resources.

We cannot say the same of the failure of supply which war may occasion. The countries from which we now receive corn may fall under hostile influence or power, and notwithstanding our boasted naval invincibility, it is not impossible the enemy may attain a temporary superiority at sea, and retain it long enough to expose us to severe distress by intercepting our supplies. We know that such apprehensions are generally considered as groundless, and treated with derision; we think improperly. Their accomplishment may not be probable, but they are not impossible, and as the evil they would occasion is of great magnitude, it is better to be provided against it. At the beginning of this century, we boasted that our superior mechanical skill and capital gave us such a decided superiority in various branches of manufacture, that no prohibitive enactments of foreign powers could prevent their introduction into their dominions. Yet Bonaparte's Berlin and Milan decrees were executed so effectually, as nearly to annihilate that commerce for several years, and it only revived at the fall of that potentate.

The policy of Britain, in regard to the trade in corn, has been very fluctuating. During more than half of the last century, we were upon the whole an exporting country, and this was considered as essential to our welfare, and encouraged by a bounty when the prices of corn fell below a specified rate. The system of bounty commenced at the revolution, and though it underwent frequent suspensions, it was not laid aside till the year 1814. During the latter part of the last century, we were generally an importing country. The corn laws, which had undergone frequent alterations and repeals, were attempted to be moulded into a more regular form, and rendered more permanent by the act of 1791, in which various prices were specified, at the lowest of which exportation was encouraged by a bounty; at the next, it was simply permitted; and at the next, it was prohibited. At the next, importation, which had been before prohibited, was permitted, but on payment of a high duty; at a higher price the duty was lowered, and at one still higher was reduced to a very low one. A method was established for ascertaining the average price, by dividing the maritime part of Britain into sixteen districts, twelve in England and four in Scotland, and the corn trade in each was regulated once a quarter, by the average price in the same for the three preceding months. Four years did not elapse before this act was suspended, on account of the deficiency of the crop, 1794, when exportation was entirely prohibited, and importation encouraged by a high bounty. In 1804, the corn laws were re-modelled, and importation regulated by the aggregate average of the maritime counties; but the scale was so favourable to importation, that it was never stopped till 1815.

In 1814, exportation was permitted in general, but without any bounty, and the bounty system has not been revived since.

In 1815, in consequence of the loud complaints of the agriculturists, the prices at which importation was permitted were raised much higher. Wheat was prohibited to be imported from our American colonies when the price per quarter was under sixty-seven shillings, and from all other places when under eighty shillings, (except for being warehoused under bond), and other kinds of grain at proportional prices. When the prices rose higher, importation was permitted duty free. This act was so operative, that there was scarcely ever any importation till the last act of 1828.

By that act there is no absolute prohibition. New regulations were appointed for ascertaining the average prices of the different kinds of grain. When wheat is from sixty-two to sixty-three shillings per quarter, it is permitted to be imported on payment of a duty of one pound four shillings and eight-pence; and for every shilling that the price rose above sixty-three shillings till sixty-seven shillings, the duty is lessened by one shilling; when the price rises above sixty-seven shillings, the duty decreases at a quicker rate—and when the price rises to seventy-three shillings or upwards, the duty is lowered to one shilling. Importation from the British colonies in America, or elsewhere out of Europe, is permitted on payment of a lower duty. Duties on barley and other kinds of grain vary by a decreasing scale as their price rises, on the same principle.

Famine is among the heaviest calamities to which human nature is liable, and though it cannot be prevented by any legislative enactment, it may sometimes be alleviated by embracing measures conducive to that effect. We at present refer to a famine inflicted by the hand of nature, through unproductive seasons, not to that which the ravages of war occasion.

The bounty system, so long adhered to, has been considered as highly useful for preventing or alleviating the evils of famine. If we raise a quantity of corn considerably more than is required for the maintenance of our population in ordinary seasons, exporting the surplus to foreign countries, when a deficient crop occurs from a bad season, we stop exportation, and, in whatever proportion the deficiency takes place, being charged on a quantity which was before more than sufficient, the evil of scarcity, if not entirely removed, is at least alleviated.

This system, however, is liable to weighty objections. It restricts the population within narrower bounds than the country, in its existing state of cultivation, can support; an effect which will be reprobated by all who consider an extensive population as constituting the strength of the society, or on any account desirable. It gives the landholders and agriculturists an advantage to which they have no title, at the expense of the rest of the community. It raises the rate of wages and expense of manufacture, and consequently depresses that important source of national industry and wealth.

These evils would result from bounties, though the money that paid them were obtained from some unknown source, without being in any way burthensome to the community. But this is not the case. The bounty must be paid by means of a tax, a measure always burthensome to a part or the whole of the community, especially in a country already so heavily taxed as Britain. This argument bears strongly against bounties of every kind, which should never be granted, except for the most urgent reasons, and with the greatest caution.

Every measure proposed as beneficial to one nation, which cannot at the same time be adopted by other nations in similar circumstances, is of a very suspicious tendency. We desire that Britain should raise a surplus of corn in ordinary years, in order to afford a resource in years of scarcity. Why should not France, Spain, and Germany, do the same? The argument applies alike to all. If they all adopt that system, how are their surpluses to be disposed of?

If, for these reasons, the measure of forcing a surplus growth of corn by bounties be laid aside, it remains to inquire whether there be any other means within human power for averting or mitigating the calamities of famine. If the failure of the crop be confined to one country, importation is an obvious and practicable remedy; but, if it extend over all accessible countries, no relief can be obtained in that way.

In ordinary seasons, at the conclusion of every harvest there is a part of the crop of the former year remaining on hand, perhaps one-fourth. A deficient crop takes place. If the deficiency does not exceed that quantity, its consumption would afford a supply to the country at the ordinary rate till the next harvest; but there would be no stock remaining to aid the following year; and though this stock on hand might be forthcoming for one year, it would leave no resource in the case of several successive bad seasons. It is likely, however, that the rise of price occasioned by the deficiency of the crop would lessen the usual quantity of consumption, and leave some part of the usual stock unconsumed at the end of the next harvest, and so afford some resource for another year; and if several plentiful years succeeded, the usual stock would be replaced.

We have stated the stock of corn on hand at the end of the succeeding harvest at one-fourth of the whole quantity required for a year's consumption, and considered that as affording considerable relief for one bad season. If the stock remaining be larger, the relief will be more considerable, and of longer duration. If it can be increased to one-half, three-fourths, or even a whole year's consumption, it would afford a resource for as long a duration of scarcity as almost ever occurs.

There is no physical impossibility in this, for grain may be preserved by proper care for more than a year, with little injury. But there are moral and political obstacles which go far to prevent a system of this kind from being carried into execution to any considerable extent. The farmer cannot afford to keep back his produce from the market. If he could, it is not his interest to do so. The corn-dealer will seldom find it a profitable measure to keep large quantities on hand. It has sometimes been suggested that granaries might be erected at the public expense, and a large quantity of corn purchased, and renewed from time to time; but the quantity kept up till a time of scarcity made it necessary to have recourse to it. If anything of this kind has ever been done, it has been on a very limited scale*; and to carry it to extent in a large country is impracticable. Among other insuperable objections, one is, that the mob would rise and plunder the granaries whenever they felt the pressure of scarcity. However, if the

* In the city of Bern public granaries are said to have been erected, capable of holding a supply to that city for several years.

principle be admitted, as we think it ought, that a large stock of corn in the country is desirable, nothing should be done to discourage any who may be inclined to contribute thereto. Instead of considering the ingrosser as a nuisance, and delivering him to the vengeance of the mob, he is rather to be accounted a useful member of society. The difficulty is how to render his employment so beneficial to himself as to induce him to persevere in it.

Corn is, in ordinary seasons, applied to other purposes besides food, in considerable quantities, and the prohibition of such applications in time of scarcity affords a considerable supply. Of these the distillery is the most considerable, and the prohibition of distilling from grain has been several times had recourse to in years of scarcity. We are far from desiring that the ordinary consumption of grain in spirits should be increased, in order to render the supply from this source more ample. The moral evils arising from the immoderate use of spirits among the lower ranks are too heavy to admit any measure that might tend to encourage their use, which ought to be discountenanced and repressed by every possible means.

The prohibition of brewing beer is a measure

that has not been as yet had recourse to. It would occasion heavier privations than that of spirits, and is also liable to other objections. Yet the calamity of famine may be so great, though in modern times it has seldom been so, as to render every measure for increasing the supply of food necessary.

When the ordinary food is composed of a variety of articles, this variety affords some protection against famine. The several kinds of grain crops are likely to suffer from the same inclement season, but the potatoe crop may escape, and afford relief in proportion to the quantity usually raised. If animal food furnish part of the nourishment of a considerable proportion of the community, it is not liable to fail; and in countries bordering on the sea, part of the ordinary food consists of fish, and this part may be expected, in the scarcest years, in ordinary abundance. In scarce years, of late, soup kitchens, at first suggested by Count Rumford, were set up in many towns, both in Britain and the continent, from motives of humanity. Though their effect is not considerable, yet, as their tendency is to procure a share of animal food for the lower ranks, prepared in the most economical manner, they are useful in some degree.

Voluntary associations have sometimes been formed among persons in affluent circumstances, in years of scarcity, for being sparing in the use of food from grain, and having recourse chiefly to other articles, which, on account of their expense, were beyond the reach of the lower ranks. Though much effect could not be expected from such associations, yet, as they indicate a humane attention to the wants of the poor, we consider them as commendable.

But the effects of these or any other expedients that can be suggested are insufficient for affording a supply of food during a severe famine, and the only effectual alleviation of that calamity is by diminished consumption. At sea, when provisions become scarce, the crew are put upon short allowance. So they should on land. At sea this restriction is enforced by the authority of the commander. But how shall we enforce it throughout a country? The only effectual way is, by suffering the price of corn to rise so high, that the lower, and even the middling ranks, may be only able to purchase a scanty subsistence. The sooner this rise of price takes place the better. Any attempts to conceal the true state of the country, or prevent the rise of price at the beginning of the season, if they had any effect at all, would do harm.

Bounties have been sometimes granted by Government on imported corn, in seasons where the crop appeared deficient. This might give a cheaper and more plentiful supply, and prevent in some measure the pressure of want; yet we doubt the propriety of such a measure. If the famine be general, the offer of a bounty must be ineffectual, for other nations are in want themselves, and have nothing to spare. If the famine be partial, the rise of prices in the country which suffers from it will afford sufficient inducement to other nations to supply what we want.

A certain extent of privation does not destroy the health of the human constitution, but if it be carried beyond that limit it does so. When the price of corn rises very high, the labouring classes cannot afford to purchase what is requisite for supporting health, and may even be exposed to starvation. In such a case relief should be given them, either in money or some kind of cheap food, by means of poor-rates, or voluntary charity. Though poor-rates are not in general desirable, the urgency of the case now supposed may require them. But this relief, whether voluntary, or arising from poor-rates, should be confined within such bounds as to afford the narrowest subsistence consistent with the health of those who receive it.

## CONCLUDING REFLECTIONS.

THE utmost extent of wealth which the state of human nature can attain would result from a union of the following sources;—a favourable climate, and fertile soil, cultivated to the utmost; general industry among the people, directed by skill, and aided by good machinery and division of labour; a spirit of enterprize which leads to a commercial intercourse with every nation where experience has found it profitable, but not impelled by extraneous encouragement; an exemption from foreign wars and domestic dissensions; a mild and frugal administration at home. To give these full effect, they must remain steady for a considerable length of time.

No nation ever enjoyed a combination of all these advantages, and consequently none ever attained the utmost pitch of wealth. The cultivation of the earth, the most important source of wealth, is far from being carried to the utmost perfection. In the most improved countries of Europe, there are still many uncultivated tracts susceptible of improvement. Draining, irrigation, and other important operations, are only partially practised, and the common modes of husbandry admit of much improvement.

A more splendid kind of wealth may be displayed in the metropolis of a conqueror, who has ravaged all the regions around, and collected their spoils. In regard to the general mass of wealth, the ravages of war are in the highest degree destructive. The emphatic epithet of *the Scourge of God* has been aptly bestowed on the extensive warrior. If we lay aside the consideration of what the conquered countries suffer, and only attend to the state of the conqueror's country; nay, further, if we set aside the general condition of his country, and confine our attention to the spot where the spoils of the vanquished are accumulated and displayed, our imaginations may be dazzled, but our judgment will find little to admire. Riches, thus collected, no more resemble riches acquired by industry, in advancing the happiness of the nation, than the mirth of intoxication is worthy of being compared to the permanent flow of spirits which health and activity confer.

**THE END.**